Daniel M. Herzig

AF130186

**Ranking for Web Data Search
Using On-The-Fly Data Integration**

Ranking for Web Data Search Using On-The-Fly Data Integration

by
Daniel M. Herzig

Dissertation, Karlsruher Institut für Technologie (KIT)
Fakultät für Wirtschaftswissenschaften
Tag der mündlichen Prüfung: 21. Juni 2013
Referenten: Prof. Dr. Rudi Studer
Korreferent: Prof. Dr. Hannah Bast, Universität Freiburg
Prüfer: Prof. Dr. Hartmut Schmeck
Vorsitzender: Prof. Dr. Andreas Geyer-Schulz

Impressum

 Scientific
Publishing

Karlsruher Institut für Technologie (KIT)
KIT Scientific Publishing
Straße am Forum 2
D-76131 Karlsruhe

KIT Scientific Publishing is a registered trademark of Karlsruhe
Institute of Technology. Reprint using the book cover is not allowed.

www.ksp.kit.edu

Print on Demand 2014

ISBN 978-3-7315-0136-7

Karlsruhe Institute of Technology

Ranking for Web Data Search
Using On-The-Fly Data Integration

Zur Erlangung des akademischen Grades eines

Doktors der Ingenieurwissenschaften
(Dr.-Ing.)

von der Fakultät für Wirtschaftswissenschaften
des Karlsruher Instituts für Technologie (KIT)
genehmigte Dissertation von

Daniel Markus Herzig

Tag der mündlichen Prüfung: 21. Juni 2013
Prüfungskommission:
Referent: Prof. Dr. Rudi Studer
Korreferentin: Prof. Dr. Hannah Bast, Universität Freiburg
Prüfer: Prof. Dr. Hartmut Schmeck
Vorsitzender: Prof. Dr. Andreas Geyer-Schulz

Abstract

Ranking - the algorithmic decision on how relevant an information artifact is for a given information need and the sorting of artifacts by their concluded relevancy - is an integral part of every search engine. The ranking function determines the effectiveness of search by promising that relevant results are found despite the increasing data volume on the Web. Due to the efforts of the Semantic Web community and recently also through the support of major search engines, data on the Web, which is until today primarily unstructured and textual data, is augmented and supplemented with structured data. Structured data describes and links entities, such as products, people, organizations and events, and opens new possibilities for applications and search on the Web. In particular, the question arises whether structured data helps search to keep the pledge of delivering relevant results or even allows to improve the effectiveness of search. However, structured data on the Web is heterogeneous, e.g. entities referring to the same real-world object may be described in different ways and different vocabularies may be used to express similar things. These characteristics hamper the adoption of structured Web data for search and require new methods for ranking where ambiguity and vagueness challenge the assessment of relevance.

In this thesis we investigate how structured Web data can be leveraged for ranking with the goal to improve the effectiveness of search. This principal research question is divided into four specific research questions addressing the problem of (1) evaluating search over structured Web data, (2) ranking combinations of structured and unstructured data for hybrid queries, (3) dealing with heterogeneous Web data, and (4) consolidating redundant results. We propose solutions regarding these research questions and experimentally analyze and evaluate them against the latest baselines. The results show advances beyond the state-of-the-art.

Acknowledgements

Without the support, encouragement, and advice I received from so many people while working on my research, this dissertation would not have been possible. I am thankful to all of them and I can only mention some of them here.

First, I want to thank Prof. Dr. Rudi Studer for giving me the opportunity to work on this dissertation at the Institute AIFB and in particular for his guidance, support, and advice. In this regard, I also thank Dr. Thanh Tran for the numerous discussions and the impetus to pursue my research. I am grateful to Prof. Dr. Hannah Bast for taking the Korreferat of my dissertation.

In particular, I want to thank my colleagues at AIFB for their help, feedback and support. Here, I am especially thankful to Dr.-Ing. Günter Ladwig for many discussions, suggestions and his technical assistance, the latter applies also to Dr. Philipp Sorg whom I also thank for the introduction to IR and sharing his expertise on IR, and to Dr. Denny Vrandečić for hiring me as a student assistant at AIFB and thereby stirring my interest in semantic technologies and research in general, which was the de facto starting point of this dissertation.

Furthermore, I want to thank all my co-authors and in particular the organizing team of the Semantic Search challenges, among them Dr. Harry Halpin, Dr. Jeffrey Pound and Dr. Henry S. Thompson. In this context, I am especially thankful to Dr. Peter Mika, Dr. Roi Blanco and the whole team of the Yahoo! Labs in Barcelona for giving me the opportunity to work with them. Also I thank Naimdjon Takhirov for his help and suggestions during my time in Barcelona. I learned a lot from you all!

Especially, I thank my friends and in particular my beloved family, my parents, Eberhard and Elisabeth, and my brother Thomas. Their support, motivation and advice contributed to a great extent to my work and without them I would not be where I am today.

Most of all, I thank my love Miriam for her continued support and encouragement throughout all ups and downs of my research.

Contents

Chapter 1

Introduction

Web search, the technology to find information quickly on the World Wide Web, is ubiquitous in our daily lives. Web search enables us to effectively use and take advantage of the enormous and increasing information space spanned by the Web. Through search, the access to information has never been easier than today. Each day millions of search queries are processed by web search engines over a growing number of websites, which is estimated to be more than 630 million[1] today. The information retrieval technology behind search relies so far primarily on textual data and links between websites. Web search engines crawl and index the textual data of websites and run keyword queries against their index. Besides the increase of mobil devices and other influencing factors, one major trend is changing the setting of search on the Web: The increasing amount of structured data on the Web.

Driven by the incentive to achieve higher click-through-rates due to enhanced presentations in search result pages [67] and through the efforts of the Semantic Web and Linked Data community who advocate the benefits of data reuse, discovery, and the potential for new applications, an increasing amount of structured data is published on the Web according to the Linked Data principles [67, 117, 120]. The underlying idea of the Linked Data initiative is to transfer the concept of the key ingredient that made the Web so successful - the links - to the data level and interconnect not just entire websites but single data items through links. In contrast to the hyperlinks that connect websites, the data links are typed and thereby hold information on what kind of relationship exists between the two connected entities. Further, these links allow browsing through the data by following links and discovering new data on the Web. Certainly, browsing through raw data is not very appealing to (most) human users on the Web, but the idea is targeted at machines which can leverage the structured data and use it to solve tasks for humans [19, 138]. One of those tasks is to find relevant

[1]http://news.netcraft.com/archives/2013/02/01/february-2013-web-server-survey. html last retrieved on Feb 27th 2013.

1

information in the plethora of information on the Web. Currently, information retrieval techniques are employed by search engines, because they are able to deal with large volumes of unstructured textual data. However, they do not take structured data into account and hence the question arises how structured data can be leveraged for search.

The structured data on the Web is very diverse, heterogeneous, inconsistent or even messy [82, 137]. As a consequence, common database technologies are unsuitable for querying Web data, because they are built for well-curated, edited data adhering not just strictly to a data model, but also to a well-defined data schema, which is not the case for Web data. On the contrary, the huge number of data publishers on the Web results in various and diverse ways of modeling entities. As a result, ambiguity exists for structured data which imposes another problem for search and in particular for the ranking of search results.

Hence, ranking and data integration are two joint problems for effective search leveraging the structured data on the Web. Four major challenges are faced when considering structured Web data for ranking. These challenges are stated below and will be addressed in this thesis. From each challenge, we will derive one research question and provide a corresponding contribution in this thesis.

1.1 Challenges for Ranking for Web Data Search

Challenge 1: Evaluation. Measuring and monitoring progress and advances of new technologies requires repeatable and reliable evaluation methodologies. For the new setting of structured Web data, such evaluation methods for search need to be developed and a clear evaluation framework has to be defined to measure the effectiveness of search. Previous evaluation frameworks for classical IR tasks relied on expert assessments which are expensive to obtain or even inaccessible to many researchers. A new way to acquire users for specific tasks is crowdsourcing and this challenge comprises to investigate whether crowdsourcing is a feasible mean for the evaluation of structured Web data search.

Challenge 2: Hybrid data. Textual data is the primary form of data on the Web and increasingly supplemented by structured data. Search technology needs to deal with this hybrid data setting consisting of textual and structured data elements and has to consider both types of data. Further, structured elements may also be part of the query and may be taken into account when ranking search results.

Challenge 3: Heterogeneity. The structured data exhibited on the Web is typically heterogenous at the schema and the data level. Crossing differences at the schema and data level is essential to exploit the numerous Web data sources for search. Moreover, resolving the differences for each data source through manual data integration is costly, in particular on the Web where datasets are large and may change frequently.

Challenge 4: Redundancy. Exploiting the data from different sources and using them simultaneously for search, requires to cope with overlapping and redundant information in order to return concise and relevant results to users. Entities from different datasets may refer to the same real-world object, but are described using different schema attributes and values. Hence, data integration methods addressing redundancy and suitable ranking methods are necessary for effective search.

The above four challenges are different, but related parts of the overall research question of this thesis. In the next section we will clearly formulate this principal research question and break it down into four research questions, each derived from one of the above challenges.

3

1.2 Research Questions

The principal research question of this thesis is:

How can ranking techniques leverage structured Web data for effective search?

This broad research question entails the four main challenges as stated above and each of these challenges leads to one specific research question. Derived from each specific research question are hypotheses that are investigated in experiments. The challenges and the respective questions are consequences of each other and subsequently addressed in the remainder of this thesis:

Research Question 1. *Can crowd-sourced judges evaluate search over structured Web data in a repeatable and reliable way?*

The first research question is derived from Challenge 1 *Evaluation* and concerns the research methodology. It is a precondition for the subsequent work and is consequently examined first. Measuring the effectiveness of search in terms of the quality of its ranking requires repeatable and reliable evaluation methods. Rankings are assessed through relevance judgements that are usually obtained from experts. We investigate whether crowd-sourced judges can take on the task of assessing search results in a reliable and repeatable way and define an evaluation framework for the new structured Web data search in Chapter 3.

Research Question 2. *How can results consisting of structured and unstructured data be ranked by relevance for hybrid queries?*

Moving towards the core of the primary research questions, we address Challenge 2 with the above research question that was initial asked in the thesis proposal [76] leading to this work. Existing ranking techniques are based on the textual data on the Web that is now augmented with structured elements. Hence, the above question arises how the combination of both data types can be used for ranking. Further, structured data allows also structured querying in contrast to keyword queries and therefore the question is extended also to the query aspect. How can hybrid queries be considered in the ranking technique? We will investigated this research question in Chapter 4.

Research Question 3. *How can heterogenous web data from remote data sources be integrated into the local search process despite schema and data-level differences without prior data integration?*

Structured Web data originates from numerous sources across the Web and as stated in Challenge 3 is heterogenous on the schema and data level. Existing Web applications built on top of a local dataset may profit from external data. However, the heterogeneity of Web data prohibits ad-hoc integration of remote data. Especially, vertical search, i.e. the website or topic specific search, may profit by integrating complementary and additional data into the search process. However, data sources on the Web may change quickly and efforts for data integration must be kept small. Hence, we tackle this data integration problem caused by the heterogeneity of the data and address it from the search process perspective as raised by the following question that will be answered in Chapter 5.

Research Question 4. *Can we detect co-referent entities during the search process over multiple data sources without using training examples, i.e. in an unsupervised way and does consolidation of co-referent entities increase the effectiveness of search by considering co-references in the ranking procedure?*

The challenge of *Redundancy* is a direct consequence of search over several data sources. The advantage of covering more data sources may not just introduce complementary and additional but also redundant results that may diminish the benefits. Hence, overcoming heterogeneity alone is not enough. Consolidation of redundant results needs also to be addressed. This research question will be investigated in Chapter 6.

1.3 Scope of this Thesis

The topics covered in this thesis are spanned by the above research questions. The focus of the work is on the effectiveness of search, which aims at new ranking functions for the hybrid and heterogenous Web data setting and makes use of query-time data integration methods. The efficiency of search, primarily determined through indexing and query processing, is important and indispensable for the application of search, but outside the scope of this thesis. We will mention runtimes and general considerations of efficiency, but do not consider them in detail in the remainder of the thesis. The interested reader is referred to [99] for the corresponding work in this realm.

1.4 Research Paradigm and Methodology

The aforementioned research questions are addressed in this thesis through quantitive methods and empirical experimentation. In information system research, the paradigm underlying our research is known as *design science* [81]. *Design science* aims at solving relevant problems through design and creation of new, innovative artifacts providing solutions to the respective problems, rigorously evaluating these artifacts with respect to clear contributions and communicating the findings [81]. Guideline for documenting the results was Zobel (2004) [170], who defines writing, citation and style guidelines for computer science.

We designed and implemented new artifacts, each addressing a concrete problem formulated as a research question. Our artifacts are implementations of proposed solutions to the given problems and are designed based on clearly stated hypotheses. Each artifact is evaluated empirically through experimentation in controlled settings to assess its contributions with respect to the hypotheses. The standard evaluation methodology for traditional information retrieval systems is the so called *cranfield methodology* [42, 43]. Since we extend the information retrieval problem to structured Web data, we first work on extending this evaluation methodology accordingly to this new setting in Chapter 3 and apply the general methodology for the subsequent problems.

1.5 Contributions of this Thesis

This thesis comprises four main contributions which constitute the scientific accomplishment of the author. Each contribution results from the investigation of one research question and is detailed in its own chapter:

Contribution 1. *Evaluation Framework for Search over Structured Web Data based on Crowd-sourced Relevance Assessments*

We present an evaluation framework consisting of query sets, dataset, and relevance judgements obtained through crowd-sourcing. The framework is investigated with respect to repeatability and reliability and was applied in the Semantic Search Challenge in 2010 and 2011. We discussed the framework, its features and application previously in our papers [25, 26, 70]. A comprehensive discussion of our work will appear in [24]. In Chapter 3, we present a revised version of our work.

Contribution 2. *Ranking Model for Hybrid Queries over Hybrid Data*

We propose a general principled language model-based approach called *HybRank*, which enables the use of keywords, structured or hybrid queries to formulate information needs and incorporate them into the ranking of results including documents, structured data or their combination. We employ graph-structured models based on the RDF and SPARQL standard for both data and queries. In experiments using established benchmarks, which involve both document and data retrieval tasks, we show the best configuration of our approach using hybrid queries yields improvements of up to 23% upon state-of-the-art baselines. Contribution 2 is presented in Chapter 4. The general concepts and nature of the model is applied in the following chapters to address the subsequent challenges.

Contribution 3. *Heterogenous Web Data Search using On-The-Fly Data Integration*

We perform a systematic study of the two main prevailing strategies towards searching external heterogeneous data sources, keyword search and query rewriting through data integration. We propose a new approach based on language models that combines the advantages of both strategies. Our approach uses keyword search to cross schema differences and does not rely on upfront data integration. Further, we build a query-specific *Entity Relevance Model* (ERM) and employ it for computing mappings on the fly and leverage its structure also for ranking. Based on large-scale experiments using real-world datasets, we observe that the data integration approach consistently provides better results than keyword search. Our hybrid approach yields best results, outperforming keyword search by 120% and the data integration baseline by 54% on average in terms of Mean Average Precision. We have discussed this contribution in previously published papers [79, 80] and present a revised version of them in Chapter 5.

Contribution 4. *Federated Entity Search using On-The-Fly Consolidation*

We address the challenge of *Redundancy* for *federated entity search in uncooperative environments* on the Web and present an approach for entity consolidation at query time. Our novel method for entity consolidation uses the same conceptual framework as the aforementioned contributions, i.e. language models for representing entities and ranking and also a language model oriented metric for computing the similarity between entities. Our approach is completely unsupervised, which is a requirement for an uncooperative setting where training data is not available. We show how entity representation in combination with structured relevance models can be used to obtain a combined ranking of results returned from several sources. In the experiments, we employ real-world Web queries and data sources and investigate the effects of federated search in combination with consolidation. We show that our approach exceeds a state-of-the-art preference aggregation method for federated search [154] and show the advantages of consolidation for search in the federated search setting.

These four contributions collectively address the principal research question stated in Section 1.2 and show how structured data can be leveraged for ranking in order to increase the effectiveness of search.

1.6 Guide to the Reader

This thesis comprises seven chapters. Besides chapter 2, which provides the foundations and defines the main concepts used in the remainder, all following chapters are self-contained and cover one of the research question stated before. Each chapter starts with an introduction of the problem, restates the investigated research question, thereof derived hypotheses, and the contribution elaborated in this chapter. Then follows an overview of the proposed approach before it is discussed in detail and investigated in experiments. Related work and existing approaches are discussed in each chapter. The cited references are given at the end of the thesis in the bibliography. The thesis is structured as follows:

- **Chapter 2.** A brief introduction to the Web and data on the Web, as well as basic principles, techniques and definitions used in this thesis are explained in this chapter. Readers familiar to this research area may proceed to the following chapters.

- **Chapter 3.** We discuss an evaluation methodology for search over structured Web data and elaborate on an evaluation framework using crowdsourcing. This framework is investigated with respect to its reliability and repeatability.

- **Chapter 4.** We discuss a ranking model for hybrid queries and examine its performance for a document and a data retrieval task.

- **Chapter 5.** In this chapter, we investigate how external structured data sources can be integrated into the search process.

- **Chapter 6.** In this chapter, we show how several structured data sources can be queried simultaneously and how co-referent results are consolidated at query time. Further, we investigate the effects of federated search and of result consolidation on retrieval performance in this setting.

- **Chapter 7.** This chapter summarizes the thesis' results, concludes with a discussion on the results with respect to the addressed research question and gives an outlook on future research directions.

- **Bibliography.** All references cited in this thesis are listed here in alphabetical order by the surname of the first author followed by the lists of Figures, Tables, and Abbreviations.

Chapter 2

Foundations

In this chapter we introduce the areas of research and basic concepts, clarify how certain terms are used and define the terminology of this thesis. Definitions that are only used within one chapter and specific to the chapter's topic are given in the corresponding chapter. First, we elaborate on the Web of Data and introduce the main standards and practices. Second, we discuss search on the Web and the fundamental concepts applied for ranking. Thereafter, we discuss evaluation metrics used in the experiments throughout the thesis.

2.1 Web of Data

Before we dwell into standards and definitions, we take a look at the bigger picture and consider the *World Wide Web* as a whole, which we will refer to as the *Web* in the remainder. In the early 1990s, when the Web spread through increasing public access, the content available was foremost text based websites. Over time, more and more Web applications, rather simple at the beginning, appeared on the Web and provided information and services. These applications make data accessible through the Web that is stored in their databases. Collectively, the data hidden in these databases and only accessible through specific applications has been coined the *Deep Web*. In particular, the data of the Deep Web is not accessible to search engine crawlers or other applications. If the data was published on the Web then often inside HTML documents cluttered with layout or other markup information, which made the reuse even harder. On the contrary, clean structured data enables sophisticated processing of data. In order to make data reusable and to connect the scattered, isolated data silos on the Web, the idea of the Linked Data initiative is to transfer the concepts of linking data items instead of websites and thereby form the *Web of Data*. In a nutshell, the idea is to evolve the Web into a global data space [75]. The data published on the Web following this idea increases rapidly. Figure 2.1 illustrates interlinked datasets published as Linked Open Data. Each circle represents one data source on the Web and the arcs between the circles indicate the existing links between the data sources as of September 2011.

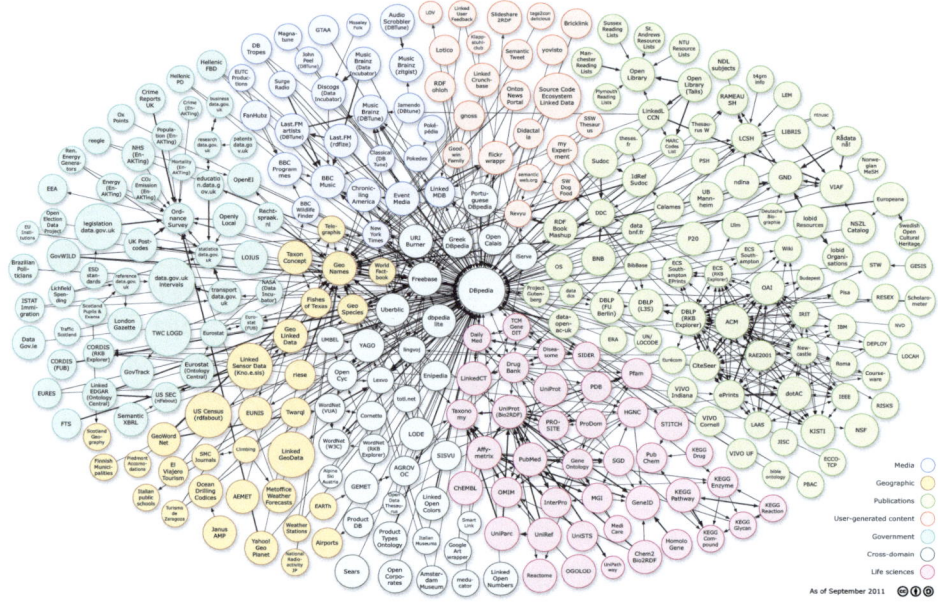

Figure 2.1: The Linking Open Data cloud[1]. Each circle represents one data source on the Web and the arcs between them indicate links between the linked data sources. The background color denote the domain of the data source.

2.1.1 RDF

Originally, the Resource Description Framework (RDF) [93, 112] was designed to describe meta data on the Web. Over time it developed into a cornerstone of the Semantic Web and is now the primary data model of the Semantic Web. The RDF data model is a directed, labeled graph with well-defined, formal semantics, which allows formal reasoning and inference. Its basic building blocks are statements in the form of ⟨*subject*, *predicate*, *objects*⟩, which are called *triples*. Each element of a triple is an *RDF Term*. An *RDF Term* is either a IRI, a Literal or a blank node. An Internationalized Resource

Identifier (IRI) is a generalized Uniform Resource Identifier (URI) [18]. A Literal is a data value, such as a string, a number, a geo coordinate, a date or others. A blank node is a local identifier within a defined scope. Given these elements, an RDF graph is defined as follows:

Definition 2.1 (RDF Graph). *An RDF Graph $G = (N, E)$ is a directed and labeled graph consisting of a set of nodes N and a set of edges E. The set of nodes N is a disjoint union of IRIs N_E, literals N_L, and blank nodes N_B, i.e. $N = N_E \cup N_L \cup N_B$. The set of edges E is a disjoint union $E = E_E \cup E_L$ of edges representing connections between identifiers, i.e. $a(e_i, e_j) \in E_E$, iff $e_i, e_j \in \{N_E \cup N_B\}$, and connections between identifiers and literals, i.e. $a(e_i, e_j) \in E_L$, iff $e_i \in \{N_E \cup N_B\}$ and $e_j \in N_L$.*

Figure 2.2 shows an example of an RDF graph describing two persons and two movies. Each arc together with the starting and targeting node represents one RDF triple.

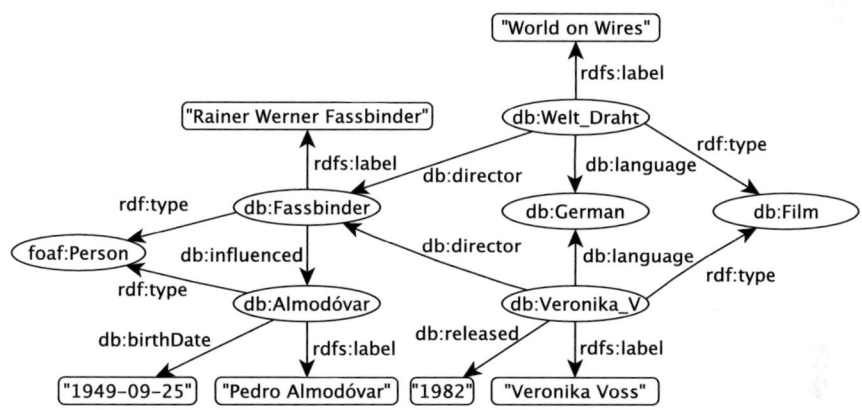

Figure 2.2: RDF Graph consisting of seven IRIs (elliptic shape), six literal values (rectangle shape) and labeled arcs denoting the relationships between the nodes. This graph describes two persons and two movies along with their attributes and relations between them.

RDF can be serialized in different notations. The most common syntaxes are *N-Triples* [63], *RDF/XML* [16], and *Turtle* [17]. RDF is a very general and flexible data model, which subsumes many other data models, e.g. the tree shaped data model of XML and the relational data model used in

---

[1]Linking Open Data cloud diagram by Richard Cyganiak and Anja Jentzsch. `http://lod-cloud.net/`, last retrieved on Feb 28th 2013.

relation databases [5] can also be expressed using RDF. This is an important features, because in general methods developed for RDF are also applicable for all subsumed data models. An extension of RDF introducing a fourth column to a triple and hence called *N-Quads*[2] has got wide usage within the Semantic Web community. The optional fourth column is used usually to store the context of the triple, e.g. provenance information about the triple.

Structured and Unstructured Data. We will refer to data published using RDF as well as data adhering to other standards, such as microformats[3], as *structured data* as opposed to *unstructured data*, which we use for data following no defined data model, i.e. usually unstructured data refers to texts in natural language.

The problems we will address in this thesis are situated in Web data scenarios and therefore the data of most interest to us is RDF data as defined before. However, for reasons of generality and simplicity, we employ a generic graph-based data model that omits specific RDF features such as blank nodes, because the use of blank nodes is still under discussion and they are not essential for the methods explained later. In order to keep a general terminology, we will use the terms data graph, entity, literal and attributes, respectively properties, and these notions correspond to their counterparts in RDF, i.e. entity nodes are RDF resources, literal nodes correspond to RDF literals, attributes are RDF properties, and edges stand for RDF triples. We now explicitly define the terms frequently used in the remainder and illustrate the definition with an example below:

Definition 2.2 (Entity). *Given a data graph G, according to Definition 2.1, we refer to each $e \in N_E$ as an entity.*

Definition 2.3 (Entity Description). *Given a data graph G, we call the bag of attribute-value edges $A(e_i) = \{a(e_i, e_j) \in E | e_i, e_j \in N_E \cup N_L\}$ the description of the entity e_i, and each $a \in A(e_i)$ is called an attribute of e_i.*

Definition 2.4 (Entity Model). *The set of distinct attribute labels of an entity e_i, i.e. $A'(e_i) = \{a | a(e_i, e_j) \in A(e_i)\}$, is called the model of e_i.*

Example 2.1 (Entity, Description, Model). *The data graph in Figure 2.2 contains seven entities, e.g. the entity* Welt_Draht. *This entity has four attributes, e.g. the attribute* language *with the value* German, *i.e.* language(Welt_Draht, German).

---

[2]http://sw.deri.org/2008/07/n-quads/, last retrieved on Feb 28th 2013
[3]http://microformats.org/ last retrieved on Feb 28 2013.

The description A of this entity consists of all four attributes A(Welt_Draht) = {label, director, language, type}. *Since this entity has only one edge per attribute type, its model A' is identical to its description A. Note, we have omitted the namespace prefix db in this example for simplicity reasons.*

2.1.2 SPARQL

SPARQL [72] is the standard query language for RDF data and specified as a W3C Recommendation[4]. Just like SQL for relational databases, SPARQL allows to formulate formal, precise, and crisp queries to retrieve information from RDF data in a database-like way. The SPARQL recommendation specifies various operators, filters, and expressions which allow expressive querying and updating of data also over multiple data sources. The most integral part of SPARQL and sufficient for the remainder of this thesis is the *Basic graph pattern (BGP)*. A basic graph pattern consists of a set of triple patterns. A triple pattern is a triple, where each of the three positions can hold a variable instead of an RDF Term. Figure 2.3 illustrates one example SPARQL query in syntax and as graphical notation. Given the data in Figure 2.2, this query would return the node db:Veronika_V for variable ?x.

  Structured and unstructured queries. In this thesis, we refer to a query expressed in a formal query language, e.g. SPARQL, or consisting of structural elements, e.g. attribute-value pairs, as a *structured query* whereas we use the term *unstructured query* synonymously with *keyword query*, i.e. a query consisting only of keywords.

2.1.3 Linked Data

RDF and SPARQL are definitions, but do not specify how they should be used when publishing data on the Web and in particular do not point out one of the strength of the RDF data model, which is linking data across domains and data sources. In this respect, Tim Berners-Lee wrote in his Design Issues[5]: "The Semantic Web isn't just about putting data on the web. It is about making links, so that a person or machine can explore the web of data". Emphasizing the aspect of linking data is driven by the previous

---

[4]Version 1.1 is still a *Proposed Recommendation* as of Dec 27th 2012.

[5]http://www.w3.org/DesignIssues/LinkedData.html last retrieved on Dec 27 2012.

SELECT ?x WHERE {
   ?x   rdf:type   db:Film .
   ?x   db:director   db:Fassbinder
   ?x   db:released   "1982" .
}

(a) syntax   (b) schematic

Figure 2.3: SPARQL query retrieving all *x* that are of the *type Film*, have the *director Fassbinder*, and are *released* in *1982*. The same query is displayed in syntax form and as a graphical visualization. *db* and *rdf* denote namespaces.

experience of the World Wide Web, where links are an integral building block allowing users to discover new content coined "surfing the Web". Transferring the same idea to data on the Web, Tim Berners-Lee defined the following four rules, which become known as the *Linked Data Principles*:

1. Use URIs as names for things.

2. Use HTTP URIs so that people can look up those names.

3. When someone looks up a URI, provide useful information, using the standards (RDF, SPARQL).

4. Include links to other URIs, so that they can discover more things.

The first principles requires proper identifiers using the Uniform Resource Identifiers [18], respectively IRIs as defined above. There might be several or even numerous identifiers for the very same entity. However, the identifiers are unambiguous and the second principle allows to clarify what the identifier refers to by dereferencing the URI via an HTTP lookup. Principle three suggests to use standards so that the returned data can easily be interpreted. The nature of the *linked* data is expressed in the fourth principle, which encourages to link to other URIs.

Linked *Open* Data. Considerable attention in recent years, not just in the academic but also in the public discourse, got the idea of *Open Data* referring to data accessible under an open license such as CC-BY[6]. Data following the above principles and available under an open license are referred to as *Linked Open Data*.

---

[6]http://creativecommons.org/licenses/by/2.0/, last retrieved on Dec 27 2012.

2.1.4 Heterogenous Web Data

The RDF as well as the Linked Data principles are standards for modeling and publishing data on the Web. However, users can use their own vocabulary to model and describe their data. Although the reuse of vocabularies is an often applied good practice, the data on the Web exhibits a diverse usage of vocabularies and concepts. Figure 2.4 illustrates an example of three entities modeled in RDF using different schema vocabularies as well as different ways to express the same content on the data level, e.g. the left entity e_a uses the attribute *Actors* to link to a literal contains the names of actors, whereas entity e_d uses *starring* to link to entities representing actors. Moreover, real Web data suffers also from nonconforming or erroneous usage of standards requiring error tolerant methods in practice. However, we disregard this latter aspect and will address the inherent heterogeneity of Web data.

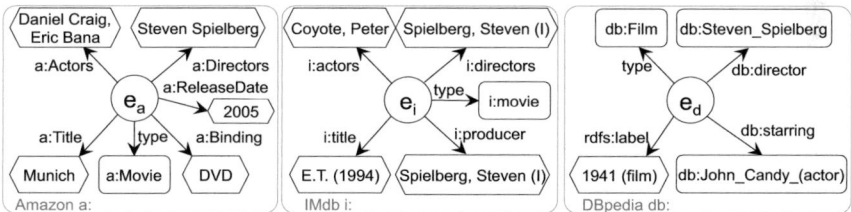

Figure 2.4: Data heterogeneity on the Web. Entities from three different Web datasets are represented differently at the schema level (e.g. *actors* vs. *starring*) and data level (e.g. *Spielberg, Steven* vs. *Steven Spielberg*).

2.2 Search

The term *search* is used in different contexts in computer science. The classical use of the term *search* in computer science refers to the discipline of algorithmic discovery of items in previously unseen data, e.g. the search for a character in a string or for a node in a network. Knuth profoundly elaborated algorithms and their features for search in this context [94].

Information Retrieval (IR). The main field of research of this thesis is *information retrieval* and we refer to the term *search* in this context. Here, *search* means the retrieval of textual artifacts commonly referred to as documents, i.e. unstructured data in our parlance, from large collections for a given information need. The aim of an IR system is to satisfy the information need, which is usually expressed through a keyword query. Keyword queries may be imprecise and ambiguous and an IR system faces additionally the challenges of keyword mismatch and information overload.

Data retrieval. According to Baeza-Yates and Ribeiro-Neto [7] IR is different to *data retrieval* in the sense that data retrieval, as applied for example in relation databases (DB), is a precise and crisp technique using well-defined data structures and semantics. Missing or erroneously retrieving a data object is considered a failure for a data retrieval system, whereas an IR system aims at satisfying an often imprecisely described information need with best effort results through ranked results.

DB&IR. Based on the observation that many applications need aspects of both worlds, DB and IR, the endeavor to combine them, known as DB&IR integration, got increasing attention in both communities [13, 34, 160, 161]. Some times DB&IR is used to refer to XML retrieval [4], because it is regarded as semistructured data and shares structured as well as unstructured aspects. However, we understand DB&IR in a broader sense and not specified through a particular technology such as XML. This thesis, although primarily located in the field of IR and Semantic Web research, follows this notion and aims to contribute towards the goal of DB&IR integration through what we call *Web data search*.

2.2.1 Web Data Search

The most prominent use case of IR techniques and known to virtually everybody using the web is *web search*. Web search comprises all aspects of information retrieval and additionally requires crawling data from the Web and taking web specific features, such as the link structure of the Web, into account. The result of a web search is a list of links (with short summaries) pointing to websites that may satisfy the information need.

In Chapter 1 and at the beginning of this section, we have described how structured data is published on the Web and that the textual data is supplemented with more and more structured data on the Web. Given this new setting, we define the task of searching over this combination of data and in particular considering the structured data as *Web data search*:

Definition 2.5 (Web Data Search).
Web data search is the task of addressing an information need with Web data consisting of interlinked artifacts comprising structured and/or unstructured data.

Web data search shares the same nature with information retrieval in the sense that it aims to satisfy information needs through ranked retrieval and does not guarantee the crispness and correctness of data retrieval in the database sense. However, the results returned for a search request are neither a list of links nor documents, but data combinations that may directly satisfy the information need. Further, the structured elements may not only be considered on the data level for Web data search, but also on the query level. Augmenting keyword queries with structure information is one optional aspect of Web data search.

If we focus on structured elements of Web data or even exclusively apply them for search, we will use the term *structured Web Data search* to emphasize this setting.

2.2.2 Semantic Search

Semantic Search as described in our previous work [68, 150] is defined as a search process using a semantic model that captures entities their attributes and relations between entities. This semantic model is used in the search process to abstract from the syntactic level to the level of meaning through interpreting search requests and data resources with the help of the model. Typical implementations of such a model are established on the basis of an RDF graph and often all search approaches build on top of RDF are referred to as semantic search. However, semantic search does not necessarily entail a Web context although many approaches to semantic search build on top of the standards and techniques developed in the Semantic Web community, such as RDF, but also OWL [64] and other formats of ontologies [145].

In this thesis, we make use of structured Web Data that complies with RDF and use structured models built from entities and their attributes in combination with relevance feedback to interpret information needs against the these models. Hence, our work is in the realm of semantic search. However, we do not use advanced techniques to infer the meaning of queries which could be conducted using reasoning on RDF. Therefore we refer to our work as *(structured) Web data search* and regard it as a basis for more advanced semantic search techniques.

2.2.3 Ranking

While the term *search* refers to the entire search process in our opinion, from collecting data, indexing, retrieval, ranking, presentation and to result refinement, the term *ranking* is one integral part of any kind of *search* and a core method determining the effectiveness of the process. We define ranking in this thesis as follows:

Definition 2.6 (Ranking). *Ranking is the algorithmic decision on how relevant an information artifact is for a given information need and the sorting of artifacts by their concluded relevancy.*

Whether an information artifact is relevant to the information need or not can only be decided by the human user. The computational ranking algorithm tries to approximate the users's perception of relevance by estimating the relevance of artifacts, in order to first present the most relevant ones to the user. Relevance is an abstract concept comprising many aspects such as aboutness, importance, topicality, freshness, correctness, comprehensiveness, and depends also to some extent on how the artifact is presented to the user in terms of understandability. A more in depth discussion of relevance can be found in [100].

2.2.4 Relevance Feedback

Relevance feedback refers to a query reformulation technique. The underlying idea is to modify the initial user query into a modified query so that more relevant documents are returned by the retrieval system. Relevance feedback was first introduced by [134] as cited in [7] and has been applied since then in many retrieval tasks and systems [135] and proved to be an effective technique [71]. Relevance feedback is a two step process. First, the initial user query is received by the system and then relevance feedback is obtained and used to reformulate the query, which is then processed to obtain the final results. The obtained feedback is used to reformulate the query, which is usually a query expansion by adding additional terms obtained from the feedback.

Two main types of approaches are distinguished for obtaining relevance feedback [7]: explicit feedback and implicit feedback. Explicit feedback is the feedback, if the users is explicitly involved in the feedback process, e.g. by selecting relevant documents or through the usage of user clicks on documents. Implicit feedback refers to feedback processes without user involvement. For implicit feedback, often also referred to as *pseudo relevance feedback*, the system acquires feedback from either external resources, such as thesauri, or from extracting feedback from the top-ranked results obtained for the initial user query.

In this thesis, only the latter type of *Pseudo Relevance Feedback (PRF)* is applied and we refer to *pseudo relevance feedback* when using the notion relevance feedback without further specification.

Relevance feedback techniques have been proposed for all major retrieval models, such as the boolean retrieval model or the probabilistic retrieval model [135]. In the context of this thesis, the relevance feedback for language models [101, 164] is most important and provides the basis for the retrieval techniques discussed in the remainder of the thesis. Besides the feedback consisting of terms, which is common for document retrieval tasks, the notion of *structural feedback* is important in this thesis. We define *structural feedback* as the feedback consisting of information on the structure of the data in contrast to the usual feedback on the content of data. A first approach of using structured information for retrieval using relevance based language models has been proposed by [102]. A more detailed discussion of relevance feedback for language models and of [101, 102] will be provided in Chapter 4.

2.2.5 Language Models

Statistical Language Models are basic concepts of computational linguistics and have been applied for natural language processing [110], speech recognition [89] and since the late 1990 also for information retrieval [129, 163]. Language models are used to model sequences of words with statistical means. For a given sequence of words, a language model tries to estimate the next word following that given sequence. Depending on the length of the sequence that are considered in the model, the models are called *unigram*, *bigram*,... or in general *n-gram language models*. Unigram language models assume that each word occurs independently and disregard the context. Although this is a strong assumption, these models are usually applied for information retrieval task, since higher order models are more complex and have shown only slight improvements over unigram models [62, 144]. For the remainder of this thesis, we will use the term language model to refer to unigram language models.

Formally, a language model θ is a multinomial distribution[7] over a vocabulary $\mathcal{V}$ assigning a probability $P(w|\theta)$ to each word $w \in \mathcal{V}$ of the vocabulary. The underlying probability space consists of a sample space Ω, which are all possible words, a set of the events $\mathcal{V}$, which are the words of the vocabulary

---

[7]There is also work on multiple Bernoulli and Poisson models, which are not applied in this thesis. We refer the interest reader to [163].

$\mathcal{V}$, and the language model θ assigning a probability to the words of the vocabulary with $\sum_{w \in \mathcal{V}} P(w|\theta) = 1$. Language models can also be understood as finite automata [111], which generate words with the corresponding probabilities. The notion of a language model generating a word is based on the view of a language model as an automata.

Regarding the notation, we use the subscript to denote the corpus for which a language model is estimated, e.g. θ_Q is the language model estimated for query Q. Whenever it is obvious that the language model is meant and not the corpus itself, we may drop the θ later in the thesis and simply write $P(w|Q)$ instead of $P(w|\theta_Q)$ in order to keep equations simple and easy to read.

Maximum Likelihood Estimation. Language models assign probabilities to words and there are several ways how these probabilities can be estimated [110]. The most common estimation technique applied in IR is the *maximum likelihood estimation*. The maximum likelihood estimation uses the relative frequency of events observed in the training corpus, e.g. a document, as their probability. Since this method sets the probability to zero for all events unseen in the training corpus and assigns the whole probability mass to the observed events, it is called maximum likelihood estimation.

Smoothing. When applying the maximum likelihood estimation in practice, a lot of events may occur that are not part of a model and are consequently treated with a probability of zero which causes undesired effects. This problem of data sparseness is addressed for language models by *smoothing*, which assigns some probability mass to unseen events. Furthermore, language models for IR are usually sampled from rather small corpora, such as documents or queries, and therefore their estimates are rather coarse. Several smoothing methods for language models have been proposed, the most wide spread techniques and used in this thesis are Jelinek-Mercer Smoothing, also called interpolation, and Dirichlet Prior Smoothing [163, 165]. Both techniques use a background model θ_C, which is usually sampled from the entire document collection and therefore often called collection model. Analogously, to the document model above a collection model can be sampled using the relative frequency of a word in the entire collection: $P(w|\theta_C) = \frac{c(w,C)}{|C|}$, where $c(w,C)$ denotes the count of w in the collection C.

When smoothing a document model using the Jelinek-Mercer interpolation, a parameter $\lambda \in (0,1)$ controls the influence of the collection model on the smoothed document model, see Equation 2.1:

$$P(w|\theta_D) = (1 - \lambda)\frac{c(w,D)}{|D|} + \lambda P(w|\theta_C) \qquad (2.1)$$

The Dirichlet Prior smoothing uses the parameter μ to set the amount of smoothing, see Equation 2.2. This method differs from the above by taking the length of the document $|D|$ into account, given a constant μ. Consequently, the influence of the collection model is greater for shorter documents and smaller for longer documents. The parameter μ is set to values around 2000 for document retrieval [165]. Note that for each value of μ an equivalent λ exists, so that both methods yield the same outcome, e.g. for $\lambda = 0.5 \Leftrightarrow \mu = |D|$.

$$P(w|\theta_D) = \frac{c(w,D) + \mu P(w|\theta_C)}{|D| + \mu} \qquad (2.2)$$

The advantage of Jelinek-Mercer method is that the parameter λ is more intuitive and hence easier to tune, where as the Dirichlet approach has the advantage of adapting to the document length. Which method performs better for IR depends surprisingly on verbosity and length of the queries [165].

Language models for Information Retrieval. In essence, there are three ways to apply language models for IR, in order to rank documents for a given user query [111]. The three different types are illustrated in Figure 2.5 and briefly discussed in the following:

(1) When a language model is sampled for each document in the collection, the documents can be ranked with respect to a user query in the order of how likely their models generate the query terms. The document whose model is most likely to produce the query terms is ranked first. This kind of ranking using language models is called *query likelihood*.

(2) Analogously, a language model can be constructed for the query and used to rank documents in the order how likely the terms of a document are generated by that query model, which is called *document likelihood*.

(3) A third way is to construct language models for both, query and documents, and compare the models. The general assumption is that the closer (or the more similar) a document model is to the query model, the more relevant is the document and the higher is its rank. The comparison of query and document model is essentially the comparison of two probability density functions. Many metrics for measuring the difference of two probability

density functions have been proposed [33]. We will discuss those applied in this thesis in the following paragraph.

We will adapt the third way of comparing models against each other in the remainder of this thesis, because we build on the work of relevance feedback using language models [101, 164], which uses the query model to incorporate the feedback and compares them against the document models.

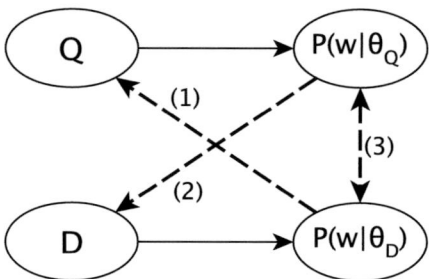

Figure 2.5: Language Models approaches for IR: (1) Query likelihood, (2) Document likelihood, (3) Model comparison (Figure from [111])

2.2.6 Measuring the difference between Language Models

Language Models are essentially discrete probability distributions over a vocabulary and therefore comparing two language models is the task of measuring the difference between two probability distributions. Many different methods have been proposed for the comparison of probability distributions using their probability density functions [33]. Most commonly applied for IR tasks are following three techniques, which will be applied later in this thesis:

Kullback-Leibler Divergence (KLD).   The KLD (also known as *relative entropy*) is a common measure in information theory and originally used to assess the quality of encodings by measuring the difference between a modeled probability distribution used to approximate a true probability distribution [110]. The KLD is not a metric (therefore called "divergence"), because it is asymmetric and also does not satisfy the triangle inequality [110]. Consequently, the values of KLD are not comparable for different combinations of distributions. Still, it allows to determine an ordinal scale with respect to one probability distribution, which is enough for ranking in IR, where the probability distributions of the documents are compared against the one of the query.

Given two language models θ_Q and θ_D, i.e. discrete probability distributions over the vocabulary V, the KLD is defined in Equation 2.3:

$$
\begin{aligned}
KLD(\theta_Q||\theta_D) &= \sum_{w \in V} P(w|\theta_Q) \log_2 \frac{P(w|\theta_Q)}{P(w|\theta_D)} \quad (2.3) \\
&= \sum_{w \in V} P(w|\theta_Q) \log_2 P(w|\theta_Q) - \sum_{w \in V} P(w|\theta_Q) \log_2 P(w|\theta_D) \quad (2.4)
\end{aligned}
$$

When inspecting Equation 2.4, we observe that the first (left) sum depends only on the query model θ_Q. Hence, it has no influence on the ranking order of documents and can be omitted. The remaining second (right) sum is known as the cross entropy and often used instead of the KLD, because it produces an equivalent ranking.

Cross Entropy (H). The cross entropy between two discrete probability distributions θ_Q and θ_D is defined in Equation 2.5:

$$
H(\theta_Q||\theta_D) = - \sum_{w \in V} P(w|\theta_Q) \log_2 P(w|\theta_D) \quad (2.5)
$$

Jensen-Shannon Divergence (JSD). The Jensen-Shannon divergence is based on the *Kullback-Leibler divergence* (KLD). The JSD however has the advantages of being symmetric, bounded ($0 \leq JSD \leq 1$), smoothed and its square root is a metric [61, 127]. Hence, we will apply $\sqrt{JSD}$ later in this thesis whenever we need a metric in order to compare scores.

Given the probability distributions θ_Q, θ_D and $\theta_R = \frac{1}{2}\theta_Q + \frac{1}{2}\theta_D$, the JSD is defined in Equation 2.6:

$$
JSD(\theta_Q||\theta_D) = \frac{1}{2}KLD(\theta_Q||\theta_R) + \frac{1}{2}KLD(\theta_D||\theta_R) \quad (2.6)
$$

2.3 Metrics

We address the research questions of this thesis through empirical experimentation. In following section, we briefly discuss the metrics used in the experiments. First, we discuss the ranking metrics and then metrics to assess the inter-rater agreement used to determine the quality of relevance assessments.

2.3.1 Ranking Metrics

Assessing the effectiveness of ranking functions is the most common evaluation task in IR and central to this thesis. The metrics discussed here take values in $(0,1)$ with 1 denoting the best performance. All metrics are computed with `trec_eval`[8], the official tool of the TREC campaigns [157]. We briefly discuss the metrics used later in the experiments. For further metrics and a more detailed discussion, we refer the reader to Manning et. al. [111]. We discuss the metrics and illustrate them with a simple example. In this Example 2.2 and the remainder of this section we use the term *item* to denote the units of retrieval. In the standard retrieval scenario an item is a document. However, an item may also be an entity (Chapter 3, 4, and 5), an annotated document (Chapter 4), or sets of entities (Chapter 4 and 6). The general evaluation method remains the same. Each item is assessed for its relevancy and given these relevance assessments the metrics below are computed to evaluate the ranking effectiveness. Relevance assessments can be binary, i.e. either *relevant* or *non-relevant*. However, also more fine grained relevance scales have been investigated [92] and we will apply a three point scale in Chapter 3. When applying binary metrics for graded relevance assessments, the grades have to be partitioned into a relevant and non-relevant grades, i.e. a binary set.

Example 2.2 (Ranking metrics). *Figure 2.6 illustrates two ranked result lists. Each list holds the items retrieved for a query in the ranked order. Relevant items have a gray and non-relevant ones a white background. The ranked list of query q_1 holds five items ($n_1 = 5$) of which only the one on rank 2 is relevant. For query q_2 the ranked lists contains four items ($n_2 = 4$). Further, we assume that the retrieval system missed some relevant items, which are displayed below the ranked list. For query q_1 the system did not retrieve two relevant items and for q_2 the system missed one relevant item. Hence, in total there are three relevant items for query q_1, $|R_1| = 3$, and $|R_2| = 4$ relevant items for q_2. We continue this example by computing the discussed metrics for this example in the remainder of this section.*

Precision at Rank k (P@k). Precision at Rank k (P@k) is the fraction of relevant items from the top of the ranked list until rank k. A specific variation is

---

[8]`http://trec.nist.gov/trec_eval`, Version 9.0, last retrieved on April 5th 2013.

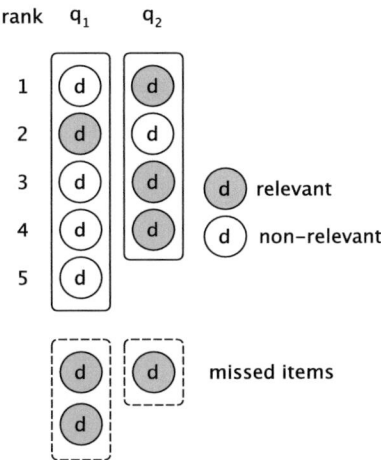

Figure 2.6: Illustration of the two ranked result lists of Example 2.2. The ranked result list for query q_1 contains five items with only one item (gray) on rank 2 being relevant. The ranked result list for query q_2 contains four items of which three are relevant. Below the lists are the items displayed that are missed by the retrieval system.

the *$\mathcal{R}$-precision (P@$\mathcal{R}$)* that is the precision at rank $\mathcal{R}$ where $\mathcal{R} = |R_i|$ is the total count of relevant items for query q_i. Precision without a specified k is the fraction of relevant items in the entire set of retrieved items. Precision is a binary measure and does not take the rank of the items into account, which can be observed in the example below. For both queries the precision at 2 has the same value, although the rank order of the first two items is different as illustrated in Figure 2.6.

Continuing Example 2.2, we compute the precision values as follows:
For query q_1: P@2 $= \frac{1}{2}$, P@4 $= \frac{1}{4}$, $\mathcal{R}$-precision $=$ P@3 $= \frac{1}{3}$, Precision $= \frac{1}{5}$
For query q_2: P@2 $= \frac{1}{2}$, P@4 $= \frac{3}{4}$, $\mathcal{R}$-precision $=$ P@4 $= \frac{3}{4}$, Precision $= \frac{3}{4}$

Recall metric (Recall). Recall is the fraction of relevant items retrieved from all relevant items. The recall has the same value as the *$\mathcal{R}$-precision*. For large datasets it is hard, if not infeasible, to determine all relevant items for a query. In practice, only results up to a certain rank r are assessed or results of several systems are pooled and then assessed. Analogously to precision, recall can also be computed for the first k ranks.

Continuing Example 2.2, we compute the recall values as follows:
For query q_1: recall $= \frac{1}{3}$
For query q_2: recall $= \frac{3}{4}$

Mean Reciprocal Rank (MRR).   Mean Reciprocal Rank (MRR) is the reciprocal rank (RR) of the first relevant item averaged over all queries $q \in Q$, see Equation 2.7. MRR is a binary metric and obviously MRR takes the rank into account, however only at one point of the ranked list.

$$MRR(Q) = \frac{1}{|Q|} \sum_{q \in Q} \frac{1}{relrank(q)} \tag{2.7}$$

with $relrank(q)$ being the rank of the first relevant item retrieved for query q.

Continuing Example 2.2, we compute the MRR values as follows:
For query q_1: RR $= \frac{1}{2}$
For query q_2: RR $= 1$
For the query set $Q = \{q_1, q_2\}$: MRR $= \frac{1}{2}(\frac{1}{2} + 1) = 0.75$

Mean Average Precision (MAP).   Mean Average Precision (MAP) is a widely used, binary measure that takes the entire list into account and averages over a set of queries. MAP is defined in Equation 2.8, where R_i is the set of relevant items for query $q_i \in Q$, $\mathbb{1}_{R_i}(k)$ is an indicator function denoting whether the item on rank k is relevant, $P@k$ is the precision at rank k as defined before:

$$MAP(Q) = \frac{1}{|Q|} \sum_{i=1}^{|Q|} \frac{1}{|R_i|} \sum_{k=1}^{n_i} P@k \cdot \mathbb{1}_{R_i}(k) \tag{2.8}$$

Continuing Example 2.2, we compute the MAP values as follows:
For query q_1: AP $= \frac{1}{3}(\frac{1}{2}) = \frac{1}{6}$
For query q_2: AP $= \frac{1}{4}(1 + \frac{2}{3} + \frac{3}{4}) = \frac{29}{48}$
For the query set $Q = \{q_1, q_2\}$: MAP $= \frac{1}{2}(\frac{1}{6} + \frac{29}{48}) = \frac{37}{96} = 0.3854$

Normalized Discounted Cumulative Gain (NDCG).   Normalized Discounted Cumulative Gain (NDCG) is an evaluation metrics that takes the entire ranked list and also graded relevance assessments into account [87].

The metrics sums the gain (usually the relevance grade) for each item discounted by the rank of the item and normalizes the sum against an ideal ranking that perfectly ranks the items by gain with the highest gain first. NDCG is currently the state-of-the-art metric and increasingly replaces MAP as the primary metric of official evaluation campaigns such as TREC[9] [157]. NDCG is defined in Equation 2.9 with $iDCG$ being the ideal DCG value of a perfectly ranked list, $gain(k)$ is the gain of the item on rank k, which is discounted by $log_2(1+k)$. Note, there are several variations of NDCG in the literature using different gain and discount functions. We apply NDCG as described in [87] and implemented in `trec_eval`[8] :

$$NDCG = \frac{1}{iDCG} \sum_{k=1}^{n} \frac{gain(k)}{log_2(1+k)} \tag{2.9}$$

Continuing Example 2.2, we assume the gain function in Equation 2.10. In this example we use a binary relevance scale for simplicity reasons (which is by coincident identical to the indicator function used above). However, a graded relevance scale with more gain levels can be applied as well.

$$gain(k) = \begin{cases} 1 & \text{if the item on rank } k \text{ is relevant} \\ 0 & \text{if the item on rank } k \text{ is not relevant} \end{cases} \tag{2.10}$$

Continuing Example 2.2, we compute the NDCG values using the above gain function. First, we compute the observed discounted cumulative gain (DCG) and second, the ideal (iDCG):

For query q_1:
$DCG_1 = \frac{1}{log_2(1+2)}) = 0.6309$
$iDCG = 1 + \frac{1}{log_2(1+2)} + \frac{1}{log_2(1+3)} = 2.1309$
$NDCG_{q_1} = \frac{0.6309}{2.1309} = 0.2961$

For query q_2:
$DCG = 1 + \frac{1}{log_2(1+3)} + \frac{1}{log_2(1+4)} = 1.9306$
$iDCG = 1 + \frac{1}{log_2(1+2)} + \frac{1}{log_2(1+3)} + \frac{1}{log_2(1+4)} = 2.5616$
$NDCG_{q_2} = \frac{1.9306}{2.5616} = 0.7537$

For the query $Q = \{q_1, q_2\}$:
$NDCG_Q = \frac{1}{2}(0.2961 + 0.7537) = 0.5249$

---

[9]`http://trec.nist.gov` last retrieved on April 4th 2013

2.3.2 Inter-rater Reliability

The aforementioned ranking metrics are based on relevance assessments. These relevance assessments are obtained from raters (also called judges) who inspect the items and then decide the relevance grade on a given scale, e.g. whether an item is *not relevant, somewhat relevant,* or *highly relevant* as shown in Figure 6.5a. A common way to ensure that the results are reliable is to ask several raters to assess one item. Given several assessments for one item, one final aggregated assessment is usually obtained by *majority vote.* However, in order to be certain whether the assessments are reliable, i.e. consistent, an analysis of all obtained assessments is needed. In the following, we briefly discuss the most common statistical reliability measures.

κ**-Statistics.** Widely used to assess the agreement of raters are the so called κ-statistics. An early and the simplest measure is Cohen's κ [46], which determines the agreement between two raters, who judged both all items. A $\kappa > 0$ indicates agreement and $\kappa = 1$ would be perfect agreement, whereas $\kappa < 0$ denote disagreement. There is no definitive meaning to the actual κ-values between 0 and 1. In practice values of around $\kappa \approx 0.5$ are considered to be moderate and acceptable agreement. A drawback of Cohen's κ is the limitation to two raters and in practice it is often not feasible that each judge rates all items, in particular for large evaluation tasks. This shortcoming is solved by Fleiss's κ [60], which allows several judges and does not assume that each judge rates all items. However, Fleiss's κ assumes a fixed number of assessments per item. We will later in Chapter 3 report values for these measure, because they are widely used in the literature. However, both measure fall short on several accounts such as proper consideration of absences of ratings and systematic bias of raters that are discussed in detail by Krippendorff [96].

Krippendorff's α. Krippendorff's α is a flexible reliability measure applicable regardless of the number of raters, items and assessments per item. In particular, it can deal with the absence and varying counts of assessments per item. There are variations of Krippendorff's α for nominal, ordinal, interval, circular and other metrics for rating categories [97], which allows to compare α values across different numbers of raters, items and relevance grades [96], which is an advantage over the previous κ measures. Also, the measure allows to detect agreement ($\alpha > 0$) as well as opposite assessments ($\alpha < 0$), in general values of $\alpha > 0.66$ can be considered as acceptable agreement [74].

Chapter 3

A Framework for Evaluation of Search over Structured Web Data

Measuring progress of system design requires a rigorous evaluation methodology which quantifies the performance of the systems with respect to a given research question and thereby allows to compare the systems and to monitor advances. Essential characteristics of a sound evaluation methodology are reliability and repeatability, which allow to draw conclusions on the observed results and to apply the methodology later in time again to reproduce the results. Given these features, an evaluation framework instantiating such an methodology will only be effective in terms of establishing reference results, if it is accepted and widely employed by the community of practice. In this chapter, we address the research question how search over structured web data can be evaluated and present an evaluation framework, which builds upon the standard methodology of Information Retrieval, the so called *Cranfield* methodology [42, 43], instantiates the concepts of Pound et al. [130] for evaluating object search, has the remarkable features of using crowd-sourcing to obtain relevance judgements and has been employed in the Semantic Search Challenge 2010 and 2011. The presented evaluation framework is investigated with respect to reliability and repeatability and in particular on the feasibility of using crowd-sourcing to obtain judgements. Our results show that the proposed evaluation framework is indeed reliable and repeatable and that crowdsourcing is not just feasible, but also fast and inexpensive.

Outline. The introduction to evaluation in Section 3.1 leads to the research question, the hypotheses, and an outline of the contributions presented this chapter in Section 3.2. We discuss related work in Section 3.3, before we present the evaluation framework in Section 3.4 where we discuss its details and components. How the evaluation framework can be instantiated is detailed in Section 3.5, where we also examine its reliability and repeatability. In Section 3.6, we report on the Semantic Search Challenge, held in 2010 and 2011, and show the applicability of our evaluation framework in practice. Finally, we conclude this chapter on evaluation methodology in Section 3.7.

3.1 Introduction

There exist a wide range of semantic search solutions targeting different tasks – from using semantics captured in structured data for enhancing document representation and *document retrieval* [32, 38, 39, 146] to processing keyword search queries and natural language questions directly over structured data [65, 126, 149].

In general, the term 'semantic search' is highly contested, primarily because of the perpetual and endemic ambiguity around the term 'semantics.' While 'search' is understood to be some form of information retrieval, 'semantics' typically refers to the interpretation of some syntactic structure to another structure, the 'semantic' structure, that more explicitly defines the meaning that is implicit in the surface syntax. Already in the early days of information retrieval (IR) research, *thesauri* capturing senses of words in the form of concepts and their relationships were used [156]. More recently, the large and increasing amount of structured data that are embedded in Web pages or available as publicly accessible datasets constitute another popular type of semantic structure. The advantage here is that these data are commonly represented in *RDF* (Resource Description Framework), a standard knowledge representation formalism recommended by the W3C. RDF is a flexible graph-structured model that can capture the semantics embodied in information networks, social networks as well as (semi-)structured data in databases. Data represented in RDF is composed of subject-predicate-object *triples*, where the subject is an identifier for a resource (e.g. a real-world object), the predicate an identifier for a relationship, and the object is either an identifier of another resource or some information given as a concrete value (e.g. a string or data-typed value). As opposed to the wide range of proprietary models that have been used to capture semantics in the past, RDF provides a standardized vehicle for representation, exchange and usage, resulting in a large and increasing amount of publicly and Web-accessible data that can be used for search (e.g. Linked Data).

The explicit semantics captured by these structures have been used by semantic search systems for different tasks (e.g. document and data retrieval). More specifically, it can be used for enhancing the representation of the information needs (queries) and resources (documents, objects). While this helps dealing with the core task of search, i.e., *matching* information needs against resources, it has been shown that semantics can be beneficial throughout the broader *search process* [150], from the specification of the needs in terms of queries to matching queries against resources and ranking results, to refining the information needs and up to the presentation and analysis of results.

While there is active research in this field of semantic search, it has been concluded in plenary discussions at the Semantic Search 2009 workshop that the lack of *standardized evaluation* has become a serious bottleneck to further progress in this field. One of the principle reasons for the lack of a standardized evaluation campaign is the *cost* of creating a new and realistically sized "gold-standard" dataset and conducting annual evaluation campaign was considered too high by the community.

In response to this conclusion, we elaborate on an approach for *semantic search evaluation* that is based on crowdsourcing. In this work we show that crowdsourcing-based evaluation is not only *affordable* but in particular, it satisfies the criteria of *reliability* and *repeatability* that are essential for a standardized evaluation framework. We organized public evaluation campaigns over two years at the SemSearch workshops and tested the proposed evaluation framework. While the main ideas behind our crowdsourcing-based evaluation may be extended and generalized to the general case (i.e., other semantic search tasks), the kind of semantic search we have focused on in the last two campaigns were keyword search over structured data in RDF. We were motivated by the increasing need to locate particular information quickly and effectively and in a way that is accessible to non-expert users. In particular, the semantic search task of interest is similar to the classic ad-hoc document retrieval retrieval task, where the goal is to retrieve a ranked list of (text) documents from a fixed corpus in response to free-form keyword queries. In accordance to ad-hoc document retrieval, we define the semantic search task of *ad-hoc object retrieval* [130], where the goal is to retrieve a ranked list of objects (also referred to as resources or entities) from a collection of RDF documents in response to free-form keyword queries. The unit of retrieval is thus individual entities and not RDF documents, and so the task differs from classic textual information retrieval insofar as the primary unit is structured data rather than unstructured textual data. In particular, we focus on the tasks of *entity search*, which is about one specific named entity, and *list search*, which is about a set of entities.

3.2 Research Question and Contribution

Given the need of a standardized, reliable and repeatable evaluation framework for search over RDF data, the main research question of this chapter is:

Research Question 1. *Can crowd-sourced judges evaluate search over structured Web data in a repeatable and reliable way?*

To address this research question, we propose an evaluation framework in this chapter and examine it with respect to the following two hypotheses:

Hypothesis 1.1. *Evaluation results obtained through crowdsourced relevance assessments are repeatable, i.e. the same level of agreement between judges is observed at different points in time and the ordering of systems based on evaluation metrics computed with these relevance assessments remains the same.*

As mentioned earlier, repeatability is a crucial attribute of an evaluation methodology. In the context of an evaluation campaign when measuring the performance of different systems or when measuring the progress from an earlier version of a system to a newer version, it is required that the ranking of the systems remains the same. In our context, repeatability means that crowd-sourced judges produce the same relevance assessment at different points in time. Since we can not assume that the very same judges will perform the task again, we have to examine, if the judges are interchangeable.

Hypothesis 1.2. *Evaluation results obtained through crowdsourced relevance assessments are reliable, i.e. assessments by expert judges and assessments crowd-source judges yield a high agreement, so that ordering of systems based on evaluation metrics computed with relevance assessments of either expert judges or crowdsourced judges is the same.*

This hypothesis targets on the crowdsourcing feature of our evaluation framework. Expert judges are reliable, but do untrained, anonymously recruited crowd-workers produce reliable results? Both hypotheses involve evaluation metrics, which are the basis for conclusions on retrieval effectiveness. Therefore, also different evaluation metrics will be studied in the context of the hypotheses in this chapter.

We address the above research question and hypotheses and provide the following contribution in this chapter:

Contribution 1. *Evaluation Framework for Search over Structured Web Data based on Crowd-sourced Relevance Assessments*

This contribution consists of the following three aspects:

- We present an evaluation framework consisting of query sets, dataset, and relevance judgements obtained through crowd-sourcing.
- We examine the framework with respect to repeatability and reliability and provide a detailed analysis on these attributes.
- We hosted the Semantic Search Challenge 2010 and 2011 where we demonstrated the applicability of the approach and thereby provide reference results for the scientific community.

These contributions and the evaluation framework presented in this chapter are the work of the organization committee of the Semantic Search Challenge in 2010 and 2011, i.e. the authors of the following publications [25, 26, 70]. Initially discussed was the work in [25, 26, 70] and a comprehensive discussion will be presented in [24]. This chapter contains a revised version of the previously published papers.

Contributions of the author. The author of this thesis was member of the organization committee of the Semantic Search Challenges in 2010 and 2011. Besides the tacit contributions of the author in the numerous discussions and correspondences during the development of the framework and its application in the campaigns, as well as the implicit contributions in analyzing results and documenting them in the respective publications [25, 26, 70], the author explicitly contributed by computing the IR performance metrics (except Table 3.9 and Table 3.10), analyzing the submitted systems in 2010 (Section 3.6.1), and 2011 (Section 3.6.2), and as coordinating and corresponding author of [24, 26].

3.3 Related Work on Search Evaluation

We discuss related work from the perspectives of crowdsourcing-based evaluation, semantic search evaluation and search evaluation campaigns.

3.3.1 Crowdsourcing-based Evaluation

The main difference in using crowdsourcing to "gold standard" evaluation dataset creation in campaigns like TREC [9] is that human judges are no longer a relatively small group of professional expert judges who complete an equal-sized number of assessments, but a large group of non-experts who may complete vastly differing numbers of assessments and may not actually have the required skill-set (such as command of English) to complete the task or be completing the task honestly. Earlier work in using crowdsourcing for information retrieval demonstrated quick turn-around times and the ability to have a much higher number of judges than previously thought possible [2]. This has led to a rapidly-expanding number of applications of crowdsourcing evaluation datasets to a wide range of information retrieval tasks such as XML-based retrieval [3]. Crowdsourcing has also been expanded successfully to related areas, such as machine translation [30].

In this vein, our primary contribution is in demonstrating the repeatability of crowdsourcing judgments in creating evaluation datasets, even when entirely different sets of judges are used on the same task over long periods of time, a necessary feature for running large-scale campaigns for novel information retrieval tasks on an annual basis. Previous work on crowdsourcing evaluation campaigns, such as work on replicating image labelling in ImageCLEF [124], has focused on determining the reliability of the judges over small subsets of the original campaign, but has not tested whether the evaluation campaign is repeatable over large time intervals (i.e., months or years), only inspecting differences over small amounts of time (4 days) and not comparing the judges performance over time to each other, but aggregating all judgments.

Previous work [2, 124] in general has focused on comparing crowdsourcing judgments to that of experts on existing campaigns with well-known "gold standards", not boot-strapping new evaluation campaigns for new search tasks where there are multiple competing but unevaluated search systems, such as in semantic search. Another goal of our work is to demonstrate the use of crowdsourcing for a large-scale evaluation campaign for a novel search task, which in our case is ad-hoc object retrieval over RDF. Many semantic search systems of this type, such as [65, 126, 149], have appeared in the past few years, but none have been evaluated against each other except on a very small scale. Semantic search systems are a subset of information retrieval systems, and thus it would be natural to apply existing IR benchmarks for their evaluation in a large-scale campaign.

3.3.2 Semantic Search Evaluation

Especially through the series of SemSearch workshops, we observed a strong need for a standardized evaluation framework. To the best of our knowledge, we are the first to propose an evaluation framework and methodology as well as organizing the campaigns for participants to evaluate their semantic search systems. There are two difficulties in applying the ad-hoc document retrieval methodology directly to semantic search and the object retrieval problem in particular, as identified in [130]. The first and most apparent problem is that not all semantic search engines perform document retrieval, but rather retrieve knowledge that is already encoded in RDF, where factual answers may be found by aggregating or linking knowledge across RDF data. This is a clear difference to 'entity search' tracks such as the TREC Entity Track [9] or the INEX Entity Ranking Track [91]. With respect to addressing keyword retrieval on structured data, there is also existing work in the database literature (e.g., [106]), but this field of research has not produced a common evaluation methodology that we could have adapted. Second, in semantic search the unit of retrieval and thus the way to evaluate the results is dependent on the type of query. In turn, the types of queries supported may vary from search engine to search engine. By reducing the broad problem of semantic search to that of keyword-based ad-hoc object retrieval (i.e. retrieving objects given in RDF with relevant factual assertions connected as a property by a single link), we could invite multiple systems to our campaign, as most semantic search systems have this base-line feature. More complex query and result processing relies upon first retrieving a baseline of relevant objects, and so this baseline should be evaluated first.

3.3.3 Evaluation Campaigns

The Semantic Search Challenge differs from other evaluation campaigns on entity search. In comparison to the TREC 2010 Entity Track [10], the SemSearch Challenge searches over structured data in RDF rather than text in unstructured web-pages and features more complex queries. Likewise, in comparison to the INEX Entity-Ranking task [50], SemSearch focusses on RDF as opposed to XML as a data-format, and searches for relevance over entire RDF descriptions, not passages extracted from XML. Unlike the QALD-1 Question Answering over Linked Data [153] task, our queries were not composed of hand-crafted natural language questions built around particular limited datasets such as DBPedia and MusicBrainz (i.e. RDF exports of Wikipedia and music-related information), but of both simple and complex real-world queries from actual query logs. The use of queries from actual Web search logs is also a major difference between our competition and all aforementioned competitions such as TREC and INitiative for the Evaluation of XML retrieval (INEX). Keyword search over structured data gets also more attention in the database community [113] and an evaluation framework was recently proposed [45], but an standardized evaluation campaign is not yet available.

3.4 Evaluation Framework

In the Information Retrieval community the *Cranfield* methodology [42, 43] is the de-facto standard for the performance evaluation of IR-systems. The standardized setting for retrieval experiments following this methodology consists of a document collection, a set of topics and relevant assessments denoting which documents are (not) relevant for a given topic. We adapted this methodology to semantic search. In this section, we describe the data collection used in our evaluation framework and the query sets, which we developed for the Semantic Search Challenge in 2010 and 2011. How we obtained relevance assessments will be described in detail in Section 3.5.

3.4.1 Data Collection

A standard evaluation data collection should be not biased towards any particular system or towards a specific domain, as our goal is to evaluate general purpose entity search over RDF data. Therefore, we needed a collection of documents that would be a realistically large approximation to the amount of RDF data available 'live' on the Web and that contained relevant information for the queries, while simultaneously of a size that could be manageable by the resources of research groups. We chose the *Billion Triple Challenge (BTC)* 2009 dataset, a dataset created for the Semantic Web Challenge [23] in 2009. The dataset was created by crawling data from the web as well as combining the indexes from several semantic web search engines. The raw size of the data is 247GB uncompressed and it contains 1.4B RDF statements describing 114 million entities. The statements are composed of *quads*, where a quad is a four tuple comprising the four fields *subject, predicate, object,* as is standard in RDF, but also a URI for *context*, which basically extends a RDF triple with a new field giving a URI that the triples were retrieved from (i.e. hosted on). There was only a single a modification necessary for using this dataset for entity search evaluation which was to replace RDF blank nodes (an existential variable in RDF) with unique identifiers so that they can be indexed. Details of the dataset are given in Table 3.1.

3.4.2 Real-World Web Queries

As the kinds of queries used by semantic search engines vary dramatically (ranging from structured SPARQL queries to searching directly for URI-based identifiers), it was decided to focus first on keyword-based search.

Billion Triple Challenge 2009 Dataset	
RDF triples	1.4 billion
Size	247GB uncompressed
Download	`http://km.aifb.kit.edu/ws/dataset_semsearch2010`
Description	`http://vmlion25.deri.ie/`

Table 3.1: Statistics on the data collection

Keyword-based search is the most commonly used query paradigm, and supported by most semantic search engines. The type of result expected varies and thus the way to assess relevance depend on the type of the query. For example, a query such as *plumbers in mason ohio* is looking for instances of a class of objects, while a query like *parcel 104 santa clara* is looking for information for one particular object, in this case a certain restaurant. Pound et al. [130] proposed a classification of queries by expected result type, and for our evaluation we have decided to focus on object-queries, i.e. queries demonstrated by the latter example, where the user is seeking information on a particular object. Note that for this type of queries there might be other objects mentioned in the query other than the main object, such as *santa clara* in the above case. However, it is clear that the focus of the query is the restaurant named *parcel 104*, and not the city of Santa Clara as a whole.

We were looking for a set of object-queries that would be unbiased towards any existing semantic search engine. First, although the search engine logs of various semantic search engines were gathered, it was determined that the kinds of queries varied quite a lot, with many of the query logs of semantic search engines revealing idiosyncratic research tests by robots rather than real-world queries by actual users. Since one of the claims of semantic search is that it can help general purpose ad-hoc information retrieval on the Semantic Web, we have decided to use queries from actual users of hypertext Web search engines. As these queries would be from hypertext Web search engines, they would not be biased towards any semantic search engine. We had some initial concerns if within the scope of the dataset it would be possible to provide relevant results for each of the queries. However, this possible weakness also doubled as a strength, as the testing of a real query sample from actual users would determine whether or not a billion triples from the Semantic Web realistically could help answer the information needs of actual users, as opposed to purely researchers [69].

Queryset 2010

In order to support our evaluation, Yahoo! released a new query set as part of their WebScope program[1], called the *Yahoo! Search Query Log Tiny Sample v1.0*, which contains 4,500 queries sampled from the company's United States query log from January, 2009. One limitation of this dataset is that it contains only queries that have been posed by at least three different (not necessarily authenticated) users, which removes some of the heterogeneity of the log, for example in terms of spelling mistakes. While realistic, we considered this a hard query set to solve. Given the well-known differences between the top of the power-law distribution of queries and the long-tail, we used an additional log of queries from the Microsoft Live Search containing queries that were repeated by at least 10 different users[2]. We expected these queries to be easier to answer.

We have selected a sample of 42 entity-queries from the Yahoo! query log by classifying queries manually as described in [130]. We have selected a sample of 50 queries from the Microsoft log. In this case we have pre-filtered queries automatically with the Edinburgh MUC named entity recognizer [118], a gazetteer and rule-based named-entity recognizer that has shown to have very high precision in competitions. Both sets were combined into a single, alphabetically ordered list, so that participants were not aware which queries belonged to which set, or in fact that there were two sets of queries. The 2010 query set is available at `http://km.aifb.kit.edu/ws/semsearch10/Files/finalqueries`. Ten random queries of the set are shown in Table 3.2.

Querysets 2011

In 2011, the Semantic Search Challenge comprised two tracks. The Entity Search track is identical in nature to the 2010 challenge. However, we created a new set of queries for the entity search task based on the Yahoo! Search Query Tiny Sample v1.0 dataset. We selected 50 queries which name an entity explicitly and may also provide some additional context about it, as described in [130].

In the case of the List Search track, the second track of the 2011 challenge, we hand-picked 50 queries from the Yahoo query log as well as from True-

---

[1]`http://webscope.sandbox.yahoo.com/`, last retrieved on April 10th 2013

[2]This query log was used with permission from Microsoft Research and as the result of a Microsoft 'Beyond Search' prize awarded to Harry Halpin.

---

james caldwell high school
44 magnum hunting
american embassy nairobi
city of virginia beach
laura bush
pierce county washington
university of north dakota
kaz vaporizer
david suchet
fitzgerald auto mall chambersburg pa
mst3000

Table 3.2: Example queries from the 2010 Entity Query Set.

Knowledge 'recent' queries.[3] The queries describe a closed set of entities, have a relatively small number of possible answers (less than 12) which are unlikely to change.

Although many competitions use queries generated manually by the participants, it is unlikely that those queries are representative of the kinds of entity-based queries used on the Web. Therefore, we manually selected queries by randomly selecting from the query logs and then manually checked that at least one relevant answer existed on the current web of linked data.

Table 3.3 shows examples from the query sets for both tracks. The entire query sets are available for download.[4]

3.5 Reliability and Repeatability of the Evaluation Framework

Advances in information retrieval have long been driven by evaluation campaigns using standardized collections of datasets, query workloads, and most importantly, result relevance judgments. TREC (Text REtrieval Conference) [155] is a forerunner in IR evaluations, but campaigns also take place in specialized forums like INEX (INitiative for the Evaluation of XML Retrieval) [91] and CLEF (Cross Language Evaluation Forum). The

---

[3] http://www.trueknowledge.com/recent/ last retrieved on April 10th 2013
[4] http://semsearch.yahoo.com/datasets.php last retrieved on April 10th 2013

08 toyota tundra	gods who dwelt on Mount Olympus
Hugh Downs	Arab states of the Persian Gulf
MADRID	astronauts who landed on the Moon
New England Coffee	Axis powers of World War II
PINK PANTHER 2	books of the Jewish canon
concord steel	boroughs of New York City
YMCA Tampa	Branches of the US military
ashley wagner	continents in the world
nokia e73	standard axioms of set theory
bounce city humble tx	manfred von richthofen parents
University of York	matt berry tv series
(a) Entity Search track	(b) List Search track

Table 3.3: Example queries of both tracks of the 2011 Semantic Seach Challenge.

main premises of these campaigns is that a limited and controlled set of human *experts* decide the correctness of a given set of results, which will be used as a ground truth for evaluating the performance of different systems [155]. Early evaluation campaigns targeted relatively narrow domains and used small collections, where evaluations using a small number of queries provided robust results. Moving to the open domain of the Web resulted in significantly larger heterogeneity of data sources and an increase in the potential information needs (and so diverse tasks) that need to be evaluated. Current research in campaigns (like TREC) and information retrieval evaluation in general focus primarily on the following goals:

Repeatability. As observed by Harter [73], there can be substantial variation among different expert judges performing the same task. If evaluation is to drive the next generation of search technologies, it is important to validate that relevance assignment is a repeatable process. This fundamental requirement exacerbates the scalability problem, because the agreement between assessors needs to be tested not only for each new search task, but also for each set of judges that have been employed (Agreement is a measure of the extent to which judges are interchangeable). However, outsiders who would like to validate an experiment will typically not have access to the original judges (or those judges may not be available or willing to repeat experiments at later times).

Reliability. The expert judges employed by campaigns such as TREC [157] are expected to be sufficiently reliable to produce a ground truth for evaluation. However, setting up new "tracks" for novel search tasks is often not feasible or expedient, due to the time and effort it takes to set up such tracks and the limited resources of the organizers. In such cases, researchers need to set up their own evaluation and seek replacements for experts, training others to be judges of their work, where training is often nothing more than providing a description of the task.

How can researchers create repeatable and reliable evaluation campaigns that scale over the number of new tasks brought about by the Web? An increasingly popular way of evaluating novel search tasks is the approach known as *crowdsourcing*. Crowdsourcing is a method of obtaining human input for a given task by distributing that task over a large population of unidentified human workers. In the case of building a search evaluation collection, crowdsourcing means distributing relevance judgments of pooled results over this crowd. The advantage of the crowd is that it is always available, it is accessible to most people at a relatively small cost, and the workforce scales elastically with increasing evaluation demands. Further, platforms such as Amazon Mechanical Turk (MT)[5] provide integrated frameworks for running crowdsourced tasks with minimal effort. We show how crowdsourcing can help execute an evaluation campaign for a search task that has not yet been sufficiently addressed to become part of a large evaluation effort such as TREC: ad-hoc Web object retrieval [130], for which we created a standard dataset and queries for the task of object retrieval using real-world data, and the way we employed Mechanical Turk to elicit high quality judgments from the noise of unreliable workers in the crowd. The queries, index used, and results of the evaluation campaign are also publicly available for use in the evaluation of web-object retrieval systems.[6]

There are two research questions that must be answered for crowdsourcing to be used systematically in evaluation campaigns. First, are evaluation campaigns with crowdsourced workers **repeatable**, such that the resulting ranking of systems is the same for different pools of crowdsourced judges over a period of time? Second, are crowdsourced workers **reliable**, such that differences between experts and crowdsourced workers do not change the resulting ranking of the systems? As our primary contribution, we experimentally demonstrate the repeatability of our search system evaluation experiment using crowdsourcing. We also test the reliability of judges who are not task or topic-experts, which has been questioned in previous work [8], as crowdsourced workers do not have access to the original infor-

---

[5]http://www.mturk.com last retrieved on April 10th 2013
[6]http://semsearch.yahoo.com last retrieved on April 10th 2013

mation need and may lack specialized training or background knowledge possessed by experts. The case of Mechanical Turk provides an extreme where the judges are not only likely to be untrained and non-expert, but they also sign up for payment and so have an incentive to "cheat" in order to gain monetary reward. Therefore, we repeat our evaluation and assess whether the results from the original campaign can be reproduced after six months with a new set of crowdsourced judges, and whether those results correspond to what we would have obtained using a more traditional methodology employing expert judges. We also explore the effect of different numbers of judges per result on the quality of judgments. Finally, we analyze the robustness of three popular information retrieval metrics under crowdsourced judgments. The metrics studied are discounted cumulative gain (NDCG), mean average precision (MAP), and precision at k (P@k), which we introduced in Section 2.3.1. To the best of our knowledge, we are the first to analyze the repeatability of crowdsourcing in a real-world evaluation campaign.

3.5.1 Crowdsourcing Judgments

In this Section, we report how we used Amazon Mechanical Turk to assess the relevance of search results and describe the different sets of assessments we obtained for the evaluation. Using Mechanical Turk, a task - called Human Intelligence Task (HIT) - are presented to a pool of human judges known as 'workers' who do the task in return for very small payments. Amazon provides a web-based interface for the workers that keeps track of their decisions and their payments. Because *anyone* can sign up to be a worker, we had to present each result for judgement in a way comprehensible to non-expert human judges. It was not an option to present the data in the native syntactic format of RDF such as RDF/XML or N-Triples, because they are too complex for average users, especially with the use of URIs as opposed to natural language terms for identifiers in RDF. In practice, semantic search systems use widely varying presentations of search results, sometimes tailored to particular domains. However, the rendering of results could possibly affect the valuation given by a judge. Allowing each participant to provide their own rendering would make it difficult to separate the measurement of ranking performance from effects of presentation, and would also eliminate the ability to pool results which reduces the total number of judgments needed.

For the purpose of evaluation, we have created a rendering algorithm to present the results in a concise, yet human-readable manner without domain-dependent customizations (see Figure 3.1). First, for each subject URI, all properties and objects were retrieved. Then the last rightmost hierarchical component of the property URI, often referred to as the local name, was used as the label of the property after tokenization. For example, the property `http://www.w3.org/1999/02/22-rdf-syntax-ns/type` was presented to the judge simply as `type`. A maximum of twelve object properties were displayed to the judge, with a preference being given to a few well-known property types defined in the RDF and RDF Schema namespaces, followed by custom-defined properties presented in the order retrieved from the dataset. In order to keep the amount of information given constant across judges and facilitate timely completion of the task, the URIs were not clickable and the judges were instructed to assess using only the information rendered, as to make the task of ad-hoc object retrieval directly comparable to tasks such as ad-hoc document retrieval. During the evaluation, we encountered the problem that some of the retrieved URIs only appear as objects, resulting in an empty display. Of the 6,158 URIs, a small minority of URIs (372) had triples only in the object position. For the current evaluation, we have ignored these results. Workers were given three options to judge each result: "Excellent - describes the query target specifically and exclusively", "Not bad - mostly about the target", and "Poor - not about the target, or mentions it only in passing." Note that we used the human-friendly labels "Excellent", "Not bad" and "Poor" for relevant, somewhat relevant and irrelevant results. We did not provide instructions to emphasize any particular properties (such as the "categories" in Figure 3.1), leaving the judgment to be based on general purpose judgment combining background knowledge about the entities and all of the displayed information. In the following, any grade higher than "Poor" will be considered as "Relevant" for metrics that compute performance values over binary relevance judgments (MAP and P@10).

3.5.2 Quality Assurance and Costs of Evaluation

In order to ensure quality in the presence of possible low-quality workers, each HIT consisted of 12 query-result pairs for relevance judgments. Of the 12 results, 10 were real results drawn from the participants' submissions, and 2 were gold-standard results randomly placed in the list of results. These gold-standard results were results from queries distinct from those used by the workers and have been manually judged earlier by an expert in RDF and information retrieval as being obviously 'relevant' or 'irrelevant'. For each HIT, there was both a gold-standard relevant and gold-standard irrelevant

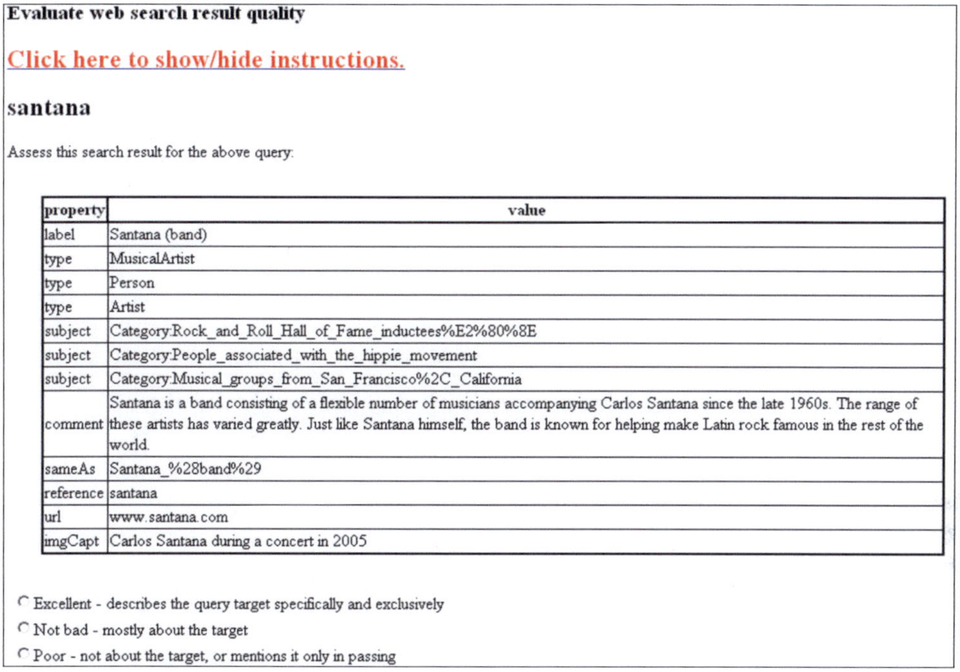

Evaluate web search result quality

Click here to show/hide instructions.

santana

Assess this search result for the above query:

property	value
label	Santana (band)
type	MusicalArtist
type	Person
type	Artist
subject	Category:Rock_and_Roll_Hall_of_Fame_inductees%E2%80%8E
subject	Category:People_associated_with_the_hippie_movement
subject	Category:Musical_groups_from_San_Francisco%2C_California
comment	Santana is a band consisting of a flexible number of musicians accompanying Carlos Santana since the late 1960s. The range of these artists has varied greatly. Just like Santana himself, the band is known for helping make Latin rock famous in the rest of the world.
sameAs	Santana_%28band%29
reference	santana
url	www.santana.com
imgCapt	Carlos Santana during a concert in 2005

○ Excellent - describes the query target specifically and exclusively

○ Not bad - mostly about the target

○ Poor - not about the target, or mentions it only in passing

Figure 3.1: Example of a human intelligent task (HIT) for semantic search evaluation.

result included. These gold-standard results enabled the detection of workers who were not properly doing their task, as can be done by monitoring the average performance of judges on the gold-standard results hidden in their HITs. It is a common occurrence when using paid crowdsourcing systems for bogus workers to try to 'game' the system in order to gain money quickly without investing effort in the task, either by using automated bots or simply answering uniformly or randomly. Note that while we chose our gold-standards manually since we were evaluating a new task, one could in future campaigns use result with high inter-annotator agreement as new gold standards. Amazon Mechanical Turk allows payment to be withheld at the discretion of the creator of the HIT if they believe the task has not been done properly.

Before publishing the final tasks, we had done small-scale experiments with varying rewards for the workers. Mason and Watts have already determined previously that increased financial incentives increase the quantity, but not the quality, of work performed by participants [114]. Thus our approach was to lower the payment to workers down to the price where the speed of picking up the published tasks was still acceptable. When our results were published via Amazon Mechanical Turk, workers were paid $0.20 per HIT. In the first experiment reported here 65 workers in total participated in judging a total of 579 HITs or 1737 assignments (3 assignments per HIT), covering 5786 submitted results and 1158 gold-standard checks. (Note that of these only a subset of 4209 results and 842 checks is relevant here, being those which were also evaluated in MT2 and EXP, see below). Three workers were detected to be answering uniformly or randomly, and their work (a total of 95 assignments) was rejected and their assignments returned to the pool for another worker to complete. Two minutes were allotted for completing each HIT. On average the HITs were completed in 1 minute, with only two complaints that the allotted time was too short. This means that workers could earn $6-$12 an hour by participating in the evaluation. The entire competition was judged within 2 days, for a total cost of $347.16. We consider this both fast and cost-effective.

To study repeatability of our evaluation campaign we have re-evaluated the relevance of the search results returned by our test systems using a second set of workers. This second experiment has been performed six months after the initial evaluation using the exact same procedure. In the following, we will refer to the original set of assessments as MT1 and the repeated set of assessments as MT2. For MT1 there were 64 judges in total. The top four judges did 131 HITs and did not differ from the experts on the gold-standard items, with the overall percentage of mistakes over the 2176 gold-standard items in those 1088 HITs was 3.2%. For MT2 there were 69 judges in total. The top five judges did 165 HITs and did not differ at all from experts on the gold-standard items, and the overall percentage of mistakes in the 1662 gold-standard items in those 831 HITs was 4.5%. For future campaigns items with a high inter-annotator reliability could be used as additional gold-standard items.

To study the reliability of our crowdsourced judgments, we also created an "Set of relevance assessments by experts (EXP)" set of relevance judgments over standard HITs that were not gold-standard items. Unlike repeatability, reliability concerns the ability of Mechanical Turk to reproduce a ground truth provided by experts. In our case, the authors of [25] have provided the ground truth by re-evaluating the same subset used in MT2. As this is a significant effort, we have used only one judge per HIT for re-evaluating the entire set of 4209 results, in 421 HITs of 10 results (leaving out the known-good and known-bad gold-standard check items). The resulting dataset is referred to as EXP herein.

For all of MT1, MT2, and EXP, we report here on the exact same set of queries and results. Some participants submitted more than one set of results (outputs from their system in differing configurations), of which we used the best submission of each of the competitor systems for testing repeatability. In total there were 6 competing systems with one submission each, which will be described in Section 3.6.1. Each result of every submission was judged by 3 crowdsourced workers, with systems results being judged up to rank 10 of each query, given that it was a new unstudied task. We broke ties by taking the majority vote, except where the three judges each gave a different judgment, in which case we chose the middle, "Not Bad" assessment. In EXP, as mentioned above, each result was judged by a single expert, but a subset of 30 results were judged by three experts to determine intra-expert reliability.

Although the procedure for MT2 was the same as for MT1, the intervening six months appear to have seen a significant change in the worker pool: monitoring worker time-to-complete and performance on the known-good and known-bad gold-standard results revealed a total of 14 bogus workers for MT2, who completed a total of 1471 assignments between them before they were detected and blocked and their assignments returned to the pool. This change from 5% of assignments rejected in MT1 to 54% of assignments rejected in MT2 may indicate a significant increase in the number of bogus workers, and underlines the importance of including known-good and known-bad data in every HIT.

3.5.3 Analysis of Results

In our experiments, we investigate the hypotheses on repeatability and reliability as stated before in Section 3.2 and use as parameters the ranking metrics (MAP, NDCG, P@10), the number of assessors per item and the relevance scale. Further, we examine which of these ranking metrics are more robust to changing the pool of workers and when replacing experts with workers. Regarding the number of assessors per item, we study whether more assessments per item yield better results and whether the results hold for a binary and ternary relevance scale.

Repeatability. As previously discussed, in IR evaluation the notion of repeatability is tied to measuring the extent to which judges are interchangeable. The argumentation goes that if we show that judges from a particular pool of assessors are inter-changeable, the experiment can be repeated with any subset of judges from the pool: the judges will agree on the relevancy of items to be judged, which will be reflected in the metrics to be computed, and the eventual ranking of the competing systems.

The most common measures of inter-annotator agreement in IR evaluations are Cohen's κ for the case of two judges and Fleiss's κ for the case of multiple judges, which we introduced in Section 2.3.2. Since the two κ metrics are commonly used in IR literature, we use them in our experiments. While we report inter-annotator agreement, we note that the applicability of standard metrics to the case of crowdsourced workers can be questioned. The reason is that although we have a fixed number of workers for each HIT, in the crowdsourcing scenario the workers select the tasks, and thus they are not necessarily the *same* workers who assess each item. Figure 3.2 shows the number of items judged by each worker in our first experiment with Mechanical Turk. In the case of traditional expert-based evaluation, this distribution would be flat as each expert would assess the same items. In our case, each worker may assess a different number of the total set of HITs. Some workers assess a large number of HITs, with the most diligent worker going through 273 HITs, while a long tail of workers worked on a single task only. This long tail is especially problematic since there is much less data about these workers on which to base reliability tests.

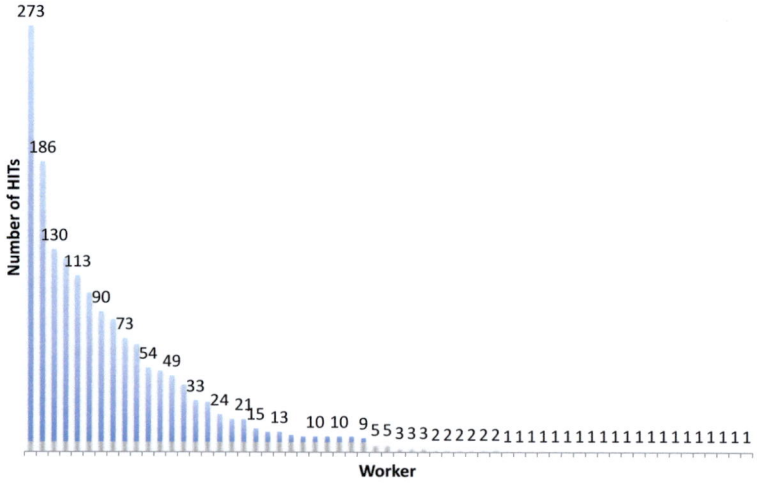

Figure 3.2: Workers ordered by decreasing number of items assessed.

Based on our knowledge of the related work, it seems that there is not yet consensus as to how to account for this deficiency [31] and the question of reliability is sometimes ignored altogether [55]. We believe the most prudent way to proceed is to report the distribution of Fleiss' κ values considering all HITs as individual assessments of a small number of 12 items. In Figure 3.3 we show this distribution for our first and second experiment. As the Figure shows, the level of agreement is very similar. The average and standard deviation are 0.36±0.18 for the first experiment (MT1) versus 0.36±0.21 for MT2. In fact, the difference between the average agreement appears at the fourth digit, strongly supporting the idea of a homogeneous pool of workers. We achieve slightly higher levels of agreement for binary relevance (with somewhat relevant and relevant judgments counted both as relevant), 0.44±0.22 and 0.47±0.25. There is thus no marked difference between a three-point scale and a binary scale, meaning that it was feasible to judge this task on a three-point scale.

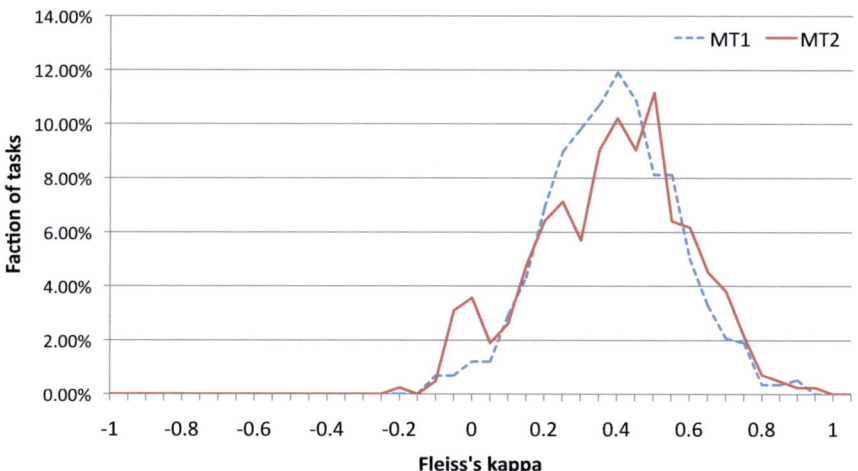

Figure 3.3: Distribution of the agreement in terms of Fleiss's κ between workers within a HIT for the two sets MT1 and MT2.

Agreement numbers are not easy to interpret even in the context of related work, and agreement is only a proxy for a repeatable evaluation: what we are ultimately after is whether different pools of workers used in different experiments lead to the same results in terms of evaluation metrics, and ultimately the same ordering of the evaluated systems. Figure 3.4 shows Mean Average Precision (MAP) scores for the different systems using the two different evaluation sets obtained via Mechanical Turk (MT1 and MT2). The results are also included in Table 3.4. We can see that the scores are close in value, and in fact there is no change to the rank-order of the systems. The result holds for both binary and ternary scale, and for both MAP, P@10 and NDCG. Broadly, this confirms our hypothesis that crowdsourced ad-hoc evaluation is repeatable. The relative change in scores reported in Table 3.4 across the two sets MT1 and MT2, for all systems is on average 7.85% for MAP, 4.24% for NDCG and 6.87% for P@10. This gives us a first indication that two systems would need to be very close in performance in order to change places in the ranking produced by repeated experiments.

In fact, crowdsourced evaluation gives surprisingly robust results with just a single assessment per item. We have tested this by subsampling, i.e. selecting randomly a single assessment for each item from the six assessments we have collected in total. We have repeated this a 100 times and computed the min, max, mean and standard deviation of our metrics. Figure 3.5a shows the min, max, and the range of one standard deviation from the mean for each system, using MAP as the metric. This figure furthermore shows that even one standard deviation intervals provide different ranges for the different systems and effectively separate them. Though the score of a system in a particular sample may surpass the score of an overall inferior system, such cases would be rare. Note that there is a particular robustness to crowdsourced evaluation. Though conventional wisdom would certainly be against running an evaluation with a possibly unreliable single judge, in the case of crowdsourcing the assessments will not come from one single judge for all the results, but multiple different workers. These workers may be individually unreliable, but each will judge only small number of items. When considering three judges, see Figure 3.5b, the systems are even more clearly separated by their retrieval performances in terms of MAP and intervals around the mean get even tighter. The decrease of standard deviation around the mean is also shown in Figure 3.6. This Figure shows for different metrics the standard deviation around the mean on the vertical axis and different numbers of workers on the horizontal axis. We see that P@10 benefits the most from increasing the number of workers and that adding more workers decreases the standard deviation between workers.

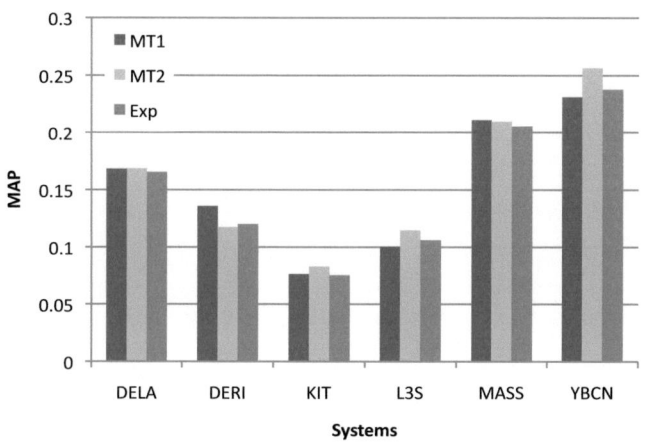

Figure 3.4: Mean average precision (MAP) for the systems using different assessment sets.

	MAP			NDCG			P@10		
System	MT1	MT2	EXP	MT1	MT2	EXP	MT1	MT2	EXP
YBCN	0.23	0.26	0.24	0.35	0.38	0.33	0.48	0.54	0.45
MASS	0.21	0.21	0.21	0.34	0.34	0.33	0.48	0.51	0.40
DELA	0.17	0.17	0.17	0.29	0.27	0.28	0.41	0.43	0.35
DERI	0.14	0.12	0.12	0.24	0.24	0.22	0.39	0.36	0.30
L3S	0.10	0.11	0.11	0.20	0.21	0.20	0.28	0.30	0.24
KIT	0.08	0.08	0.08	0.15	0.14	0.15	0.26	0.28	0.23

Table 3.4: Evaluation results for the two crowdsourced evaluation sets (MT1, MT2) and the expert's evaluation set (EXP) using the metrics MAP, NDCG, and P@10.

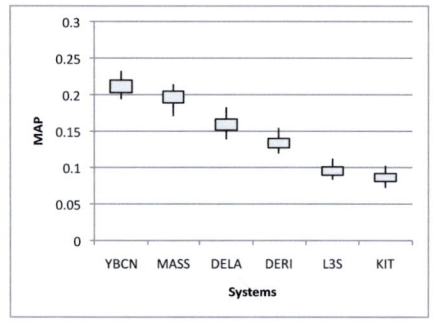 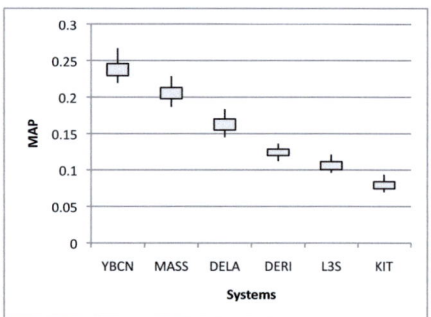

(a) One worker assessment per item.   (b) Three worker assessments per item.

Figure 3.5: Mean average precision (MAP) for different numbers of crowd-sourced assessments.

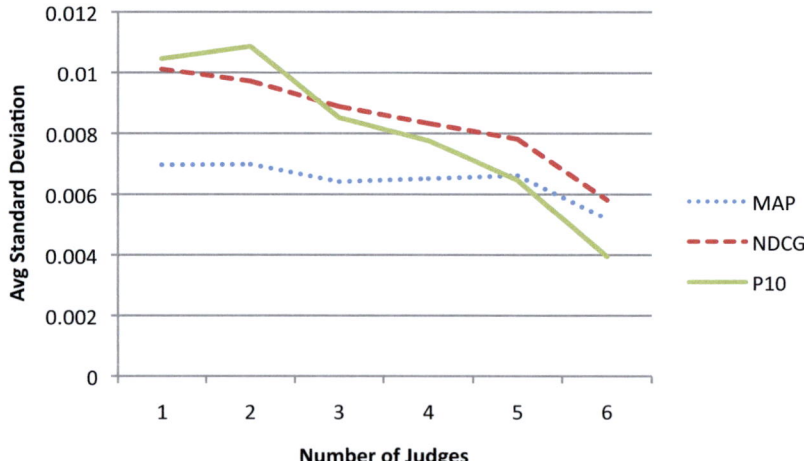

Figure 3.6: Average standard deviation around the mean for different metrics and for different numbers of crowdsourced judges.

Reliability. Repeatable evaluations require that each evaluation be reliable, and while work such as Alonso et al. [3] has shown that crowdsourced judges can be reliable in information retrieval tasks, we should show that this reliability holds over repeated experiments. We measured the agreement between expert judges on a subset of the items (30 HITs). In this case, the average and standard deviation of Fleiss's κ for the two- and three-point scales are 0.57 ± 0.18 and 0.56 ± 0.16, respectively. The level of agreement is thus higher for expert judges, with comparable deviation. For expert judges, there is practically no difference between the two- and three-point scales, meaning that expert judges had much less trouble using the middle judgment.

The most basic statistic we can look at is the difference in scoring patterns of experts and non-experts. Moving on to comparing expert reliability with crowdsourced judgements from MT1 and MT2, Table 3.5 shows that again different sets of workers behave very similarly, though different from the experts on the whole. Fleiss's κ is similar with 0.412 between MT1 and experts, and 0.417 between MT2 and experts. In particular, experts are more pessimistic in their scoring, marking irrelevant many of the items that the workers would consider somewhat relevant.

This effect is also visible in Figure 3.7, which shows how the worker assessed items compared to the experts for the three assessment options, e.g. the most left bar shows that items, which were judged as relevant by the experts, are judged by more than 60% of the crowdsourced judges also as relevant. Whereas the two worker sets display similar behavior compared to each to other, the difference towards more positive assessments compared to the experts can be observed. This may suggest that crowdsourced judgments cannot replace expert evaluations. Based on comments and the data, the source of this effect is likely the fact that experts understood "describes the query target specifically and exclusively" to be much of a more sharp distinction about objects than workers. An expert would note that the IMDB article about a movie featuring actor David Suchet would not be considered 'relevant', while workers would often judge that result as relevant if the query asked for David Suchet.

Looking at agreement rate in other settings, such as κ of 0.55 at TREC 2005 on sentence relevance at TREC 2004 Novelty Trac [141], our experts are clearly reliable, with agreement ratings of 0.57 (binary scale) and 0.56 (ternary scale). Yet then the reliability of non-expert crowdsourced judges of 0.36 in our experiment then appears to be less than ideal. However, does it change the ranking of the systems? This would be the ideal test of how far reliability has to degrade in order to impact an evaluation campaign.

Set	Total items	Irrelevant	Somewhat R.	Relevant
MT1	4209	2593	970	646
MT2	4209	2497	975	737
EXP	4209	2847	640	722

Table 3.5: Scoring patterns in different evaluation sets.

Even if the level of agreement is higher amongst expert judges, if the ranking of the systems does not change when non-experts are employed, then a crowdsourcing approach is still reliable enough for the task (even if their reliability is strictly speaking relatively lower than expert judges). The relative change in scores when going from experts to workers (moving from EXP to three-samples of MT1 and MT2), for all systems in average, and using three judgments, is 1.8% for MAP, 3.5% for NDCG and 12.8% for P@10 (see also Table 3.4). These are comparable changes to what we have seen when moving from one worker set to another, but the changes are mostly positive, with notable increases in P@10 when changing from experts to workers. In particular, the increase in somewhat relevant scores explains the increase of the binary P@10 measure. Somewhat relevant results (counted as relevant for the binary measures) that are coming in at lower ranks boost P@10 more than MAP and NDCG, which are less sensitive to changes in the lower ranks. While the reliability of non-expert judges is lower than expert judges, the reliability of non-expert judges is still sufficient for ranking systems in the evaluation.

Figure 3.4 visualizes the performance values for MAP for the different systems using the two MT evaluation sets and the expert judgments. The values are not only close, but in fact again the obtained values for the experts produce the same rank-order of the systems as with any of the MT evaluation sets.

As in the case of repeatability, we might ask whether crowdsourced assessments become more reliable when adding more judges. We have already shown in Figure 3.6 that increasing the number of workers decreases their standard deviation and increases the reliability of workers, and this trend seems to continue beyond 6 workers. Figure 3.8 shows the deviation resulting from using the workers' assessments instead of the expert assessments, in particular the average relative change in our metrics for subsamples, for different numbers of workers. We can see a clear benefit to using three workers instead of 1 or 2 workers, but there is comparatively less benefit from employing more than three judges. Figure 3.9 shows the same for

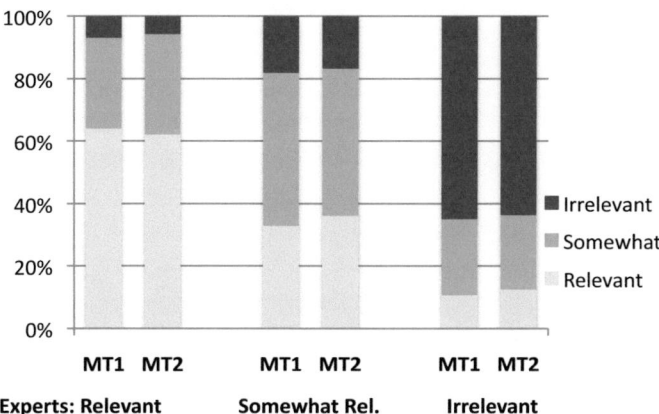

Figure 3.7: Assessments of the two workers' sets given the experts' assessments for the three assessment options.

MAP and NDCG using the average values of Kendall's τ between the subsamples of worker judgments and the expert assessments. This value of τ is already very close to one for three judges independent of the metric. While intra-worker reliability increases as the number of workers increase, adding more than three workers will lead to a higher number of disagreements with expert judges.

3.5.4 Conclusions on Reliability and Repeatability

With the advent of crowdsourcing platforms, creating a "gold standard" evaluation dataset of relevance judgments for new kinds of search tasks is now cheap, scalable, and easy to deploy. We have shown how to quickly boot-strap a repeatable evaluation campaign for a search task that has not previously been systematically evaluated, such as the object information retrieval task in semantic search, using Mechanical Turk.

Regarding the *repeatability* of such crowdsourced judgments, we have shown that the level of agreement is the same for two pools of crowdsourced judges even when the evaluation is repeated after six months. Repeating an evaluation using crowdsourcing after six months led to the same result in evaluation metrics and the rank-order of the systems being unchanged.Concerning the *reliability* of crowdsourced judgments, we have observed that experts in general rate more results negative than crowdsourced judges. This is likely due to the object retrieval task and the time

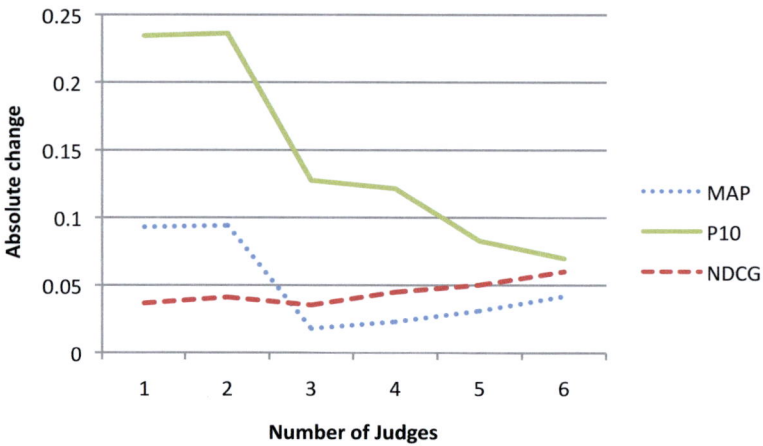

Figure 3.8: Average deviation of sample means from the expert assessments.

pressure on workers, as experts were more adept at discriminating between queries exclusively about an object to ones simply mentioning an object given time limits. However, the rank ordering of systems does not change when moving from experts to crowdsourced workers for the given systems. Three judges seems to be a sufficient number and, surprisingly, increasing the number of crowdsourced judges has little effect unless the systems are particularly close. As regards evaluation metrics, *P@10* is more brittle than measures such as *MAP* and *nDCG* and so benefits most from collecting additional judgments.

We have successfully shown how a number of real-world and research semantic search systems can be evaluated in a repeatable and reliable manner via creating a new evaluation campaign using crowdsourcing. While the study here has focused on agreement between judges and workers over time and holding the items (queries and results) constant, future research needs to study the agreement between judges and workers on a per-item basis. For example, how does the ambiguity of entity queries effect reliability and repeatability? So the next study should also take into account if these results hold over different kinds of items, so the "Semantic Search" evaluation campaign will be broadened to deal with new kinds of semantic search tasks featuring different keyword queries and more expressive and complex queries beyond keywords. Of course, the methodology demonstrated in this

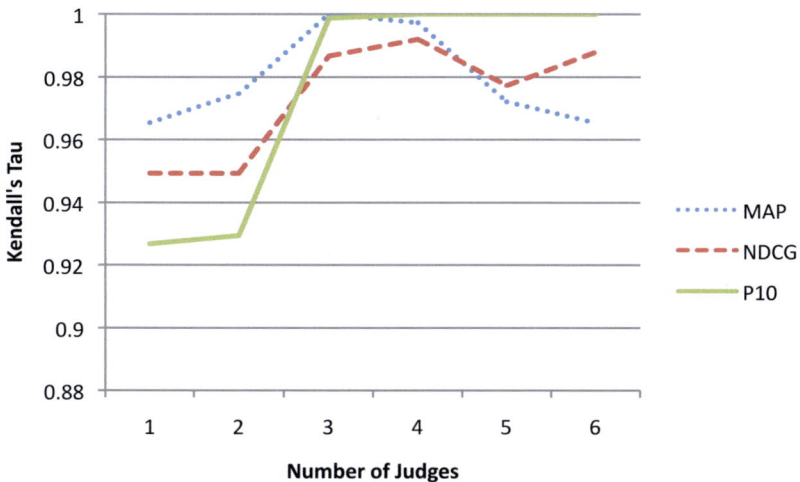

Figure 3.9: Kendall's τ between workers and experts for different number of assessments per item.

work should be repeated for these new tasks if the task goes beyond entity retrieval. Crowdsourced evaluation can lead to new tasks being evaluated quickly with reliable and repeatable evaluations. It also aids in having much larger corpora and query workloads for these campaigns. Most importantly, as the crowdsourced results are reliable and repeatable for this task at any time, evaluation campaigns can now run *continuously* (by using a standard community-driven evaluation web service) rather than annually. Our results support fast and scalable "just-in-time" evaluation of new search tasks, with empirically demonstrated repeatability and reliability.

3.6 Semantic Search Challenge

We applied the evaluation framework in the Semantic Search Challenge 2010 and 2011, which were held as part of the Semantic Search Workshop at WWW2010 and WWW2011. The main difference between the challenges is that that 2011 challenge comprised also a List Search Track in addition to the Entity Search Track.

3.6.1 Semantic Search Challenge 2010

In the following, we describe the participating systems and discuss the results of the Semantic Search Challenge 2010 as reported in [70].

Entity Search Track. The Entity Search track aims to evaluate a typical search task on the web, i.e. keyword search where the keyword(s) is generally the name of the entity. Entities are ranked according to the degree to which they are relevant to the keyword query. Originally, we have called this track the "Ad-hoc Object retrieval" track [70]. In order to be terminologically consistent in this thesis and also to use the term meanwhile established in the research community, we call it here *Entity Search* track. This task was part of the Semantic Search Challenge 2010 and also in 2011.

Participating Systems 2010.

For the evaluation campaign, each semantic search engine was allowed to produce up to three different submissions ('runs'), to allow the participants to try different parameters or features. A submission consisted of an ordered list of URIs for each query. In total, we received 14 different runs from six different semantic search engines. The six participants were DERI (Digital Enterprise Research Institute), University of Delaware (Delaware), Karlsruhe Institute of Technology (KIT), University of Massachusetts (UMass), L3S-Research Center Hannover (L3S), and Yahoo! Research Barcelona (Yahoo! BCN). A brief description of each system is given below, and detailed descriptions are available at
`http://km.aifb.kit.edu/ws/semsearch10/#eva`.

All systems used inverted indexes for managing the data. The differences between the systems can be characterized by two major aspects:

- The internal model used for representing entities.
- The kind of retrieval model applied for matching and ranking.

We will now first discuss these two aspects and then discuss the specific characteristics of the participated systems and their differences. For entity representation, RDF triples having the same URI as subject have been included and that URI is used as the entity identifier. Only the **DERI** and the **L3S** deviate from this representation, as described below. More specifically, the entity description comprises attribute and relation triples as well as provenance information. While attributes are associated with literal values, relation triples establish a connection between one entity and one another.

Both the attributes and the literal values associated with them are incorporated and stored on the index. The entities of relation triples are in fact identifiers. Unlike literal values, they are not directly used for matching but this additional information has been considered valuable for ranking. Provenance is a general notion that can include different kinds of information. For the problem of entity search, participated systems used two different types of provenances. On the one hand, RDF triples in the provided dataset are associated with an additional context value. This value is in fact an identifier, which captures the origin of the triples, e.g. from where it was crawled. This provenance information is called here the 'context'. One the other hand, the URI of every RDF resource is a long string, from which the domain can be extracted. This kind of provenance information is called 'domain'. Clearly, the domain is different to the context because URIs with the same domain can be used in different contexts. Systems can be distinguished along this dimension, i.e., what specific aspects of the entity they took into account.

The retrieval model, i.e. matching and rankings [111], is clearly related to the aspect of entity representation. From the descriptions of the systems, we can derive three main types of approaches: (1) the purely 'text based' approach which relies on the 'bag-of-words' representation of entities and applies ranking that is based on TF/IDF [136], BM25 [133], or language models [165]. This type of approaches is centered around the use of terms and particularly, weights of terms derived from statistics computed for the text corpus. (2) Weighting properties separately is done by approaches that use models like BM25F [132] to capture the structure of documents (and entities in this case) using a list of fields or alternatively, using mixture language models, which weight certain aspects of an entity differently. Since this type of approaches do not consider entities as being flat as opposed to the text-based ones but actually decompose them according to their structure, we call them 'structure-based'. (3) While with this one, the structure information is used for ranking results for a specific query, there are also approaches that leverage the structure to derive query independent scores, e.g. using PageRank. We refer to them as 'query-independent structure-based' (Q-I-structured-based) approaches. To be more precise, the three types discussed here actually capture different aspects of a retrieval model. A concrete approach in fact uses a combination of of these aspects.

Based on the distinction introduced above, Table 3.6 gives an overview of the systems and their characteristics as follows:

- *attribute-value:* Are the attribute-values of the triples used in the entity representation (yes +/no−) ?

Participant		Delaware			DERI			KIT	L3S	UMass			Yahoo! BCN		
	Run	sub28-Okapi	sub28-Dir	sub28-AX	sub27-dpr	sub27-dlc	sub27-gpr	sub32	sub29	sub31-run1	sub31-run2	sub31-run3	sub30-RES.1	sub30-RES.2	sub30-RES.3
Entity representation Attribute values		+	+	+	+	+	+	+	-	+	+	+	+	+	+
Relations		-	-	-	+	+	+	-	-	-	-	-	-	-	-
Domain		-	-	-	+	+	+	-	+	-	-	-	+	+	+
Context		-	-	-	+	+	+	-	-	-	-	-	-	-	
Retrieval model Text based		+	+	+	+	+	+	-	+	+	+	-	-	-	-
Structure-based		-	-	-	-	-	-	+	-	-	-	+	+	+	+
Q-I-Structure-based		-	-	-	+	+	+	-	-	-	-	-	+	+	+

Table 3.6: Overview of systems, internal entity representation and retrieval
model applied in the 2010 challenge

- *relations:* Are the relations to other entities considered (yes + / no
  −)? The relations are potentially exploitable for ranking, because they
  form the data graph by linking to other entities. If this information
  is not taken into account, the relations usually treated as additional
  attribute-value pairs.

- *domain:* Is the domain information used (yes + / no −) ? Entities of a
  certain domain are some times boosted, because certain domains are
  considered a-priori as relevant or of high quality. Often entities from
  dbpedia.org are considered for a-priori boosting.

- *context:* Is the context information included in the entity representation
  (yes + / no −) ? This information can be used as well to favor certain
  sources.

Delaware:

Entity representation: The system from Delaware took all triples having
the same subject URI as the description of an entity. However, the resulting
structure of the entity as well as the triple structure were then neglected.
Terms extracted from the triples are simply put into one 'bag-of-words' and
indexed as one document.

Retrieval model: Three existing retrieval models were applied for the different runs, namely Okapi for **sub28-Okapi**, language models with Dirichlet
priors smoothing **sub28-Dir**, and an axiomatic approach for **sub28-AX**.

DERI:

Entity representation: The Sindice system from DERI applied a different notion of entity. All triples having the same subject and also the same context constitute one entity description. Thus, the same subject that appears in two different contexts might be represented internally as two distinct entities. Further, the system considered relations to other entities, context information, and URI tokens for the representation of entities.

Retrieval model: The context information, as well as the relations between entities are used to compute query independent PageRank-style scores. Different parameter configurations have been tested for each run, resulting in different scores. For processing specific queries, these scores were combined with query dependent TF/IDF-style scores for matches on predicates, entities and values.

KIT:

Entity representation: The system by KIT considered literal values of attributes and separately those of the *rdfs:label* attribute as the entity description. All other triples that can be found in the RDF data for an entity were ignored.

Retrieval model: The results were ranked based on a mixture language model inspired score, which combines the ratio of all query terms to the number of term matches on one literal and discounts each term according to its global frequency.

L3S:

Entity representation: The system by L3S takes a different approach to entity representation. Each unique URI, appearing as subject or entity in the dataset, is seen as an entity. Only information captured by this URI is used for representing the entity. Namely, based on the observation that some URIs contain useful strings, a URI was splitted into parts. These parts were taken as a 'bag-of-words' description of the entity and indexed as one document. Thereby, some provenance information is taken into account, i.e., the domain extracted from the URI.

Retrieval model: A TF/IDF-based ranking combined with using cosine similarity to compute the degree of matching between terms of the query and terms extracted from the entity URI was used here.

UMass:

Entity representation: All triples having the same subject URI were taken as the description of an entity. For the first two runs, **sub31-run1** and **sub31-run2**, the values of these triples are just seen as a 'bag-of-words' and no structure information was taken into account. For the third run, **sub31-run3**, the entity representation was divided into four fields, one field containing all values of the attribute *title*, one for values of the attribute *name*, a more specific one for values of the attribute *dbpedia : title* and one field containing the values for all the attributes.

Retrieval model: Existing retrieval models were applied, namely the query likelihood model for **sub31-run1** and the Markov random field model for **sub31-run2**. For **sub31-run3**, the fields were weighted separately with specific boosts applied to *dbpedia : title, name,* and *title*.

Yahoo! BCN:

Entity representation: Every URI appearing at the subject position of the triples is regarded as one entity and is represented as one virtual document that might have up to 300 fields, one field per attribute. A subset of the attributes were manually classified into one of the three classes *important, neutral,* and *unimportant* and boosts applied respectively. The Yahoo! system took the provenance of the URIs into account. However, not the context but the domain of the URI was considered and similarly to the attributes, it was classified into three classes. Relations and structure information that can be derived from them were not taken into account.

Retrieval model: The system created by Yahoo! [27] uses an approach for field-based scoring that is similar to BM25F. Matching terms were weighted using a local, per property, term frequency as well as a global term frequency. A boost was applied based on the number of query terms matched. In addition, a prior was calculated for each domain and multiplied to the final score. The three submitted runs represent different configurations of these parameters.

2010 Entity Track Evaluation Results

The top 10 results per query were evaluated, and after pooling the results of all the submissions, there was a total of 6,158 unique query-result pairs. Note this was out of a total of 12,880 potential query result pairs, showing that pooling was definitely required. Some systems submitted duplicate results for one query. We considered the first occurrence for the evaluation and took all following as not relevant. Further, some submissions contained ties, i.e. several results for one query had the same score. Although there exist tie-aware versions of our metrics [115], the *trec_eval* software[7] we used

---

[7]http://trec.nist.gov/trec_eval/ last retrieved on April 10th 2013

Participant	Run	P@10	MAP	NDCG
Yahoo! BCN	sub30-RES.3	0.4924	0.1919	0.3137
UMass	sub31-run3	0.4826	0.1769	0.3073
Yahoo! BCN	sub30-RES.2	0.4185	0.1524	0.2697
UMass	sub31-run2	0.4239	0.1507	0.2695
Yahoo! BCN	sub30-RES.1	0.4163	0.1529	0.2689
Delaware	sub28-Okapi	0.4228	0.1412	0.2591
Delaware	sub28-AX	0.4359	0.1458	0.2549
UMass	sub31-run1	0.3717	0.1228	0.2272
DERI	sub27-dpr	0.3891	0.1088	0.2172
DERI	sub27-dlc	0.3891	0.1088	0.2171
Delaware	sub28-Dir	0.3652	0.1109	0.2140
DERI	sub27-gpr	0.3793	0.1040	0.2106
L3S	sub29	0.2848	0.0854	0.1861
KIT	sub32	0.2641	0.0631	0.1305

Table 3.7: Results of submitted Semantic Search engines in 2010.

to compute the scores can not deal with ties in a correct way. Therefore we broke the ties by assigning scores to the involved result according to the order of occurrences in the submitted file.

Table 3.7 shows the evaluation results for the submitted runs. The third run submitted by Yahoo!, together with the third run of the UMass system, gave the best results.

It was interesting to observe that the top two runs achieve similar levels of performance with retrieving very different sets of results. The overlap between these two runs as measured by Kendall's τ is only 0.11. By looking at the results in detail, we see that **sub31-run3** has a strong prior on returning results from a single domain, dbpedia.org, with 93.8% of all results from this domain. DBpedia, which is an extraction of the structured data contained in Wikipedia, is a broad-coverage dataset with high quality results and thus the authors have decided to bias the ranking toward results from this domain. The competing run **sub30-RES3** returns only 40.6% of results from this domain, which explains the low overlap. The performance difference is also visible in Figure 3.12, which shows the NDCG per query for both runs. Also we can observe that **sub30-RES3** exceeds **sub31-run3** for 40 of 92 queries.

Figure 3.10 shows the per-query performance for queries from the Microsoft and Figure 3.11 for the queries from the Yahoo! log. Both Figures show the boundary of the first and third quartiles using error bars. It is noticeable that the Yahoo! set is indeed more difficult for the search engines

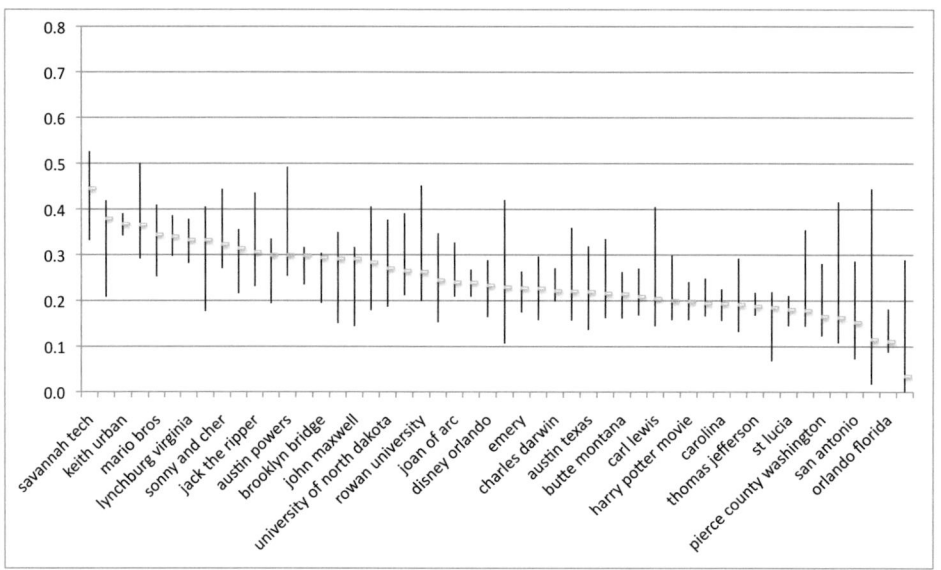

Figure 3.10: Average NDCG for queries from the Microsoft query set.

to process, with larger variations of NDCG across both queries and across systems. The performance on queries from the Microsoft log, which are more frequent queries, shows less variation among queries and between systems processing the same queries. This confirms that popular queries are not only easier, but more alike in difficulty.

Discussion of the 2010 Challenge

The systems submitted to the evaluation represent an array of approaches to semantic search, as shown by the diversity of results. Most participants started with well-known baselines from Information Retrieval. When applied to entity search on RDF graphs these techniques yield workable results almost out-of-the-box, although a differential weighting of properties has been key to achieving top results (see the runs from **Yahoo! BCN** and **UMass**).

Besides assigning different weights to properties, the use of 'semantics' or the meaning of the data has been limited. All the participating systems focused on indexing only the subjects of the triples by creating virtual documents for each subject, which is understandable given the task. However, we would consider relations between entities as one of the strong character-

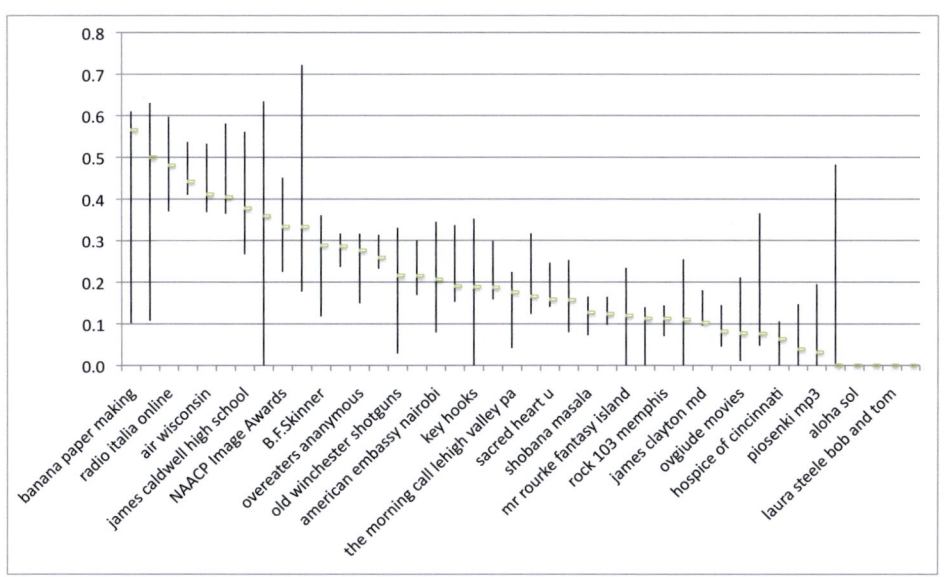

Figure 3.11: Average NDCG for queries from the Yahoo! query set.

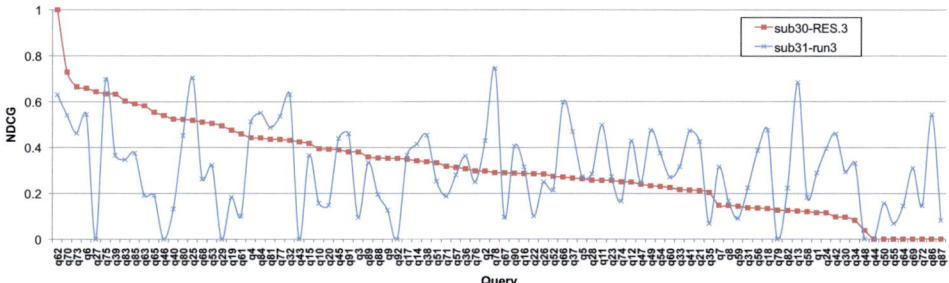

Figure 3.12: Comparison between runs **sub30-RES3** and **sub31-run3** in terms of NDCG per query for the Entity Track 2010.

istics of the RDF data model, and the usefulness of graph-based approaches to ranking will still need to be validated in the future. Note that in the context of RDF, graph-based ranking can be applied to both the graph of entities as well as the graph of information sources. Similarly, we found that keyword queries were taken as such, and despite our expectations they were not interpreted or enhanced with any kind of annotations or structures. The possibilities for query interpretation using background knowledge (such as ontologies and large knowledge bases) or the data itself is another characteristic of semantic search that will need to be explored in the future. The lack of some of these advanced features is explained partly by the short time that was available, and partly by the fact that this was the first evaluation of this kind, and therefore no training data was available for the participants.

3.6.2 Semantic Search Challenge 2011

As described in Section 3.6.1 the evaluation in 2010 was centered around the task of entity search. This choice was driven by the observation that over 40% of queries in real query logs fall into this category [130], largely because users have learned that search engine relevance decreases with longer queries and have grown accustomed to reducing their query (at least initially) to the name of an entity. However, the major feedback and criticism of the 2010 SemSearch Challenge was that by limiting the evaluation to keyword search for named entities the evaluation excluded more complex searches that would hypothetically be enabled by semantic search over RDF. Therefore, the 2011 SemSearch competition introduced a second track, the "List Search" track, that focused on queries where one or more entities could fulfill the criteria given to a search engine. Therefore, the Semantic Search Challenge 2011 comprised two different tracks, the Entity Search Track, just like in 2010, and the List Search Track.

Participating Systems in the Entity Track 2011

Four teams participated in both tracks. These teams were University of Delaware (**UDel**), Digital Enterprise Research Institute (**DERI**), International Institute of Information Technology Hyderabad (**IIIT Hyd**), and Norwegian University of Science and Technology (**NTNU**). Dhirubhai Ambani Institute of Information and Communication Technology (**DA-IICT**) participated additionally in the List Search Track.

Each team was allowed to enter up to three different submissions per track, in order to experiment with different system configurations.In total, 10 runs were submitted for the Entity Search Track and 11 runs for the List Search Track.

In the following sections, we briefly describe and characterize the systems for each track and report on their performance. Detailed system descriptions are available at the Challenge website[8]. We use the same characteristics as in the previous section to categorize the systems and provide an overview in Table 3.8.

---

[8]http://semsearch.yahoo.com last retrieved on April 10th 2013

Overview of Evaluated Systems Entity Track 2011

Participant		UDel		DERI			NTNU		
	Run	VO	Prox	1	2	3	Olav	Harald	Godfrid
Entity representation	attribute-value	+	+	+	+	+	+	+	+
	relations	-	-	-	-	+	-	-	+
	domain	+	-	-	+	+	+	+	+
	context	-	-	+	+	+	-	-	-
Retrieval model	Text-based	+	+	+	+	+	+	+	+
	Structure-based	-	-	+	+	+	-	+	+
	Q-I-structure	-	-	-	-	+	-	-	-

Table 3.8: Overview of systems, internal entity representation and retrieval
model applied in the 2011 Entity Search track

UDel:

Entity representation: All quads having the same subject URI constituted
one entity. Terms extracted from these quads are simply put into one
'bag-of-words' and indexed as one document.

Retrieval model: An axiomatic retrieval function was applied by University of Delaware [59]. For run **UDel-Prox**, query term proximity
was added to the model, which favors documents having the query
terms within a sliding window of 15 terms. The third run **UDel-VO**
promotes entities whose URI has a direct match to a query term.

DERI:

Entity representation: In contrast to the other systems, the Sindice system
from DERI took all quads having the same subject and the same context
as the description of an entity. Only entity descriptions comprising
more than 3 quads were considered. This entity description is internally
represented as a labeled tree data model with an entity node as the root,
and subsequent attribute and value nodes. In addition, run **DERI-3**
used the entire graph structure, so exploiting the relationships of any
given entity when ranking.

Retrieval model: BM25MF, an extension of BM25F, which allows fields
to have multiple values was used by Sindice to rank entities for all
runs. The second and winning run, **DERI-2**, applied additionally
query specific weights, namely query coverage and value coverage.

These weights indicate how well the query terms are covered by a root node, respectively value node, in the internal data model. The more query terms are covered by a node, the more weight is contributed to this node. In addition, query independent weights were assigned to attributes, whose URI contain certain keywords, e.g. *label*, *title*, *sameas*, and *name*. Run **DERI-3** used additionally the relations to compute query independent scores based on the graph structure.

IIIT Hyd:

Did not provide a system description.

NTNU:

Entity representation: NTNU used the *DBPedia* dataset in addition to the BTC to represent entities. An entity is represented by three sub-models, the first comprises all name variants of this entity in DBPedia, the second considers several attributes from DBPedia for this entity, and the third uses the data from BTC about this entity. On the syntactic level, all triples having the same subject URI were used for the models based on DBPedia. For run **NTNU-Olav**, the model based on the BTC used only literal entities and regarded them as one flat text representation. For the runs **NTNU-Harald** and **NTNU-Godfrid**, the model had two fields, the name field which contained values of attributes that mentioned the name of the entity, while all other attributes were put into the content field.

Retrieval model: Mixture language models were used to incorporate the different entity models in the retrieval function, while weights were applied for specific attributes of DBPedia. Run **NTNU-Godfrid** used *sameAs* (an equivalence link on the Semantic Web) relations to propagate scores, in order to rank directly related entities higher.

2011 Entity Track Results

Discussion of the 2011 Entity Search Track

The semantic search task of finding entities in an large RDF graph has been addressed by a spectrum of different approaches in this challenge as shown by the diversity of the results. The basis for most system are still the well known Information Retrieval techniques, which yields acceptable results. However, the winning system from DERI is a specialized system, which adapted IR methods and tailored them to RDF. The key feature for success, shared by the two top ranked systems in the 2011 challenge, is to take the proximity or coverage of query terms on individual attribute values into

Participant	Run	P10	P5	MAP
DERI	2	0.260	0.332	**0.2346**
UDel	Prox	0.260	0.337	**0.2167**
NTNU	Harald	0.222	0.280	**0.2072**
NTNU	Godfrid	0.224	0.272	**0.2063**
NTNU	Olav	0.220	0.276	**0.2050**
UDel	VO	0.194	0.248	**0.1858**
DERI	1	0.218	0.292	**0.1835**
DERI	3	0.188	0.252	**0.1635**
IIIT Hyd	1	0.130	0.148	**0.0876**
IIIT Hyd	2	0.142	0.132	**0.0870**

Table 3.9: Results of the 2011 Entity Search Track.

account. This is a consequent development step over last 2010 challenge, where weighting properties individually was the key feature for success. The general observation is that considering the particular pieces of the structured data yields higher performance over unstructured, text-based retrieval. This shows that search can benefit from considering structure information.

Similar to the 2010 challenge, one of the main and promising features of the RDF data model, namely the ability to express and type the relations between entities was only used by one run from DERI, which did not exceed the other runs. Whether relations are actually not helpful for entity search on large scale datasets or whether the usage of the relations is not yet understood remains to be investigated in the future.

2011 List Search Track Evaluation

The List Search Track comprises queries that describe sets of entities, but where the relevant entities are not named explicitly in the query. This track was designed to encourage participating systems to exploit relations between entities and type information of entities, therefore raising the complexity of the queries. The information need is expressed by a number of keywords (minimum three) that describe criteria that need to be matched by the returned results. The goal is to rank higher the entities that match the criteria than entities that do not match the criteria. Examples of the queries used in the two tracks are shown in Table 3.3 and described in the Section 3.4.2.

For the List Search track, the workers were presented additionally with a reference list of correct entities in addition to the criteria itself, which was obtained through manual searching by the organizers. This was done as the queries were of such difficulty that many assessors may not know the answers themselves.

In general the teams participated with the same systems in the List Search Track and adapted them only slightly to this new task, although the most high-performing system was specially designed for the List Track. The modifications are mostly on query analysis and interpretation, because the queries were not just keywords but more complex descriptions in natural language, as described in Section 3.4.2. The modifications as well as the additional system are described in the next section followed by the results for this track.

Participating Systems in the List Search Track

Delaware:

> The team from Delaware applied an NLP parser to process the queries for run **UDelRun1**, in order to find the target type of the entities. Only entities belonging to this type were considered as results. For the runs **UDelRun2** and **UDelRun3** the type information was manually expanded, because the automatic processing failed in some cases. Instead of the axiomatic retrieval function, model-based relevance feedback was applied for run **UDelRun3** [164].

DERI:

> DERI participated with an identical system configuration in the List Search Track.

NTNU:

> NTNU participated with a system especially designed for this track. The system used only the Wikipedia dataset and mapped the results to entities in the BTC collection. The queries were analyzed and potentially reformulated using the Wikipedia Miner software [119], in order to find the primary entity of the query. The query was run against an index of Wikipedia abstracts to get a candidate list of Wikipedia articles. The outgoing links from these articles were expanded and the resulting articles were also added to the candidate list. Scores are added if an article occurs multiple times and articles with a direct relation to the principal entity are boosted. In contrast to run **NTNU-1**, the runs **NTNU-2** and **NTNU-3** used an additional boosting for articles belonging to a Wikipedia set that had more than a certain fraction of its set of members in the candidate list. Run **NTNU-3** also applied an additional boost based on *sameAs* links.

DA-IICT:

The system by DA-IICT used a text-based approach built on Terrier [128] which favored entities according to the number of query terms present in their textual description. Due to data loss, the queries were only run against a part of the BTC data collection.

List Search Track Results

The retrieval performance for the submitted runs are shown in Table 3.10. The metrics were computed the same ways as for the Entity Track. There are on average 13 relevant entities per query with a standard deviation of 12.8. The participating systems could not find relevant entities for 6 queries. These were the queries with numbers $q15$, $q23$, $q27$, $q28$, $q45$ and $q48$, for example $q15$: "henry ii's brothers and sisters".

Participant	Run	P@10	P@5	MAP
NTNU	3	0.354	0.356	0.2790
NTNU	2	0.348	0.372	0.2594
NTNU	1	0.204	0.200	0.1625
DERI	1	0.210	0.220	0.1591
DERI	3	0.186	0.216	0.1526
DERI	2	0.192	0.216	0.1505
UDel	1	0.170	0.200	0.1079
UDel	2	0.162	0.152	0.0999
IIIT Hyd	1	0.072	0.076	0.0328
IIIT Hyd	2	0.072	0.076	0.0328
DA-IICT	1	0.014	0.012	0.0050

Table 3.10: Results of the 2011 List Search Track.

Discussion of the 2011 List Search Track

The List Search Track proved to be a hard task and may require different techniques compared to the Entity Search Track. Since this track was new, most teams participated with their systems built for the Entity Search Track and adapted to the task mainly by analyzing and interpreting the query. Still, the performances show that solutions can be delivered, although there is still room for improvement. The winning system by NTNU did not use the BTC data collection, but was built on the Wikipedia corpus and exploited the links between articles, demonstrating that the plain links between articles are a valuable resource for search. Ideally, such algorithms could eventually be adopted to more general-purpose RDF structured data outside that of Wikipedia.

Discussion of the 2011 Semantic Search Challenge

The Semantic Search Challenge started in 2010 with the task of entity search from RDF data crawled from the Web. Though this task is seemingly simple, because the query contains the name of the entity, it features many of the problems in semantic search, including the potential ambiguity of short-form queries, the varying degrees of relevance by which an entity can be related to the one named in the query and the general quality issues inherent to Web data. The List Search Track introduced in 2011 presented an even harder problem, i.e. queries that don't explicitly name an entity, but rather describe the set of matching entities.

There are a number of open questions that may impact the end-user benefits of semantic search engines and would still need to be investigated. For example, the retrieval engines above do not attempt to remove duplicates, and may return different, redundant descriptions of the same entity multiple times. A semantic search engine should remove such duplicates or merge them. We will address this problem later in Chapter 6. Similarly, the user experience is largely impacted by the explanations given by the search engines. Similar to how current text search engines generate summaries and highlight keyword matches, a semantic search engine should attempt to summarize information from an RDF graph and highlight why a particular result is an answer to the user's query.

3.7 Conclusion

Summary. The topic of semantic search has attracted large interests both from industry and research, resulting in a variety of solutions that target different tasks. There is however no standardized evaluation framework that helps to monitor and stimulate the progress in this field. We define the two standard tasks of entity search and entity list search, which are commonly supported by semantic search systems. Starting with these tasks, we run evaluation campaigns organized in the context of the series of Semantic Search workshops to assess the state-of-the-art in semantic search with respect two these basic tasks. Aiming at affordable, repeatable and reliable evaluation, we provide a crowdsourcing-based evaluation methodology alongside with a semantic search evaluation framework consisting of real-world queries and datasets. This work discusses the tasks, the framework, the performances achieved by the systems participated in the campaigns, and the repeatability and reliability of the proposed methodology. We observed that not only evaluation was reliable and repeatable but also, experiments could be performed with acceptable cost.

Conclusions. We investigated the Research Question 1. From this research question, two hypotheses are derived and examined in our experiments. Hypothesis 1.1 assumed the repeatability of our approach. Repeatability means here that the crowd-sourced relevance assessment yield the same result when evaluated at different points in time by different non-expert judges. We have investigated the agreement between the different sets of judges and based on the high agreement, we regard the above hypothesis as confirmed. This first hypothesis is a necessary condition, for the following Hypothesis 1.2 on reliability. As mentioned before, the framework has to be repeatable in order to be reliable. However, reliable here means also that the anonymous judges, which are not trained and perhaps not familiar with the Web of data or any of the applied concepts, understand the task and produce assessments of a quality close enough to those judged by experts. In our experiments, we have examined the number of judges required to achieve a stable consensus and also the agreement between expert and crowd-sourced judges and observed an agreement between these groups that allow us to consider also the above hypothesis as confirmed.

Besides analyzing our evaluation framework with respect to the above hypotheses, we have shown the applicability of the framework in two evaluation campaigns. Hence, we consider the provided evaluation framework as a basis platform, which invites researchers to participate and several studies have already used our framework [27, 40, 47, 148], which shows the general acceptance by the research community.

Outlook. So far, the methodology has been tested only with respect to two tasks, entity search and list search. Consequently, a further direction of research is to extend it to cover other retrieval scenarios, for example such as search for documents with embedded RDF or search for relations between entities. Moreover, an open question is whether the evaluation process can be further automatized by detecting outlier judges or classifying problematic results, where no consensus can be achieved.

Chapter 4

A Ranking Model for Hybrid Search Queries over Textual and Structured Data

Advances in entity recognition as well as the incentive provided by search engine providers to return a more enhanced result presentation for Web pages with structured data annotations, lead to an increasing amount of structured data embedded in documents on the Web. Also at the level of queries, structure information can be made available in addition to keywords, which might be obtained through query annotation tools or expressed manually by means of hybrid query languages. While efficient solutions for managing these hybrid data and queries exist, there is a lack of search solutions that support the effective ranking of results in this setting. In particular, existing search solutions focus either on document or structured data search, and use either term-based or structured representations of queries for ranking. In this work, we present a general principled ranking model based on the use of language models, which enables the use of keywords, structured, or hybrid queries to express information needs and ranks results comprising documents, structured data, or their combination. In experiments using established benchmarks, which involve both document and structured data search tasks, we show that our approach using hybrid queries yields up to 23% improvements upon existing ranking approaches.

Outline. We start this chapter with an introduction in Section 4.1 and state the research question, the hypotheses and the contribution of this chapter in Section 4.2. In Section 4.3 we define the notions of hybrid query and hybrid data and discuss existing ranking strategies. How we use hybrid queries and data in our ranking approach is explained in Section 4.4. Related work is discussed in Section 4.5 and related and prior approaches are used in our evaluation. Our experimental results are presented and discussed in Section 4.6. We conclude in Section 4.7.

4.1 Introduction

Searching for information is one of the most frequent tasks on the Web as well as in corporate environments or on personal devices. Using keywords to express information needs is the dominant query paradigm applied for search, because its simplicity makes it suitable for fast, ad-hoc search and also enables lay users to find information easily. Advances in entity recognition and extraction make it possible to automatically augment keyword queries with structured information [39] and hence, it is desirable to allow also more expressive query constructs, which combine keywords with structured parts, or fully structured queries that more precisely capture the information needs. Providing these different means for querying, i.e. keywords, fully structured and *hybrid queries*, requires a ranking approach that covers this whole range and exploits the various cues (keywords and structure) to show the most relevant results to the user.

Besides having one single point of entry for all types of search requests, it is also desirable to make the entire data spectrum, ranging from unstructured textual documents to structured data, available to these search requests. This requires a ranking framework that is also capable of dealing with and exploiting different cues in the data. Handling textual data in combination with structured data, i.e. *hybrid data*, is becoming more important, because an increasing amount of structured data is published in addition to unstructured data on the Web. Providers publish structured data as Linked Data[1], or embed them in existing pages as annotations in the form of microformats or RDFa[2]. For example, Semantic MediaWiki [98], a collaborative editing web-platform, allows to publish unstructured and structured data and enjoys wide spread usage on the Web [77].

However, dealing with unstructured and structured data in an integrated fashion is a problem that is not specific to the Web but also attracted large investments in the enterprise setting. In the research community, this topic also known as DB&IR integration has gained much attention, resulting in many efficient solutions for hybrid data management, as discussed in Section 2.2. For instance, there are database solutions optimized for the integrated storage of unstructured and structured data [13], languages and mechanisms for dealing with hybrid queries containing structured query patterns as well as keywords [34, 147], and indexes for retrieving hybrid query results efficiently [159]. However, there is a lack of search solutions

---

[1] `http://linkeddata.org`, last retrieved on April 10th 2013
[2] `http://www.w3.org/TR/xhtml-rdfa-primer`, last retrieved on April 10th 2013

79

that support the *effective ranking of results in this hybrid data and hybrid query scenario*.

In particular, existing ranking solutions focus either on document or structured data search. Structured data search approaches can be classified into those that given keyword queries, search for matching entity descriptions given as structured data, called *entity search* [121] or *ad-hoc object retrieval* [130], or complex relational results representing several entities and their relationships, called *Relational keyword search (RKS)* [45]. Document retrieval solutions return documents instead of structured data as results. Most related to this hybrid scenario are approaches, which deal with structured (XML) documents [167], called *Structured document retrieval (SDR)* or those, which make use of annotations, called *Annotation-based document retrieval (ADR)* [39]. In the extreme case where documents are modeled entirely as annotations, ADR amounts to a structured data search task, namely the retrieval of annotations describing documents [78, 146]. To be effective, existing approaches rely on heuristics that are specific to either one of these tasks. In fact, most ranking approaches for entity search and RKS adapt ranking solutions originally proposed for (structured) document retrieval such as BM25F, introducing special heuristics such as length and structure normalization [105] to cope with differences in the structured data case. As a result of using fine-tuned heuristics, existing approaches are not directly applicable to both tasks, i.e. they are not applicable to queries that may ask for documents, structured data or a combination of the two. Moreover, a recent benchmark study [45] has shown that the use of heuristics (as proposed for RKS [105]) may do not perform well in a larger scale experiment with a broader set of queries. In this work, we use a principled approach based on the statistical framework of language models (LMs) [129] to study ranking in both data and document retrieval scenarios.

Also at the query level, we note that existing approaches have limitations w.r.t. our hybrid setting. Possibly due to their high degree of ambiguity, the proposed ranking approaches are mainly concerned with keyword queries. That is, there is a lack of approaches that not only exploit words and structure in the data, but also words and *structure in the query* for ranking. We evaluate our ranking model using established benchmarks in a document as well as in a structured data search scenario. The applied benchmarks provide keyword queries. We automatically annotate these keyword queries to construct hybrid queries using an existing annotation service [119]. Since automatic annotations are not perfect, we additionally study the situation when users interfere. They simply remove the constructed annotations and queries considered as not relevant for their needs and use the original keywords instead. As a result, we have three different query types in our experiment, (1) *keyword* queries, (2) automatically obtained *hybrid* queries and (3) hybrid queries refined by the *user*.

4.2 Research Question and Contribution

In this chapter, we study the ranking of hybrid queries over hybrid data and address the following research question:

Research Question 2. *How can results consisting of structured and unstructured data be ranked by relevance for hybrid queries?*

We ask this question because document and structured data search tasks have been done in separate systems in the past and we aim at unifying them. Hence, our first hypothesis in this chapter is:

Hypothesis 2.1. *Extending the language model based retrieval framework to take structured information at the query and data level into account allows to address information needs of both, document and also structured data search scenarios, with a retrieval effectiveness at the same level or better than previous approaches tailored for either of the two tasks.*

This hypothesis assumes that a unified approach allows to solve both tasks with the same system. Moreover, we want to allow not just unstructured keyword queries, but also use hybrid queries for search, and further investigate the following second hypothesis in this chapter:

Hypothesis 2.2. *Hybrid queries executed over the combination of documents and structured data yield a higher precision than keyword queries.*

Regarding these two hypotheses, we propose a ranking model built on the principled LM-based framework [129].

Contribution 2. *Ranking Model for Hybrid Queries over Hybrid Data*

The contribution of this chapter towards effective ranking in the hybrid setting can be summarized as follows:

We propose a general principled LM-based ranking approach called *HybRank*, which enables the use of keywords, structured, or hybrid queries to express information needs and is able to rank results including documents, structured data, or their combination (e.g. relational results representing relationships between documents and other entities). To capture their hybrid nature, graph-structured models based on the RDF and SPARQL standards (refer to Section 2.1) are proposed for both data and queries. Nodes in the data and queries may refer to structured entities or texts modeled as bag-of-words. Language models are employed to model hybrid data and queries. The main technical difference to previous usage of LMs [22, 101, 121, 167] is the combined modeling of the unstructured as well as structured parts of the hybrid query. In experiments using established benchmarks, which involve both document and structured data search tasks, we show the best configuration of our approach using hybrid queries yields improvements of 23% upon state-of-the-art ADR, ES and RKS systems.

4.3 Overview

In this section, we discuss the problem of ranking in the hybrid setting, where queries and data may be structured, unstructured, or both. Then, we review existing works partially applicable to this setting, showing that *LMs* represent a principled and effective foundation that have been used to deal with the subproblems of ranking documents or structured data.

4.3.1 Hybrid Data and Queries

For modeling documents, entities and their relations, we use, for brevity, a simplified version of the graph-structured RDF model, as defined in Definition 2.1 without blank nodes. To capture unstructured data, we extend this model with bags of words $o \in D$, where $o = \{v_1, ..., v_i, ..., v_n\}$ and $v_i \in V$, the vocabulary of all words.

Definition 4.1 (Hybrid Data Graph). *Hybrid data is modeled as a graph $G(N, E)$, where nodes are the disjoint union of entity nodes N_E, literals L, document nodes N_D, and bags of words D, $N = N_E \cup N_D \cup L \cup D$, and edges $\mathcal{E}$ connecting the nodes $\mathcal{E} = \{\langle s, a, o \rangle \in (N_E \cup N_D) \times E \times N\}$ are called* **triples**. *Triples $\langle s, p, (o \in \cup D) \rangle$, which associate an element s with* **unstructured** *data, i.e. a bag of words $o \in \cup D$, can be distinguished from other triples $\langle s, a, (o \in N_E \cup L) \rangle$ that associate s with* **structured** *data, i.e. an IRI or a literal. In fact, a textual representation is used for every literal: for every $\langle s, a, (o \in L) \rangle$ there is a corresponding bag of words representation $\langle s, a, (o \in \cup D) \rangle$. Further, there are two special attributes, a_*, about $\in E$:*

- *$\langle s, a_*, \mathbf{o} \rangle$, where $\mathbf{o} = \bigcup_{\langle s, a, o \rangle \in \mathcal{E}} o \in D$, denotes the union of* **all bags of words** *associated with s,*

- *$\langle s, about, o \rangle$, where $s \in N_D$ and $o \in N_{EN}$, stands for* **entity annotations of** *the document s. Contrary to the usual definition, an instance of the about*

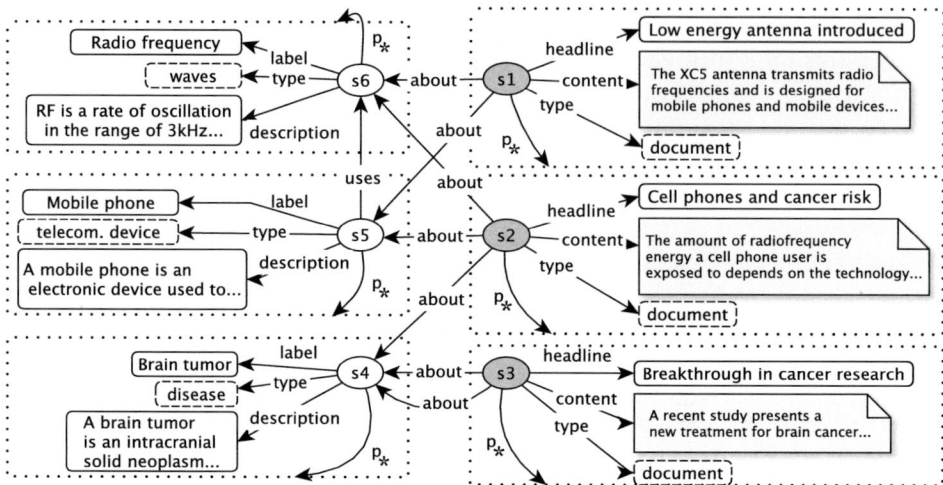

Figure 4.1: Hybrid Data Graph with document nodes N_D (gray) and entity nodes N_E (white).

triple can occur multiple times, e.g. when a document is annotated several times with the same entity.

This model simply extends the data graph model defined in Definition 2.1 with nodes that represent documents and two special relations. Hence, documents are simply treated as a particular kind of entities N_D that are associated with textual content D. In fact, both documents and other entities may be associated with bags of words and searched using the same mechanism. This is to deal with the fact that many entities captured in RDF, especially in Linked Data, are associated with long textual descriptions over attributes such as `comment` or `description`. All these textual descriptions of an entity or the textual content of a document can be combined and captured through a $\langle s, a_*, o \rangle$ triple. Annotations, the structured representation of textual descriptions, are modeled via the special triples $\langle s, about, o \rangle$.

Example 4.1 (Hybrid Data Graph). *Figure 4.1 illustrates an example of a hybrid data graph. The graph consists of three document nodes $s_1, s_2, s_3 \in N_D$, holding texts via the `content` edge. The entity annotations are expressed via the about edge from document nodes to entity nodes $s_4, s_5, s_6 \in N_{EN}$. Certainly, a document can be annotated several times with the same entity, as illustrated by the two about edges from s_3 to s_4. The nodes have edges to literals, e.g. `label` or `headline`, and edges to other entities, e.g. `uses`. Note the special a_*-edge, which comprises all textual information of one node.*

The standard model for querying Web data in RDF is SPARQL, a structured query language based on the notion of graph patterns, which we introduced in Section 2.1.2. We combine the core feature of SPARQL, basic graph pattern (BGP), with keywords to obtain Hybrid graph pattern (HGP) queries. The only difference to SPARQL BGP is that bags of words in D can also be used as constants:

Definition 4.2 (Hybrid Graph Pattern). *Let N_E be the set of IRIs, L be the set of literals, D be the set of all possible bags of words and X the set of all variables. A hybrid graph pattern is a set of triple patterns $P = \{\mathrm{p_i}, \ldots, \mathrm{p_n}\}$, where each $\mathrm{p} = \langle s, a, o \rangle \in (N_E \cup N_D \cup X) \times (E \cup X) \times N$. If $s, a, o \in X$, they are called variables, constants otherwise.*

Example 4.2 (Hybrid Query). *In Figure 4.2 we illustrate hybrid queries for different search tasks. $?x \in \mathcal{X}$ denote variables. (q_1) is the equivalent of a common keyword query, i.e. unstructured in our parlance, since it uses only a bag of words to describe the information need. (q_2) consists of exactly one triple pattern and thus, is completely structured, whereas (q_3) has one hybrid pattern, consisting of the structured element* label *and the bag of words holding the term "phone". (q_4) searches for documents and is essentially just a special kind of entity query. (q_5) and (q_6) illustrate how these patterns can be combined, e.g. query (q_5) asks for documents relevant to "treatment", which are annotated with s_4 (Brain tumor). Query (q_6) consists of a structured and a hybrid pattern and models an information need, where the searcher is interested in results on diseases related to "mobile phone".*

Modeling hybrid data and queries this way leverages the existing RDF and SPARQL standards. At the data level, no changes to the RDF semantics are needed because every bag of words in D can be treated as a special type of literals. Changes to the SPARQL semantics are needed so that besides the exact matching of literals/URIs in the query against literals/URIs in the data, IR style matching of keywords in the query against textual data can also be supported. (1) For instance, the semantics of exact matching as defined for SPARQL can further be used for structured components, i.e. the parts of the HGP which represent BGPs. For a triple pattern with a keyword component, $\langle s, a, q \rangle$, where $q \in D$ is a bag of words $q = \{q_1, \ldots, q_n\}$, there exists a mapping (a result) in the data if there are exact mappings of s and p to literals/URIs in the data, and there is a bag of words in the data that is *relevant* for o. (2) Alternatively, a vague relevance-based interpretation may be applied not only to the keyword part but also the structured part of the query so that also for that, non-exact matches varying in terms of

Entity search

q_1	$\langle ?x, a_*, \{\text{"mobile", "phone"}\}\rangle$
q_2	$\langle ?x, type, disease\rangle$
q_3	$\langle ?x, label, \{\text{"phone"}\}\rangle$

Document search

q_4	$\langle ?x, content, \{\text{"mobile", "phone", "cancer"}\}\rangle$

Relational search

q_5	$\langle ?x, content, \{\text{"treatment"}\}\rangle$
	$\langle ?x, about, s_4\rangle$
q_6	$\langle ?x_1, type, disease\rangle$
	$\langle ?x_2, about, ?x_1\rangle$
	$\langle ?x_2, a_*, \{\text{"mobile", "phone"}\}\rangle$

Figure 4.2: Hybrid Queries

relevance can be produced and considered as result candidates for ranking (this vague interpretation of structure constraints has shown to be effective for XML retrieval).

Matching vs. Ranking. More elaborated treatment of (other possible) query semantics that can be used for matching is however out of the scope of this thesis. The main problem is the ranking of complex results composed of unstructured and structured data, according to their relevance. For the purpose of ranking, internal representations of data and query based on (structured) LMs are used, which capture them as multinomial distributions over words. In the experiments, results are generated for the two semantics of the hybrid queries discussed above (exact and vague, where structured parts are also treated as keywords). That is, different semantics are used for *matching*, and the problem addressed is finding the *ranking* of matching results, which corresponds to the given relevance judgments.

4.3.2 Existing Approaches for Ranking

The ranking of results is determined by comparing the internal models of results and information needs (the latter is also called query, or more abstractly, the relevance model [101]). Different models of query and result have been proposed, among which LM represents a principled and effective way to approach the ranking problem. We will now discuss existing, particularly LM-based approaches proposed for dealing with structured and unstructured data/query that constitute the foundation of our *hybrid search* solution.

Result Modeling. A popular way to model not only documents but also entities and complex relational results is to represent them as vectors of TF-IDF term weights. For the relational case (for RKS tasks), every entity is seen as bags of words (each is associated with an entity through an attribute), and every result is a structured collection of entities. Adoption of *TF-IDF* weighting such as specific normalizations of IDF, inter-entity weights and the size of the structured result are introduced to recognize that here, every attribute-specific bag of words has its own vocabulary and thus shall be treated differently. A result is a collection and thus requires normalization beyond the single-entity level, and not only the single-entity length but also the overall size of the structured result shall have an effect on relevance [105]. For modeling structured entities [27] (ES tasks) and documents (SDR tasks) [86], *BM25F* have also been used, not only to assign attribute-specific TF-IDF weights to terms but also, to use different weights for attributes to recognize that some are more important than others in ranking entities. A recent benchmark study [45] has shown that the specific normalizations proposed for RKS [105] as well as other heuristics do not perform well when considering a broader set of queries and different types of data. As an alternative to modeling results through fine-tuned TF-IDF weights, *LM* represents a principled method based on statistical theories. An *unstructured* result s is treated as a multinomial distribution over terms $P(v|\theta_s), v \in \mathcal{V}$, and *structured* results are modeled through a collection of such LMs [80, 121]. For instance, an entity s is modeled as a linear mixture of attribute-specific language models θ_a, associated with a prior $P(a)$, i.e.

$$P(v|\theta_s) = \sum_{a \in A'(s)} P(v|\theta_a)P(a), \qquad (4.1)$$

where $A'(s)$ is the model of entity s as defined in Definition 2.4. An entity can be seen as the root while its attributes represent the leaves of a tree. For XML document retrieval, *hierarchical* models for trees with arbitrary depth have been proposed, which incorporate evidences, i.e. LMs, from children, descendants as well as parents [125]. A *relational* result $\mathbf{s}$ has been modeled as a geometric mean of the LMs of its entities, $\mathbf{s} = \{s_1, \dots, s_i, \dots, s_n\}$, i.e.

$$P(v|\theta_{\mathbf{s}}^k) = \sqrt[n]{P(v|\theta_{s_1}^k) \dots P(v|\theta_{s_n}^k)}, \qquad (4.2)$$

where one such attribute-specific model is constructed for every distinct $a^k \in A(s_i)$ of the entities $s_i \in \mathbf{s}$ [22].

Query Modeling. Also the *internal query model* used for ranking might be *structured* or *unstructured*. In XML retrieval for instance [125], ranking is based on the probability that the hierarchical result LM θ_s, generates the query q that is treated as a bag of words, i.e. based on $P(q|\theta_s) = \prod_{v \in q} P(v|\theta_s)^3$. As the query is often too short, pseudo-relevance feedback (PRF) has been used for expanding the query model. A LM-based approach to this is to construct a *relevance model* from PRF results [101]. For a keyword query $q = \{q_1, \ldots, q_n\}$, it captures the probability of observing a word v together with the query keywords, $q_1, \ldots, q_n$, in the PRF results,

$$P(v|\theta_q) \approx P(v|q_1, \ldots, q_n) = \frac{P(v, q_1, \ldots, q_n)}{P(q_1, \ldots, q_n)}. \tag{4.3}$$

Thus, the query model is a distribution that assigns non-zero probabilities not only to query words but also other words in the vocabulary that occur together with the query words. Note that compared to result modeling, not only the (PRF) results, but also the query is incorporated into the model. For RKS, also structured PRF results obtained for query keywords have been used [22]. Similar to the result modeling approach discussed before, the proposed query model comprises several models, one for every attribute in $a_k \in A(PRF) = \{a_1, \ldots, a_k, \ldots, a_m\}$ that can be found in the structured PRF results. The attribute-specific model θ_q^k estimates the probability of observing a word v together with some query keywords in q in the a_k's bag of words o of an entity $s \in PRF$, $\langle s, a_k, o \rangle \in \mathcal{E}$ (denoted by $a_k : (q, v)$). Because the query is unstructured, i.e. it is unknown which attribute a query keyword is associated with, it actually estimates the probability of observing v in a_k, given the query has been observed in any attribute (the event $a_* : q$, where a_* is the special symbol we introduced to represent any attribute in $A(s)$, in this case):

$$
\begin{aligned}
P(v|\theta_q^k) &\approx P(a_k : v | q_1, \ldots, q_n) = \frac{P(a_k : (v, q), a_* : q)}{P(a_* : q)} \\
&\approx \frac{\sum_{s \in PRF} P(v|a_k, s) \cdot \prod_{i=1}^{n} P(q_i | a_*, s)}{\sum_{s \in PRF} \prod_{i=1}^{n} P(q_i | a_*, s)}
\end{aligned}
\tag{4.4}
$$

---

[3]To be precise, it is $P(q|\theta_s) = \prod_{v \in q} P(v|\theta_s)^{tf(v,q)}$. For clarity, we assume every term v appears only once in the query, $tf(v, q) = 1$.

Hybrid Search Modeling. In summary, LMs have be used to capture both structured and unstructured results. Existing approaches use specific models for either data or document retrieval, e.g. SDR uses structured and hierarchical LMs for documents [125], ES and RKS used structured models for entities and relational results [22, 121]. Our data model captures documents as another type of entities such that in principle, models used for SDR and RKS (e.g. Eqs. 4.1+4.2) can be applied to deal with hybrid data. In particular, our work builds upon the idea behind entity modeling (Equation 4.1) using attribute-specific models associated with weights to indicate their importance. Similar to previous RKS work (Equation 4.2), a structured result is also treated as a collection of entities. However, because every entity occurs exactly once in the structured RKS result, previous work employs a set of entities. The ranking score of the final result is simply the arithmetic mean of the scores of its entities (entities have the same weight). Our work additionally considers the document retrieval case, where annotations may occur several times in the document. We propose to use the resulting counts to obtain different weights for the annotations. To account for this, parameter estimation and the combination of entity scores differ from previous works.

Crucial differences to previous work are at the query level. We note that while structured and hybrid queries are available (as inputs), they were not used for ranking (as the internal query model). For ADR tasks, structured data have been extracted not only from texts but also from queries to represent them as XML fragments [39]. However, these hybrid queries are only used for matching, i.e. finding results. Also in the SDR case, the structured component of the content-and-structure queries are used to prune results, while only its keyword (content) component is used for ranking the remaining candidate results [125, 167]. More precisely, the LMs of candidate results (e.g. Equation 4.1) are used to determine their relevance, based on the probabilities the keyword components of the query can be observed. In other words, an unstructured model of the query is used for ranking here. The query model in Equation 4.4 also captures the structure of PRF results, but assumes an unstructured query (q may appear in any attribute a_*). Our solution is also based on the use of PRF results [22, 101]. However, the proposed ranking model incorporates queries that may be composed of unstructured and structured components. That is, the internal query model is hybrid, capturing that some query keyword may appear in a_* or some specific attributes a.

4.4 HybRank

First, we give a brief overview of the ranking procedure employed by our approach before we explain the involved models in detail. For a given hybrid query q, results S are obtained from the data through matching. The aim of our procedure is to rank each individual result $\mathbf{s} \in S$ for the query q. For this ranking task a model θ_q representing the query q and a model $\theta_{\mathbf{s}}$ representing a result $\mathbf{s} \in S$ are computed. For constructing θ_q, PRF results are needed. Thus, the process is (1) matching q against the data to obtain S, (2) producing an initial ranking to focus on the k-best PRF results, (3) constructing θ_q from these PRF results, (4) constructing a model $\theta_{\mathbf{s}}$ for every $\mathbf{s} \in S$, and finally (5) compute a ranking score for each result $\mathbf{s}$ and query q using the corresponding models θ_q and $\theta_{\mathbf{s}}$. We employ the cross entropy H, as discussed in Section 2.2.6 and compute the difference for each attribute specific model, i.e. we split the query model θ_q into attribute specific models θ_q^k for each attribute $a^k \in A'(PRF)$, and analogously we split $\theta_{\mathbf{s}}$ into corresponding models $\theta_{\mathbf{s}}^k$:

$$Score(q, \mathbf{s}) = H(\theta_q || \theta_{\mathbf{s}}) = \sum_{a^k \in A'(PRF)} \sum_{v \in \mathcal{V}} P(v|\theta_q^k) log P(v|\theta_{\mathbf{s}}^k) \qquad (4.5)$$

We will now discuss the five steps and explain the models in detail.

4.4.1 Modeling Hybrid Queries

The input to our procedure is a hybrid query where the structured parts may have been constructed manually, or by means of query annotation tools as in previous work [39] or through the support of a user interface [14, 15]. Let the query be q, its structured part be $\{\langle s_1, a_1, q_1 \rangle, ..., \langle s_m, a_m, q_m \rangle\}$, and its unstructured part be $\{\langle s_{m+1}, a_*, q_{m+1} \rangle, ..., \langle s_l, a_*, q_l \rangle\}$. For the purpose of ranking, also the elements q_i in the structured part are treated as keywords, i.e. as bags of words $q_i = \{q_{1i}, ...q_{ni}\}$. We propose an attribute-specific query model θ_q^k that estimates the probability of observing a word v in a_k (in a_k's bag of words to be precise), written as $a_k{:}v$, given that (1) query keywords have been observed in specific attributes as specified by the structured part of the query, i.e. $a_1{:}q_1, ..., a_m{:}q_m$, and (2) $q_{m+1}, ..., q_l$ observed in any attribute a_* (unstructured part of the query):

$$P(v|\theta_q^k) \approx P(a_k{:}v | a_1{:}q_1, ..., a_k{:}(q_k, v), ..., a_m{:}q_m, a_*{:}(q_{m+1}, ..., q_l)) \qquad (4.6)$$

We approximate $P(v|\theta_q^k)$ analogously to Equation 4.3 as:

$$P(v|\theta_q^k) \approx \frac{P(a_1:q_1,...,a_k:(q_k,v),...,a_m:q_m,a_*:(q_{m+1},...,q_l))}{P(a_1:q_1,...,a_m:q_m,a_*:(q_{m+1},...,q_l))} \qquad (4.7)$$

and estimate it as:

$$P(v|\theta_q^k) = \frac{\sum_{s \in PRF} P(v|a_k,s)P(a_k|s)P(s)P(q|s)}{\sum_{s \in PRF} P(q|s)} \qquad (4.8)$$

$$P(q|s) = \prod_{i=1}^{m+1} P(a_i|s) \prod_{j=1,q_{ji} \in q_i}^{n} P(q_{ji}|a_i,s) \qquad (4.9)$$

The estimates above is obtained through i.i.d. sampling on structured PRF results. Note there are many differences to previous work (Equation 4.4 [22]). First, we apply weights, $P(a_k|s)$, to each attribute a_k to explicitly distinguish its importance and take the structure of the result as captured by its attributes into account. This weight, $P(a_k|s)$, denotes the probability that an attribute a_k is generated by the PRF result s. Further, the term $P(s)$ is explicitly added to make clear that the probability of observing an entity s in the PRF set is not uniform. Intuitively, $P(s)$ indicates the importance of an entity s. Finally, the term $P(q|s)$ takes the structure of the query into account and estimates the probability that given s, we observe the structure $P(a_j|s)$ (i.e. the attributes and their weights, analogous to $P(a_k|s)$) and query keywords in this structure, $P(a_{ji}|a_i,s)$. Note that as defined before, the query has $m+1$ attributes (m attributes for the structured part and one for the keyword part), and every q_i associated with an attribute has n elements. All of them are incorporated into the model through the term $P(q|s)$. The top-k PRF set of entities used for this estimation is retrieved using the given HGP, and ranked using a mechanism described in Section 4.4.3.

Example 4.3 (Hybrid Query Model). *Assume for query q_3 (Figure 4.2), we obtain the PRF results $PRF = \{s_5,s_6\}$ (see nodes in Figure 4.1). We observe five attributes in this PRF set, namely {label, type, description, uses, a_*}, and build a model for each, e.g. $\theta_{q3}^{description}$. Given this model $\theta_{q3}^{description}$, we estimate (1) the probability of observing a word v in every PRF result, (2) weighted by the probability of observing the query. For instance, we estimate the probability of observing a word, e.g. $v = $ "mobile", i.e. $P(\text{"mobile"}|\theta_{q3}^{description})$. For (1), we sum over each node in the PRF set and estimate the probabilities, e.g. for s_5, that we observe "mobile" in* *the bag of words of the description of s_5, i.e. $P(\text{"mobile"}|description, s_5)$, that we observe the attribute description for s_5, $P(description|s_5)$ and the prior probability of s_5, $P(s_5)$. For (2) the query weighting component $P(q_3|s_5)$, we estimate the probability of observing the query structure including a_* and its content, given s_5, i.e. we iterate over $a_i \in \{label, a_*\}$ (because label is the only attribute given in the query) and then over the content of these attributes. In this case, the content of both are the same, which consists only of one word ($n = 1$), $q_{label} = q_* = \{\text{"phone"}\}$.*

4.4.2 Modeling Hybrid Results

Because PRF results are incorporated, the query model proposed above already involves data. One can think of it as being composed of two components, a query-independent one capturing the probability a word v will be observed, and a query-dependent component $P(q|s)$, which ensures that v occurs together with the query. For modeling the results, the same idea applies but the query-dependent component is no longer needed.

In the general hybrid search case, the result is a set of triples $\{\langle s_1, a_1, o_1 \rangle, \ldots, \langle s_i, a_i, o_i \rangle\}, \ldots, \langle s_n, a_n, o_n \rangle\}$, where any s_i and o_i might be a document, or an entity. For ranking, the result is treated as a set of entities $\mathbf{s}$, where each $s_i \in \mathbf{s}$ is associated with a weight component $P(s_i)$. This entity set includes all s_i and o_i in the result, which represents a document or an entity. In the case they represent triples, both the subject and object of the triples are added to $\mathbf{s}$.

The result model captures the probability of observing v in the a_k's bag of words o of an entity $s_i \in \mathbf{s}$, where $\langle s_i, a_k, o \rangle$ is a triple in the result, and $\mathbf{s}$ is the set of entities, each associated with a weight component $P(s_i)$:

$$P(v|\theta_{\mathbf{s}}^k) = \sum_{s_i \in \mathbf{s}} P(s_i) P(v|a_k, s_i) P(a_k|s_i) \tag{4.10}$$

4.4.3 Computing PRF Results

Given the HGP q, we employ exact matching for the structured part, and the vague interpretation of the unstructured part as discussed before to obtain results. That is, for a triple pattern $\langle s_k, a_*, q_k \rangle$, s is a binding to the variable s_k if o, a bag of words associated with s, is relevant for the keywords q_k. This matching step is employed not only to produce the PRF set but also to obtain the set of all candidate results S that shall be ranked.

AND-semantics is the standard for interpreting SPARQL BGPs, i.e. bindings to triple patterns that share a common variable are joined so that entities matching the join variable satisfy both patterns. AND-semantics is however too strict in some cases, missing results that are relevant, as observed in our experiments. An alternative is the less "exact" OR-semantics, where instead of the join, the union is performed to combine results from different patterns. Moreover, a HGP can be treated as an unstructured query, i.e. converted to a set of keywords. However, while using keywords to obtain documents and entities (in the PRF set) is possible, the retrieval of relational results using keywords is less straightforward. In this work, we employ OR-semantics to build the PRF set as well as the set of all results S.

In the general relational case, this matching yields sets of triples as results. Entities are extracted from these structured results to produce the PRF set. As discussed, documents and entities are directly put into **s**, the set representation of a result, while reified triples are expanded to obtain their subjects and objects.

Thus, results to q can also be conceived as the union of all entity result sets **s**. Ranking the entities in this union set is needed to obtain the k-best one forming the PRF set. Note that at this point, the query model based on PRF results, θ_q, is not built yet. One way to approach this is to treat the HGP and entities as unstructured bags of words and rank them using a standard IR approach. Analogous to the modeling of results (Equation 4.10), we construct structured models of results and queries as

$$P(v|\theta_x^k) = P(v|a_k, x)P(a_k|x), \tag{4.11}$$

where x may stand for a result s or a query q. The query model used here is not estimated from PRF results but simply from the attributes and keywords given in the query. As we will see in the subsequent section, without smoothing, $P(v|\theta_q^k) > 0$ only when v is mentioned in a triple pattern in the query, i.e. there is $\langle s, a_k, q \rangle$, $v \in q$.

4.4.4 Parameter Estimation

We apply maximum likelihood estimation to obtain the language models and the general smoothing technique is Jelinek-Mercer smoothing, see Section 2.2.5 for a brief discussion of these techniques. The probability $P(v|a_k, s)$ of observing the word v given an attribute a_k and an entity s is obtained through a two-stage smoothing. First, it is smoothed by the probability of observing the word v for any attribute a_*, i.e. $P(v|a_*, s)$, and then, with the collection probability $P(v|D)$. This smoothing is controlled by the corresponding parameters λ_k, s.t. λ_* and λ_D, $\lambda_k + \lambda_* + \lambda_D = 1$:

$$
\begin{aligned}
P(v|a_k,s) &= \lambda_k P(v|a_k,s) + \lambda_* P(v|a_*,s) + \lambda_D P(v|D) \\
&= \lambda_k \frac{n(v,o_{s,k})}{|o_{s,k}|} + \lambda_* \frac{n(v,o_{s,*})}{|o_{s,*}|} \\
&\quad + \lambda_D \frac{\sum_{o \in D} n(v,o)}{\sum_{o \in D} |o|},
\end{aligned}
\tag{4.12}
$$

where $o_{s,k}$ and $o_{s,*}$ denote the bags of words of the attributes a_k and a_*, respectively, which are associated with the entity s.

In hybrid data, some entities/documents might have very few attributes, whereas other might have many. Using uniform weights for attributes often results in a bias towards results with many attributes. Thus, we introduce $P(a|s)$ to distribute the probability mass over the edges of s using Dirichlet smoothing:

$$
P(a|s) = \frac{n(a, A(s)) + \mu_a \frac{n(a,E)}{|E|}}{|A(s)| + \mu_a}
\tag{4.13}
$$

where $n(a, A(s))$ denotes the count of a in the description of s and μ_p controls the smoothing of the background of observing a in the data graph.

In previous work, a uniform prior $P(s)$ is used because a document occurs only once in the PRF results [101], and likewise, an entity occurs only once in the relational result [22]. In the hybrid case, an entity annotation may occur several times in the documents. Before, we discussed how to construct the set representation of structured results, $\mathbf{s}$. During this process, the counts $n(s,\mathbf{s})$ are kept so that $\mathbf{s}$ can also be seen as a bag of entities. Similar to equation 4.13, we estimate:

$$
P(s) = \frac{n(s,\mathbf{s}) + \mu_s \frac{n(s,\mathbf{s})}{|N_D \cup N_E|}}{|\mathbf{s}| + \mu_s}
\tag{4.14}
$$

4.4.5 HybRank Implementation

HybRank is implemented based on techniques and available implementations for language models. Additional to unstructured documents, HybRank also deals with structured data entries. However, the previous discussion on parameter estimation makes clear that for supporting both these types of data, only frequency statistics are needed (counts). An advantage of this is that these statistics can be computed offline and stored in an index for an efficient computation during runtime. As described in the related work section, language models implemented in this way have been successfully applied for information retrieval before and shown to perform well.

4.5 Related Work

We presented hybrid search as a general search direction that includes document retrieval approaches such as SDR and ADR and structured data search approaches such as ES and RKS. For ES and especially RKS, the PageRank concept has been adapted so that a *popularity* score can also be computed for entity nodes forming data graphs [85, 122]. While the original PageRank is applied to graphs capturing only one type of links (hyperlinks), these approaches address the problem of dealing with different edge types that vary in semantics. Also, *proximity-based* ranking has been applied to the structured data case, where structural proximity is defined as a window of elements in structured XML data or the length of edges in relational search results [90].

Popularity and proximity-based concepts are orthogonal to the type of ranking concerned here, which is based on a *distance* metric between the models of query and result. For this, adaptations of the vector-space model [32] and BM25F [27] as well as customized normalizations [105] of TF-IDF weights have been proposed for the structured data setting. Most related are LM-based approaches that have been adapted for keyword-based object retrieval [123], ranking results to structured SPARQL queries [55], or structured LM models for inferring values in empty fields of structured databases [102]. These and specifically the LM approaches discussed in Section 2.2 constitute the foundation for HybRank, our LM approach to hybrid search. We pointed out the differences between HybRank and these approaches: (1) In summary, existing solutions use (a) only the keyword part of the hybrid query for matching and ranking or (b) the hybrid query for matching and the keyword part for ranking. We are the first to present a solution that uses (c) the hybrid query for both *matching and ranking*. Further, we do not target either data or document retrieval, but both scenarios. (2) Orthogonal to this, approaches belonging to either of the three types (a), (b) and (c) may also exploit *PRF results* to infer the needs and to expand the query (or not). (3) Just like candidate results, only keywords or both structure and keywords might be used for *finding PRF results*. (4) Further, *ranking PRF results* is necessary because only the top results form the PRF set. The ranking strategy applied to PRF results might be different from the strategy used for ranking the final results (the latter can exploit PRF results for query modeling).

In the next experimental section, we will compare HybRank against the related LM-based approaches as discussed before, which can be distinguished w.r.t. these dimensions as follows. *Relevance-based Language Model (RM)* represents a state-of-the-art document retrieval baseline [101], which uses the unstructured query to obtain PRF results and to construct the relevance model as an unstructured query model (Equation 4.3). This query model is then matched against unstructured models of results to rank candidate documents retrieved via keywords. *ADR* is the annotation-based baseline, which implements the idea behind the work based on XML fragments [39]. The implementation used in our experiments later uses RM for ranking. The difference to RM is that it retrieves candidate documents using hybrid queries. Inputs to ADR are documents and queries, which were annotated using a standard data extraction tool [119]. *RKS* [22] is the third approach, which can be used to rank entities and relational results in general. It uses keyword queries to retrieve structured PRF results. A structured model of these results is combined with the unstructured query to obtain the query model (Equation 4.4). As opposed to RKS, *HybRank* uses hybrid queries to retrieve and a structured approach (i.e. structured model of the query and result) to rank PRF results (Equation 4.11). Further, the structured model of results is combined with the hybrid query for ranking final results (Equation 4.8).

4.6 Experiments

In this section we present the experimental results and compare them to the previously described approaches *RM*, *ADR* and *RKS*. We use well established evaluation benchmarks for our experiment and augment them with structured annotations to obtain hybrid data and queries. We used the wikify service of the Wikipedia Miner [119] to annotate queries and documents with Wikipedia entities, and then follow the mappings between Wikipedia and DBpedia[4] entities to retrieve more structured data. We performed experiments in two settings, one where keyword queries and unstructured documents are transformed to hybrid queries and data using the annotation service. In the other setting, the keyword queries are annotated and then executed against hybrid data that is directly given. In summary, the results

---

[4]http://dbpedia.org, last retrieved on April 11 2013

of both these document and structured data search experiments suggest that using hybrid queries can produce better results than using keyword queries, especially when embedded structure information is not only used for matching but also for ranking as supported by our HybRank approach.

Hybrid Queries. Both evaluation benchmarks used for our experiments contain keyword query sets. For these keyword queries, we obtain entity annotations (Wikipedia articles) and through correspondences between them and DBpedia entities, more structured data about these entities can be obtained as illustrated in Figure 4.4 and Figure 4.5. We use common attributes associated with DBpedia entities including *label* and *name* to automatically construct hybrid queries (the sets of attributes are fixed beforehand , but vary in the different experiments here that involve datasets from different domains). For each entity annotation s obtained for a keyword query q a hybrid triple pattern $\langle x,a,o \rangle$ is constructed, where x is a variable, $x \in \mathcal{X}$, $o \in D$ is a bag of words containing the terms extracted from the values of p. The final hybrid query contains triple patterns constructed from annotations as $\langle x,a,o \rangle$ as discussed, or just keywords in the form of $\langle x,a_*,q \rangle$. Examples of keyword queries and corresponding hybrid queries are shown in Table 4.1 and Table 4.9.

For both the document and structured data search experiments, we experimented with three types of query sets, (1) *keyword*, (2) *hybrid* queries constructed automatically as explained above, or through additional (3) *user* involvement. The third type aims to mimic a scenario with user interactions. The system automatically computes the query annotations and presents them to the users who decide whether they represent the intended information need (as described in the benchmarks) or not. We apply the most simple mechanism where the user (one of the authors) simply rejects annotations, if they do not fit to the information need, and uses the keyword query only, or to accept the automatically generated hybrid query as-is. It has been shown that regular Web users can judge whether an entity fits to an information need [25]. Hence, we regard the use of this simple interaction mechanism, where users can accept certain query annotations and reject others as a feasible scenario. Applying more complex user interaction could be a promising path for future work that could further improve the quality of hybrid queries.

Query ID	Keyword query	Hybrid query
TREC 303	*Hubble Telescope Achievements*	$\langle ?x, content, \{"hubble", "telescope", "achievements"\}\rangle$ $\langle ?x_1, label, \{"hubble", "telescope", "space"\}\rangle$
TREC 307*	*New Hydroelectric Projects*	$\langle ?x, content, \{"new", "hydroelectric", "projects"\}\rangle$ $\langle ?x_1, label, \{"hydroelectricity"\}\rangle$
TREC 310	*Radio Waves and Brain Cancer*	$\langle ?x, content, \{"radio", "waves", "brain", "cancer"\}\rangle$ $\langle ?x_1, label, \{"radio"\}\rangle$ $\langle ?x_2, label, \{"wave"\}\rangle$ $\langle ?x_3, label, \{"brain", "tumor"\}\rangle$
TREC 314	*Marine Vegetation*	$\langle ?x, content, \{"marine", "vegetation"\}\rangle$ $\langle ?x_1, label, \{"marine", "ocean"\}\rangle$ $\langle ?x_2, label, \{"vegetation"\}\rangle$
TREC 322	*International Art Crime*	$\langle ?x, content, \{"international", "art", "crime"\}\rangle$ $\langle ?x_1, label, \{"art"\}\rangle$ $\langle ?x_2, label, \{"crime"\}\rangle$

* in the *user* scenario, annotations were rejected.

Table 4.1: Five example queries of TREC HARD 2005 query set and corresponding hybrid queries.

4.6.1 Document Retrieval using Annotations

We studied our approach in the setting of the TREC 2005 HARD track [1] which uses the ACQUAINT[5] collection and 50 keyword topics.

$G(N,E)$	$|N_D|$	$|N_E|$	$|E|$
	1,033,461	8,965,171	42,665,361

Table 4.2: Hybrid Data Graph.

Data. The ACQUAINT document collection contains 1,033,461 english newswires from different sources. We annotated these documents and used the direct correspondences between the resulting entity annotations (Wikipedia articles) and DBpedia entities to augment the documents with structured data from DBpedia. All attributes that can be found in DBpedia for these entity annotations such as *label, type, comment,* and others as illustrated in Figure 4.1, are used to construct a hybrid data graph of documents, their annotations and related structured data from DBpedia. In total there are 24M annotations based on 306k different entities[6]. On average a

---

[5] AQUAINT Corpus, Linguistic Data Consortium (LDC) catalog number LDC2002T31
[6] The annotations are available at `http://aifb.kit.edu/web/dhe/data`, last retrieved on April 10th 2013

document has about 23 entity annotations and an entity is annotated in 52 documents (see details in Table 4.3). The percentages of documents with a certain number of annotations is shown in Figure 4.3a, while Figure 4.3b depicts the percentages of entities that are associated with a certain number of documents. In total the hybrid data graph consists of about 1M document nodes and 8.9M entity nodes connected by a total of 42.6M triples (see Table 4.2 for details).

Annotations	#annotations/doc	#uniq. annota./doc	#docs/annota. entity
mean$\pm\sigma$	23.3$\pm$21.5	15.5$\pm$12.9	52.4$\pm$721
max/med./min	746/18/0	479/12/0	208k/3/1

Table 4.3: Number of (unique) entity annotations per document and the number of documents an entity is associated with via an annotation.

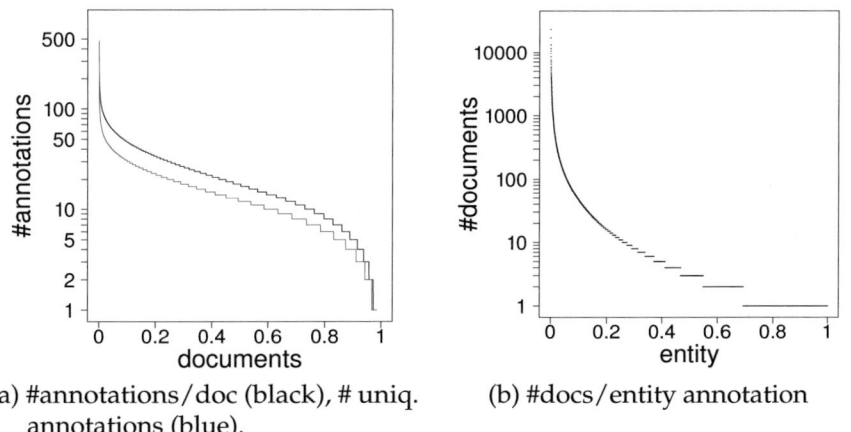

(a) #annotations/doc (black), # uniq. annotations (blue).

(b) #docs/entity annotation

Figure 4.3: Distribution of annotations over document sorted by annotation count (left) and documents over entity annotations (right).

Noting the logarithmic scale of the vertical axis of Figure 4.3 as well as the differences between average and median in Table 4.3, we can observe that relatively many documents have only few annotations compared to the average and about 1% of the documents (i.e. about 100k) have no annotations at all. Facing the retrieval task we seek to accomplish, the biggest challenge is to cope with the (potenial) absence of annotations as well as balancing the large differences in the number of annotations per document.

Queries. The *keyword* query set comprises the 50 titles of the TREC 2005 HARD topics[7], from which 50 corresponding *hybrid* queries were generated automatically. Table 4.1 shows five corresponding queries from the keyword and hybrid set. For the *user* scenario, the hybrid queries were used as candidates. If the annotations and hybrid queries did not fit the information need well, the hybrid queries were rejected and the keyword query used as a fall back instead, e.g. for query 307 (Table 4.1) the annotations were rejected, because the information need captured by the resulting hybrid query is deemed incorrect. We will discuss this later in this section in more detail. In total, 21 automatically generated hybrid queries were accepted and the others were rejected. Table 4.4 shows the number of keywords per query that is the same for all query sets. One can see that about 2.6 triple patterns are generated for every query.

Queryset	#Q	$avg|q|$	$avg|A| \pm \sigma$	$avg|p| \pm \sigma$
HARD 05 *hybrid*	50	2.64±0.66	1.62±0.69	2.62±0.69

Table 4.4: Hybrid query set: #Q number of queries, $|q|$ average number of keywords per query, $|A|$ average number of annotations per query, $|p|$ average number of hybrid triple patterns per query.

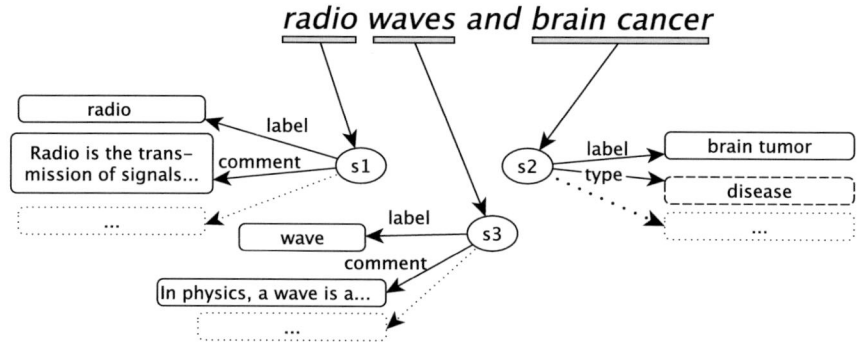

Figure 4.4: Keyword Query TREC 310 with Annotations.

Systems. We use *RM* as the state-of-the-art document retrieval system [101], whose results correspond to the TRM3 run as reported for the

---

[7]http://trec.nist.gov/data/t14_hard.html, last retrieved on April 10th 2013

HARD topics before [52]. Another system is *ADR* which uses the hybrid queries for matching only, i.e. they are used to prune the results to be ranked by the *RM* system in two ways: (1) with *OR-semantics*, ADR prunes a result if it does not match an annotation of the query; with (2) *AND-semantics* it removes a result, if it does not match all annotations of the query. Hence, they differ only, if the query has more than one annotation, which is the case for 25 of 50 queries. They are compared against our HybRank approach, which uses hybrid queries for matching, query modeling as well as for ranking.

Results. The official metric of the TREC 2005 HARD track is Precision@R (Rprec). Since we are foremost interested in the top of the ranked list, we report also Mean Reciprocal Rank (MRR), Precision@10, Mean Average Precision (MAP) and the number of queries improving (*#improved*) upon *RM* in Table 4.5.

| | RM | ADR | | | | HybRank | |
| | | OR | | AND | | | |
	keyword	*hybrid*	*user*	*hybrid*	*user*	*hybrid*	*user*
Rprec	0.2660	0.2164	0.2751	0.1606	0.2348	0.2160	**0.3284** (+23 %)
#improved		17	13	12	10	**21**	21
MRR	0.5745	0.609	0.5824	0.5176	0.5357	0.5451	**0.6337** (+10 %)
#improved		16	12	14	10	16	12
P@10	0.4300	0.394	0.4300	0.3260	0.3900	0.3800	**0.5140°** (+20%)
#improved		5	3	7	5	15	9
MAP	0.2451	0.1597	0.2404	0.1271	0.2101	0.1672	**0.2917°** (+19%)
#improved		12	8	11	8	16	15

stat. significant diff. with respect to *RM* according to paired t-test * at level .001, ° at level .05

Table 4.5: Results for annotation-based document retrieval. The number of queries which improve over *RM* is given below each metric.

Overall, HybRank improves upon RM when the user intervenes and rejects annotations, which results in 23% improvements w.r.t to *Rprec*. For the user query set, HybRank also outperforms ADR OR-semantics (the best ADR configuration), indicating that using the hybrid queries also for ranking is beneficial. We observe that given these high quality queries, most of the retrieved PRF results were relevant. Further, the structure and terms captured by these queries were successfully exploited once more for weighting the terms of the query model. Thus, as opposed to ADR, these queries have an impact not only on the retrieval of candidates (matching) but also the modeling of queries and the ranking of results, respectively.

Correspondingly, improvements critically depend on them to be of high quality.

For the hybrid queries, HybRank is comparable to ADR OR-semantics and worse than RM. Its superior results for the user set and comparable results for this hybrid set compared to ADR OR suggest that HybRank is more successful in exploiting the effect of high quality queries and also handles low quality queries relatively well. In other words, it offers a more balanced exploitation of hybrid queries. ADR OR-semantics is consistently superior than ADR AND-semantics. Requiring candidate results to match all patterns in the queries seems to be a too hard constraint that misses out relevant results. The overall low performance on these queries compared to RM captures the strong reliance of all annotation-based approaches (ADR, HybRank) on annotations.

We identify two problematic cases, where annotations can have a negative impact on performance. The first is "annotation recall". At the query level, poor recall means that the queries are not completely annotated and consequently represent the information need in an unbalanced way, e.g. the keyword query *"new hydroelectric projects'* is annotated correctly with the entity *hydroelectricity*, but there is no annotation for *"new"* and *"project"*. This skews the results towards the *"hydroelectric"* part of the query. Even when the annotations capture the information needs of the query well, the recall problem may occur at the document level. This leads to an annotation mismatch, where documents contain high quality annotations but miss those found in the query. Besides this, "annotation precision" is critical. Low precision means that annotations found in the query, respectively in the document, do not capture the meaning behind the information needs or document content. For dealing with the second problem, this work employs user queries, which can be further improved in future work through more sophisticated user interactions. The first problem occurs both in the hybrid and user query set. The better results provided by HybRank indicate that it is more effective in dealing with query-document pairs with varying number of annotations (varying levels of annotation recalls), exploiting keywords and the structure captured by annotations in a more balanced way.

4.6.2 Structured Data Search

A benchmark for RKS evaluation has been proposed [45], which we use to study our approach.

Data Graph	$|E|$	Uniq. edges
IMDb	6,298,729	18
Mondial	347,013	155
Wikipedia	605,525	9

Table 4.6: Graph statistics: Number of triples and unique edge labels per dataset.

Data. The benchmark comprises three datasets and corresponding *keyword* query sets. For the experiments, we used results pooled from 9 different RKS systems, made available by [45], including the relevant results for each query (see details in Table 4.7). The relational datasets from this benchmark are treated as data graphs (foreign keys form relation edges between entities, see Table 4.6 for details).

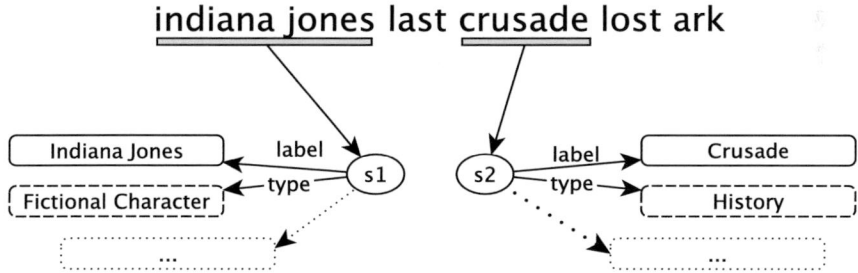

Figure 4.5: A keyword query annotated with entities s_1, s_2.

Queryset		$|Q|$	$avg|q|$	Rel. R.	Pooled R.
IMDb	*keyword*	50	2.04	4.32	2653±1159
Mondial	*keyword*	50	3.88	5.90	1782±758
Wikipedia	*keyword*	50	2.66	3.26	3072±1046

Table 4.7: Keyword query set: $|Q|$ number of queries, $|q|$ average number of keywords per query, Rel. R. average number of relevant results per query among all pooled results (Pooled R.).

Queries. Analogous to the document retrieval case, we study three different scenarios. (1) The basis is the *keyword* query set of [45], which contains 50 keyword queries for each data graph. Details of these are given in Table 4.7. (2) We annotate these keywords to obtain the *hybrid* query set. The annotations are based on Wikipedia articles and thus, are cross-domain.

Queryset		$|Q|$	$\#\varnothing$	$avg|A| \pm \sigma$	$avg|p| \pm \sigma$
IMDb	hybrid	50	10	0.92±0.57	1.5±0.58
	user	50	10	0.92±0.57	1.44±0.57
Mondial	hybrid	50	3	1.36±0.59	1.70±0.50
	user	50	11	1.20±0.78	1.60±0.53
Wikipedia	hybrid	50	1	1.6±0.69	1.74±0.75
	user	50	1	1.16±0.42	1.5±0.58

Table 4.8: Hybrid query sets: $|Q|$ number of queries, $\#\varnothing$ number of queries without annotations, $|A|$ average number of annotations, $|p|$ average number of hybrid patterns per query

However, the data graphs *Mondial* and *IMdb* are from the specific domains of geography and movies. Thus, we keep only annotations that belong to these domains, i.e. annotations that belong to the types country, province, state, river and organization for Mondial and the types movie, fictional character, film and actor for IMDb. We illustrate this in Figure 4.5. Since the type of s_2 is outside the movie domain, it is omitted and the resulting hybrid query is:

$$\{\langle ?x_1, char\_name, "indiana", "jones"\}\rangle$$

$$\langle ?x_2, a_*, \{"last", "crusade", "lost", "ark"\}\rangle\}.$$

IMDb 1	denzel washington	$\langle ?x, name, \{"denzel", "washington"\}\rangle$
IMDb 12	star wars	$\langle ?x, title, \{"star", "wars"\}\rangle$
IMDb 34	title toto i've a feeling we're not in kansas any more	$\langle ?x, a_*, \{"title", "toto", "i've", "a", "feeling", "we're", "not", "in", "kansas", "any", "more"\}\rangle$
Mondial 1	thailand	$\langle ?x, countryname, \{"thailand"\}\rangle$
Mondial 12*	niger	$\langle ?x, countryname, \{"niger"\}\rangle$
Mondial 41	iceland haiti	$\langle ?x, countryname, \{"iceland"\}\rangle$ $\langle ?x, countryname, \{"haiti"\}\rangle$
Wikipedia 1	microscope	$\langle ?x, title, \{"microscope"\}\rangle$
Wikipedia 12	1760	$\langle ?x, title, \{"1760"\}\rangle$
Wikipedia 16*	tianjin china district beijing	$\langle ?x, title, \{"tianjin"\}\rangle$ $\langle ?x, title, \{"china"\}\rangle$ $\langle ?x, title, \{"district"\}\rangle$ $\langle ?x, title, \{"beijing"\}\rangle$

Table 4.9: Example keyword queries and corresponding hybrid queries. *In the *user* Scenario, annotations were rejected.

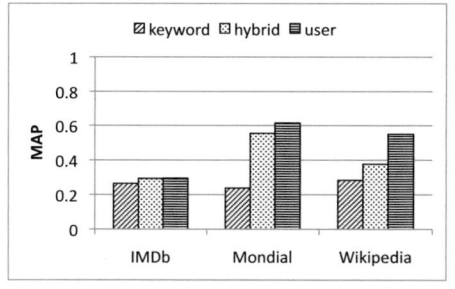

(a) Mean Average Precision

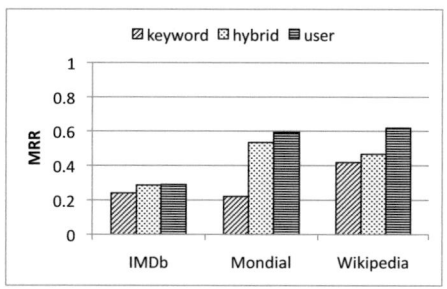

(b) Mean Reciprocal Rank

Figure 4.6: Results of the structured data search task.

As a consequence, the queries for these two data graphs have less annotations compared to the Wikipedia query set or even no annotations, e.g. for query *IMDb 34* in Table 4.9 no annotations could be found and hence the query is a purely keyword-based query in this hybrid scenario. Overall, IMDb queries have the smallest number of annotations (see Table 4.8). (3) In the *user* scenario, the hybrid queries are the starting point and then annotations not fitting to the information need are omitted and the corresponding terms treated as keywords.

Table 4.8 provides statistics on the query sets and Table 4.9 shows three queries for each data graph.

Systems. *RKS* [22] uses the proposed model for ranking but without graph-based smoothing. For comparison purposes, both RKS and our approach HybRank are set to use the standard technique for smoothing presented in Section 3.4. as well as the same values for the smoothing parameters. RKS uses the keyword queries while HybRank runs with the hybrid and user query sets.

Results. Compared to the previous task, low quality annotations is less a problem since hybrid data is directly given such that only queries have to be annotated. Figure 4.6a and Figure 4.6b display the retrieval performance in terms of Mean Average Precision and Mean Reciprocal Rank. Overall, HybRank consistently yields better performance than RKS using hybrid queries. User queries further leads to higher improvements.

Mondial queries work best because geographic entities, especially countries, are well covered by Wikipedia. Hence, there are high quality annotations available. While annotation recall is thus relative high, annotation precision could be improved. For instance, the country "Niger'" has been returned as annotation while the query seeks for "Niger" as a river. In some cases, this could be addressed by user queries, which yield better performance than hybrid queries. This potential for improving results by pruning low quality annotations is especially evident for Wikipedia, where the relative improvement achieved with user queries is the highest.

IMDb is the most problematic dataset for HybRank. As presented before, queries for this dataset have only few annotations that can be exploited. There are many queries with movie quotes in colloquial language, for which annotations could not be found or are incorrect as illustrated by query IMDb 34 in Table 4.9.

In summary, improvements can also be achieved for this scenario, especially when high quality annotations are available. Compared to the ADR problem, producing annotations here is a more easy task. Hence, even the version of HybRank that relies entirely on automatically generated hybrid queries, consistently provides superior results.

4.7 Conclusion

Summary. In this chapter, we present a study that involves both document and structured data search tasks and propose HybRank as a ranking approach for hybrid search that supports both tasks. Besides hybrid data support, HybRank also enables flexible querying, ranging from keyword queries to structured queries and in particular, supports hybrid queries. We showed how hybrid queries can be automatically constructed using annotation tools and also, with the help of users. We use established benchmarks in our experiments and have observed that the best HybRank configuration yields large and significant improvements of 23% upon state-of-the-art solutions.

Conclusions. The research conducted in this chapter was initiated by Research Question 2. We addressed this question by designing a ranking model for hybrid queries and hybrid data and conducted experiments to assess its performance. Our experiments aimed to answer the Hypotheses 2.1 and 2.2. Based on the results obtained, we showed the applicability of our ranking approach *HybRank* and were able to address the information needs in both settings as shown in Section 4.6. Hence, we accept Hypothesis 2.1 for our approach as true. The second hypothesis investigated in this chapter was Hypothesis 2.2 assuming that hybrid queries increase the effectiveness of the ranking. The conclusion on the second hypothesis depends on the recall of the annotations as discussed in Section 4.6. We have observed in the experiments that queries having annotations that do not entirely capture the information need yield better results with plain keyword search for document retrieval. However, improvements in terms of precision can be achieved for those with adequate annotations. For structured data search, the automatically created hybrid queries consistently improved upon the plain keyword queries. In summary, allowing the user to assess a hybrid query and if neccessary remove annotations ensures retrieval quality in terms of precision and given this condition, the Hypothesis 2.2 can be considered as accepted. As a consequence we suggest the future direction of research as described next.

Outlook. Our experiments showed that automatic query annotation in the way we applied it can be a crucial factor for retrieval quality. Involving the user in this step to control the quality yielded improvements, and hence explicit user feedbacks for ensuring the quality of the annotations and ultimately, the model of the information needs, is promising and worth to be investigated further.

Chapter 5

Heterogenous Web Data Search using Relevance Based On-The-Fly Data Integration

Searching over heterogeneous structured data on the Web is challenging due to *vocabulary and structure mismatches* among different data sources. In this chapter, we study two existing strategies and present a new approach to integrate additional data sources into the search process. The first strategy relies on data integration to mediate mismatches through upfront computation of mappings, based on which queries are rewritten to fit individual sources. The other extreme is keyword search, which does not require any up-front investment, but ignores structure information. Building on these strategies, we present a hybrid approach, which combines the advantages of both. Our approach does not require any upfront data integration, but also leverages the fine grained structure of the underlying data. For a structured query adhering to the vocabulary of just one source, the so-called seed query, we construct an *Entity Relevance Model (ERM)*, which captures the content and the structure of the seed query results. This ERM is then aligned on the fly with keyword search results retrieved from other sources and also used to rank these results. The outcome of our experiments using large-scale real-world datasets suggests that data integration leads to higher search effectiveness compared to keyword search and that our new hybrid approach consistently exceeds both strategies.

5

Outline. First, we motivate the subject of this chapter in Section 5.1 and then state the research question and concrete hypotheses derived from this question in Section 5.2. In Section 5.3, we formally define the research problem, give an overview of existing solutions and briefly sketches our new approach. This ranking approach using relevance based on the fly mappings is presented in detail in Section 5.4. Evaluation results are presented in Section 5.5. In Section 5.6, we discusses the related work and conclude in Section 5.7.

5.1 Introduction

A rapidly increasing amount of structured data can be found on the Web today. This development is triggered by the Linked Data movement, Semantic Web community efforts, and recently, also enjoys strong support from large companies including Google, Yahoo!, and Facebook, and governmental institutions. The amount of Linked Data alone is in the order of billions of RDF triples residing in hundreds of data sources [75]. In this chapter, we aim at supporting the exploitation of these structured Web data. In particular, we aim at extending vertical search capabilities beyond internal data to also incorporate external Web data into the retrieval process. We illustrate the problem behind it through the following scenario:

There is a company running a movie shopping website. Users can search for movies on this website via form-based interfaces and their requests are internally executed as structured queries against the company's dataset. Now, the company aims to exploit the numerous Web data sources available as Linked Data, including data provided by a partner company with similar offerings and an encyclopedia dataset that contains additional movie related information. The goal is to incorporate data from these external sources into the search processes. However, the vocabularies and structure exhibited by these target data sources are different such that issuing the same structured queries (called seed queries) against these external sources may not produce any results. Results satisfying the information needs behind these seed queries may exist but due to mismatches in structural and syntactical representation, they cannot be found.

In this chapter, we study three different strategies that are applicable to this search scenario:

(1) There are Information Retrieval (IR) solutions, which treat both the data and queries as bags of words [36, 159]. Because structure information is ignored during query processing, this strategy (called *keyword search*) often leads to non-empty results – albeit with varying quality.

(2) The alternative is to employ database solutions, where information needs are expressed as structured queries. Given the richer representation of the information needs, the structure of the underlying data can be exploited and incorporated into the matching process. While this can improve the quality of the results, this type of solutions requires upfront investment in *data integration*, i.e. computation of ontology and schema mappings and consolidation of data instances that refer to the same object (entity mappings) [35, 53, 54, 83]. Based on these mappings, results from external sources can be obtained via query rewriting [28, 169]. Integration

111

efforts are needed whenever the data changes. Moreover, integration on the Web is hard due to the large number of sources and their scale as well as their heterogeneity regarding differences at the schema and data level. We introduced the notion of data heterogeneity in Section 2.1.4 and repeat the illustrating Figure 2.4 below for the ease of reading. This figure displays entities representing movies. One can observe that three different representations of "Steven Spielberg" are used for the same real-world object. Also, different labels are used to express the same attribute and entities are described with a varying number of attributes.

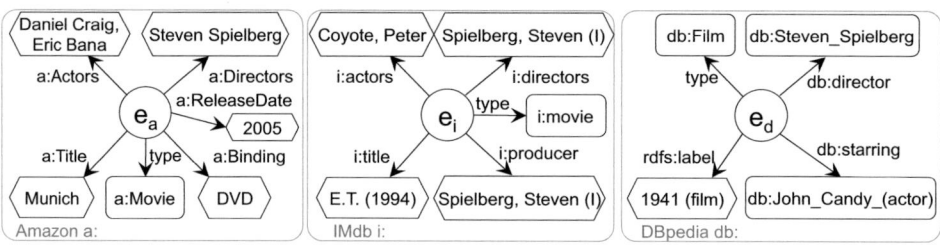

Figure 2.4: (Figure repeated) Data heterogeneity on the Web. Entities from three different Web datasets are represented differently at the schema level (e.g. *actors* vs. *starring*) and data level (e.g. *Spielberg, Steven* vs. *Steven Spielberg*).

(3) As the third category, we elaborate on a hybrid solution, which combines the flexibility of unstructured IR solutions (in the sense that no prior data integration is needed) and the expressiveness of database-style querying by incorporating the structure of the underlying data. The idea is to start with a structured seed query specified for one particular source. Based on the content and structure of the results obtained from this source, we construct an *Entity Relevance Model* (ERM) that can be seen as a compact representation of relevant results mirroring the underlying information need. Instead of relying on up-front computed mappings for rewriting the structured seed query, we treat the seed query as a keyword query and submit it against external data sources to obtain additional results. These candidates are obtained using a standard IR-based search engine. Then, we create mappings between the structure of each candidate result and the structure of the ERM on the fly. These mappings are used for an additional round of matching and ranking. Candidates which more closely match the content as well as the structure captured by the ERM are ranked higher. Thereby the

structure of the ERM and of the result candidates are incorporated into the search process. Since the same similarity metrics used for creating the mappings are reused for ranking, this on the fly integration comes essentially for free. As a result, this hybrid strategy takes not only structure information into account for more effective search, but also provides on the fly computed mappings that can support a pay-as-you-go integration paradigm where data integration is tightly embedded into the search process [108].

5.2 Research Question and Contribution

In this chapter we address the following research question:

Research Question 3. *How can heterogenous web data from remote data sources be integrated into the local search process despite schema and data-level differences without prior data integration?*

The observation which lead this question is that an increasing number of structured data sources surface on the web. Some of these data sources hold information, which is beneficial when integrated into a search process over a local dataset. However, the data exhibits the heterogeneity described in Section 2.1.4 and taken up later in this chapter. We assume that this heterogeneity can be overcome at query time without using training examples or prior data integration and state this in the following hypothesis:

Hypothesis 3.1. *Schema and data level differences can be crossed by establishing mappings at query time through measuring the similarity between attribute values of entities and in particular without prior data integration or the usage of training examples.*

As soon as we have crossed the difference, we can take advantage of the structure of the data and we assume that this allows to increase the retrieval effectiveness. This assumption is the basis for the following hypothesis:

Hypothesis 3.2. *Taking the structure of the data retrieved from remote sources into account for ranking through unsupervised on the fly alignments improves retrieval effectiveness compared to keyword search and query rewriting.*

Based the above research question and hypotheses, we will present an approach and investigate it through experiments. As a result, we provide the following contribution in this chapter:

Contribution 3. *Heterogenous Web Data Search using On-The-Fly Data Integration*

Our initial work on heterogenous web data search has been discussed at the *Consuming Linked Data Workshop* [79] and the mature paper at the *World Wide Web Conference* [80]. The work presented in this chapter is a revised version of the previously published papers. The contribution in this chapter can be summarized as follows:

- We perform a systematic study of the two main prevailing strategies towards searching external heterogeneous data sources. In particular, we show how to adopt the data integration approach to our scenario where the computation of entity mappings is challenging.

- To achieve the best of both worlds, we elaborate a hybrid approach that does not rely on upfront data integration, but uses a query-specific *Entity Relevance Model* (ERM) for searching as well as for computing mappings on the fly.

- Based on large-scale experiments using real-world datasets, we observe that the data integration approach consistently provides better results than keyword search. The hybrid approach yields best results outperforming keyword search by 120% and the data integration baseline by 54% on average in terms of Mean Average Precision as we will see in Section 5.5. Further, this hybrid approach is able to leverage upfront integration results leading to additional quality improvement, when precomputed mappings are considered. The qualitative differences between these approaches are: Keyword search and the hybrid approach do not require upfront data integration. Additionally, the hybrid approach provides on the fly computed mappings that can be used for a pay-as-you-go integration process that can exploit user feedbacks for quality improvement (as discussed in [108]).

5.3 Overview

In this section, we present the setting of the addressed problem and provide an overview of three different solutions.

Web Data Heterogeneity. Web data reside in different datasets, each represented by a data graph $G = (N, E)$ as defined in Defintion 2.1. Note, in contrast to the previous chapter, documents and the special properties (a^*)

are not relevant in this chapter and hence are not part of the model. Here, the data graph follows Defintion 2.1 and consists of entities according to the Definitions 2.2, 2.3, and 2.4. Typically, real-world Web datasets exhibit *heterogeneity* at the schema and the data level, as described earlier in Section 2.1.4. At the data level, entities in different datasets, which refer to the same real-world object, may have different descriptions. Differences at the schema level occur when the same entity is represented in different datasets using attributes with different labels (different models). Figure 2.4 exemplifies this heterogeneity exhibited by real-world datasets. Dealing with these types of heterogeneity requires data integration. For this, a large body of work on schema alignment and entity consolidation (record linkage) can be leveraged to compute mappings between data sources [53]. While mappings of varying semantics have been proposed, the most basic and commonly used one asserts that two elements (schema elements or entities) are the same (i.e. *same-as mappings*).

5.3.1 Research Problem

Given this model of Web data, structured queries can be specified to search over such datasets. The most commonly used language for querying RDF data on the Web is SPARQL [131]. One essential feature of SPARQL is the Basic Graph Pattern (BGP), as defined in Section 2.1.2, which we recap here for the ease of reading. Basically, a BGP is a set of conjunctive triple patterns, each of the form $\langle subject, predicate, object \rangle$. They represent patterns because either *predicate*, *subject* or *object* might be a variable, or is explicitly specified as a constant. Answering these queries amounts to the task of graph pattern matching, where subgraphs in the data graph matching the query pattern are returned as results. Predicates are matched against edges in the data graph, whereas bindings to subjects and objects in the query are entity or literal nodes.

One particular form of BGP with high importance are so-called *entity queries*. Essentially, they are star-shaped queries with the node in the center of the star representing the entity (entities) to be retrieved. We have already seen such a query in Figure 2.3 and will see three more examples of star-shaped queries in Figure 5.4. These queries retrieve all entities x that are of the type `movie/film`, are directed by `Fassbinder` and released in `1982`. According to a recent Web query logs study performed, queries searching for entities constitute the most common type on the Web [130]. Also, most of the current Semantic Web search engines such as Sig.ma [1] and Falcons [36] focus on answering these queries. We also focus on this type of queries in this chapter to illustrate the main ideas underlying our approach.

Problem. Based on her knowledge about the schema and data of one particular source (e.g. the one owned by the company in our scenario), it is possible for a programmer or expert user to specify complex entity queries that specifically ask for information from this source. It is however not trivial to exploit external datasets for this kind of entity search when they exhibit heterogeneity at the schema and data level as discussed before. The problem we tackle is finding relevant entities in a set of *target datasets* G_t given a *source dataset* G_s and an entity query q_s adhering to the vocabulary of G_s.

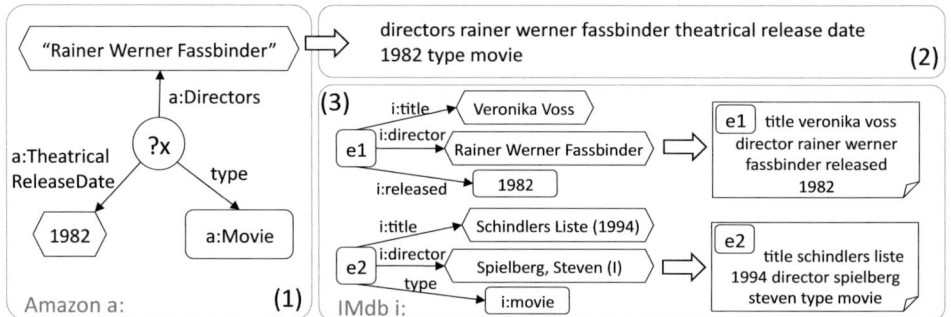

Figure 5.1: **KW:** The left part (1) shows structured query retrieving all x that are of the type `movie/film`, are directed by `Fassbinder` and released in `1982`. This query is transformed into a keyword query shown in part (2). Entities are analogously transformed into *bag of words* representations shown in (3). The keyword query is matched against these *bag of words*.

5.3.2 Solutions

Clearly, if all datasets exhibit the same schema and data representation, then q_s can directly be used to retrieve information from G_t. When this is not the case, the following different solutions can be applied.

Keyword Search (KW). The first and most widespread solution to this end is to use keyword search over so called 'bag-of-words' representations

---

[1]`http://sig.ma/` last retrieved on April 10th 2013

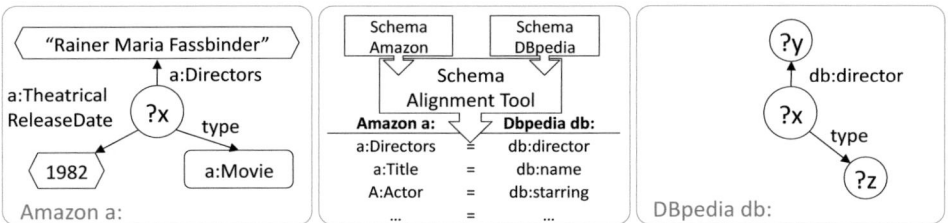

Figure 5.2: **QR**: A structured query for *Amazon* (left) is rewritten into a query for *DBpedia* (right) using the mappings obtained through an ontology alignment tool (middle). Constants of the left query are replaced with variables and missing mapping results in an "empty" triple pattern.

of entities [36, 159]. That is, the description of an entity is simply a bag of terms. A query is also represented as terms, which is then matched against the term-based representation of the entities. The strategy KW is illustrated with an example in Figure 5.1. Clearly, this approach is simple but also flexible in the sense that the same keyword query specified for G_s can also be used for G_t because results from G_t can be obtained when there are matches at the level of terms. However, this approach ignores the structure of the data and we assume that retrieval effectiveness can be increased when the structure information is exploited for ranking.

Structured Query Rewriting (QR). Another view on this retrieval problem is the database perspective. In contrast to the previous approach, structure information of the entity descriptions is taken into account and also queries are fully structured. The strategy to query over multiple datasets and to deal with data heterogeneity is here to rewrite the structured seed query q_s into a query q_t that adheres to the vocabulary of the target dataset $G_t \in \mathbb{G}_t$. In order to rewrite the query, same-as mappings are computed using entity consolidation and schema mapping tools [35, 53, 54, 83]. Given the mappings created by such tools, predicates and constants in q_s referring to attributes and entities in G_s are replaced with predicates and constants representing corresponding attributes and entities in G_t. While this strategy can exploit the fine grained structure of data and query, it relies on upfront data integration, which is problematic in the Web scenario because Web datasets are heterogeneous and evolve quickly. In an experiment on the datasets prepared for the Billion Triple Challenge[2] for instance, it has been

---

[2]http://challenge.semanticweb.org last retrieved on April 10th 2013

117

observed that state-of-the-art entity consolidation approaches [35] do not scale well to large datasets [158]. In particular, they are focused on the single-domain setting such that for these heterogeneous datasets (where many of them exhibit only small pairwise overlaps at the schema level), only a relatively small amount of correct mappings could be produced. Thus, rewriting constants using entity mappings is especially challenging in this scenario.

In fact, it has been recognized that integration at the Web scale is too complex and resource-intensive to be performed completely upfront [108]. A more practical strategy to deal with this dynamic and large-scale environment is to perform integration as you go [108], i.e. at usage time as the system evolves. In this regard, an alternative solution is to precompute schema mappings only. Then, entity mappings that are needed for a specific query are obtained at runtime. Figure 5.2 illustrate this: Schema mappings are used to rewrite the query, triple patterns for which no corresponding schema-level mappings exist are omitted, and constants are replaced with variables, because replacing the constants with the corresponding constants of the target source is infeasible, since these constants are unknown and identifying them mounts to the problem of entity search which is the original task we aim to solve. The resulting query captures only structure constraints of the original query and thus, produces possibly much more results than a query where constants are also rewritten. To achieve that, a standard IR search engine can be leveraged to limit the results to only those, which match the constants expressed as keyword queries. That is, the constants that have been replaced by variables in the first step, act as a keyword query in the second step to perform on the fly entity consolidation, i.e. to find entities in G_t, which match the entities in G_s as represented by the constants (such as "Rainer Maria Fassbinder 1982" in the example).

Our approach. In this chapter, we present a framework to address this problem of querying heterogeneous Web data using on the fly mappings computed in a pay-as-you-go fashion based on entity relevance models. This framework is instantiated involving the following four steps. (1) First, we compute an ERM from the results returned from the source dataset G_s using q_s. (2) Second, we treat q_s as keywords and using a standard IR-based search engine, we obtain result candidates from the target datasets G_t. (3) Then, a light-weight on the fly integration technique is employed, which maps the structure of result candidates to the structure of the ERM. (4) Finally, the result candidates are ranked according to their similarity to the ERM using the mappings computed at runtime.

(1)

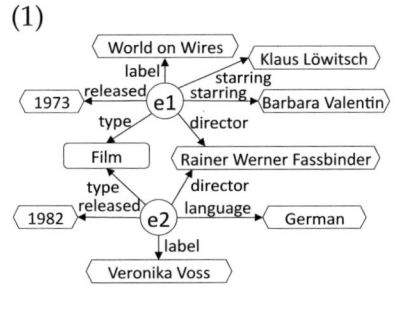

(2) *ERM*

$a_s \in A_s$	$k(a_s)$	$w : P_s(w|a_s)$
label	1	world:0.2, on:0.2, wires:0.2, ...
starring	0.5	klaus:0.25, löwitsch:0.25, barbara:0.25,...
director	1	rainer:0.33, werner:0.33, fassbinder:0.33
released	1	1973:0.5, 1982:0.5
language	0.5	german:1
type	1	film:1

(3) e_t

$a_t \in A(e_t)$	$w : P_t(w|a_t)$
i:title	e:0.33, t:0.33, 1994:0.33
i:actors	coyote:0.5, peter:0.5
i:directors	spielberg:0.33, steven:0.33, i:0.33
i:producer	spielberg:0.33, steven:0.33, i:0.33
type	movie:1

Figure 5.3: (1) Result set R_s consisting of two entities e_1, e_2 obtained for a seed query.

(2) *ERM* built from two entities e1 and e2 illustrated in (1). The ERM has a field for each attribute with label a_s. Each field is weighted with $k(a_s)$ and has a language model $P_s(w|a_s)$ defining the probability of w occurring in field a_s, e.g. "1982" occurs with a probability of 0.5 for field *released*. Note, that words result from standard tokenization of values.

(3) Model e_t representing the entity e_i of Figure 2.4 with language models for each attribute with label a_t (without smoothing for simplicity reasons).

5.4 Search Over Heterogeneous Data

In this section, we present how the entity relevance model is constructed and discuss how this model can be exploited for ranking and relevance-based on the fly data integration.

5.4.1 Entity Relevance Model

We aim at building a model that captures the structure and content of entities relevant to the information need, which is expressed in the seed entity query q_s. The proposed model is called the *Entity Relevance Model (ERM)*. The ERM builds upon the concept of language models, uses maximum likelihood estimation, Jelinek-Mercer smoothing and relevance feedback as discussed in Section 2.2.4 and the following. Further, we use the negative cross entropy to compare models as introduced in Section 2.2.6. We adopt these concepts and approaches to the problem of searching structured Web data.

Entity Relevance Model. Our goal is to model both the structure and the content of entities. The idea behind the ERM is to represent the attribute structure of entities by a set of language models, and each language model captures the content of the respective attribute. Hence, instead of using language models to represent entire documents, we use them for modeling attribute values.

The $ERM = (R_s, A_s, \mathcal{P}_s)$ is a composite model consisting of a set of entities $R_s \subseteq N_E$, a set of attributes $A_s \subseteq E$, and a set of language models $\mathcal{P}_s$. Each $P_s \in \mathcal{P}_s$ is associated with a weight defined through the function $k : \mathcal{P}_s \rightarrow [0,1]$. The entities R_s are obtained by submitting the query q_s against the source dataset G_s and used as pseudo-relevance feedback. A_s denotes the set of all distinct attribute labels that are associated with the entities R_s, i.e. $A_s = \{a | a \in A'(e), e \in R_s\}$. For each distinct attribute label $a_s \in A_s$, we compute a corresponding language model $P_s(w|a_s) \in \mathcal{P}_s$ and its weight $k(a_s)$. The language model $P_s(w|a_s)$ specifies the probability of any word $w \in V$ occurring in the nodes of data graph edges with label a_s, where V is the vocabulary of all words. Let $N(e_i, a_s)$ be the set of nodes that are connected with e_i through edges with label a_s, i.e. $N(e_i, a_s) = \{e_j | a_s(e_i, e_j) \in E\}$, we compute $P_s(w|a_s)$ from all entity descriptions for $e_i \in R_s$ as follows:

$$P_s(w|a_s) = \frac{\sum_{e_i \in R_s} \sum_{e_j \in N(e_i, a_s)} n(w, e_j)}{\sum_{e_i \in R_s} \sum_{e_j \in N(e_i, a_s)} |e_j|} \qquad (5.1)$$

where $n(w,e)$ denotes the count of word w in the node e and $|e|$ is the length of e (the number of words contained in e). The outer sum goes over the entities $e_i \in R_s$ and the inner sum goes over all values e_j of attributes with labels a_s. Thus, entity descriptions, which do not have the attribute a_s, do not contribute to $P_s(w|a_s)$. In order to capture the importance of these attribute-specific language models, we compute $k(a_s)$ as the fraction of entities having an attribute with label a_s:

$$k(a_s) = \frac{n(a_s, R_s)}{|R_s|} \qquad (5.2)$$

where the numerator denotes the number of entities having an attribute with label a_s and the denominator is the total number of entities in R_s. In summary, an ERM can be seen as a query specific model built from pseudo-relevance feedback entities retrieved for the seed query q_s. An example for an ERM constructed from two entities is illustrated in Figure 5.3 (2).

5.4.2 Search Using ERM

We tackle the problem of searching over heterogeneous data in a way similar to entity consolidation. That is, given the results $e_s \in R_s$ from the source dataset obtained for the seed query, we aim at finding entities in the target datasets which are similar to R_s. We use the ERM as the model of those relevant results. In particular, we estimate which entities e_t of G_t are relevant for the query q_s by measuring their similarity to the ERM and rank them by decreasing similarity. We model a candidate entity e_t analogously to the ERM: $e_t = (A'_t, \mathcal{P}_t)$ where A'_t is the model of e_t (Definition 2.4) and $\mathcal{P}_t$ is a set of language models. Similar to the ERM, $\mathcal{P}_t$ contains a language model $P_t(w|a_t)$ for each distinct attribute label $a_t \in A_t$. Let $N(a_t)$ be the set of value nodes of the attribute a_t, i.e. $N(a_t) = \{e_j | a_t(e_t, e_j) \in E\}$, $P_t(w|a_t)$ is estimated as follows:

$$P_t(w|a_t) = \frac{\sum_{e_j \in N(a_t)} n(w, e_j)}{\sum_{e_j \in N(a_t)} |e_j|} \tag{5.3}$$

Here, the sum goes over all values e of attributes with label a_t, $n(w, e)$ denotes that number of occurrences of w in e, and $|e|$ denotes the length of e. Figure 5.3 (3) illustrates an example.

We calculate the similarity between the *ERM* and a candidate entity e_t by measuring the difference between a language model of *ERM* and a language model of e_t using the negative cross entropy $-H$, which we defined in Equation 2.5. We sum over these differences and weight each summand by $k(a_s)$ and the parameter $\beta_{(a_s)}$:

$$Sim(ERM, e_t) = \sum_{a_s \in A_s} \beta(a_s) \cdot k(a_s) \cdot -H(P_s(w|a_s)||P_t(w|a_t)) \tag{5.4}$$

The parameter β gives us the flexibility to boost the importance of attributes that occur in the query q_s as follows:

$$\beta(a_s) = \begin{cases} 1 & \text{if } a_s \notin q_s \\ b & \text{if } a_s \in q_s, \ b \geq 1 \end{cases} \tag{5.5}$$

In particular, we apply this similarity calculation only when we know which attribute label a_s of *ERM* should be matched against which attribute a_t of e_t. We address this problem in the next section and show how the ERM can be exploited to create on the fly schema mappings, i.e. mappings between an attribute a_t and a field a_s of *ERM*. If there is no mapping

121

between a_s and a_t, then we use a "maximal difference". This difference is computed as the cross entropy between $P_s(w|a_s)$ and a language model that contains all words in the vocabulary but the ones in $P_s(w|a_s)$.

For constructing the language models of the ERM and of the candidate entities, a maximum likelihood estimation has been used, which is proportional to the count of the words in an attribute value. However, such an estimation assigns zero probabilities to those words not occurring in the attribute value. In order to address this issue, $P_t(w|a_t)$ is smoothed using a collection-wide model $c_s(w)$, which captures the probability of w occurring in the entire dataset G_s. This smoothing is controlled by the Jelinek-Mercer parameter λ, see Section 2.2.5 for more details on this smoothing technique. As a result, the negative cross entropy $-H$ is calculated over the vocabulary V of field a_s as:

$$-H(P_s||P_t) = \sum_{w \in V} P_s(w|a_s) \cdot \log(\lambda \cdot P_t(w|a_t) + (1-\lambda) \cdot c_s(w)) \qquad (5.6)$$

5.4.3 On The Fly Integration Using ERM

We want to determine which attribute of an entity needs to be compared to a given field of the ERM constructed for q_s. The ERM is not only used for search, but also exploited for this alignment task. The details for computing mappings between entity attributes $a_t \in A_t$ and ERM fields $a_s \in A_s$ are presented in Algorithm (1). The rational of the algorithm is that a field a_s is aligned to an attribute a_t when the cross entropy H between their language models is low, i.e. a mapping is established, if H is lower than a threshold t (normalized based on the highest cross entropy, line 12). The algorithm iterates over $n \cdot r$ comparisons in worst case for an ERM with n fields and an entity with $r = |A'(e_t)|$ attribute labels. Note that n and r are relatively small (see Table 5.1 and Table 5.3) because this algorithm operates only on entities that are requested as part of the search process compared to full-fledge upfront integration that takes the entire schema into account. Further, ranking requires the same computation (Equation 5.6) and thus the entropy values computed here are kept and subsequently reused for ranking. Moreover, for a faster performance, ERM fields having a weight of $k(a_s) < c$ can be pruned due to their negligible influence (see Section 5.5.6 and 5.5.7). In addition, existing mappings can be reused to reduce the number of comparisons even further.

Algorithm 1 On the fly Alignment

Input: *ERM*, Entity e_t, Threshold $t \in [0,1]$
Output: *Mappings* $A := \{(a_s, a_t) | a_s \in A_s, a_t \in A_t \cup null\}$
  1:   $A := new\ Map$
  2:   **for all** $a_s \in A_s$ **do**
  3:      $candMappings := new\ OrderedByValueMap$
  4:      **for all** $a_t \in A'(e_t)$ **do**
  5:        **if** $a_t \notin A.values$ **then**   // If not already aligned
  6:          $h \leftarrow H(P_s(w|a_s)||P_t(w|a_t))$ // see equation (5.6)
  7:          $candMappings.add(a_t, h)$
  8:        **end if**
  9:      **end for**
10:      $bestA \leftarrow candMappings.firstValue$
11:      $worstA \leftarrow candMappings.lastValue$
12:      **if** $bestA < t \cdot worstA$ **then**
13:        $a_t \leftarrow candMappings.firstKey$
14:        $A.add(a_s, a_t)$
15:      **else**
16:        $A.add(a_s, null)$ // no mapping found
17:      **end if**
18: **end for**
19: **return** A

5.5 Experiments

In this section, we report on the experiments conducted with the three solutions discussed in Section 5.3. We experimented with different parameter settings and observed that performance is stable when the employed parameters are in certain ranges (will be discussed in Section 5.5.6). Results reported in the following are obtained using the configuration: boosting $b = 10$ (Equation 5.5), pruning $c = 0.8$ (Section 5.4.3), threshold $t = 0.75$ (Section 5.4.3). The smoothing parameter λ, whose effect on retrieval performance has been studied extensively for IR tasks, was set to 0.9, a common value used in literature. We follow the *Cranfield* [41, 42] methodology for the experiments on the search effectiveness and adopt the same methodology to analyze the effectiveness of mapping computation.

5.5.1 Datasets

Our experiments were conducted with three RDF Web datasets, *DBpedia 3.5.1*, *IMdb*, and *Amazon*[3]. In every experiment, one of them serves as the source dataset and the other two represent the target datasets. DBpedia is a structured representation of Wikipedia, which contains more than 9 million entities of various types, among them about 50k entities typed as films. The IMdb and Amazon datasets are retrieved from `www.imdb.com` and `www.amazon.com` [169], and then transformed into RDF. The IMdb dataset contains information about movies and films, whereas the Amazon dataset contains product information about DVDs and VHS Videos. These three datasets are representative for our Web scenario because a vertical search application running one of these datasets (e.g. the one owned by the company in our scenario) could benefit from incorporating the other two into the search process. Further, the datasets exhibit the heterogeneity previously illustrated in Figure 2.4. Table 5.1 provides for each dataset the number of entities, the number of distinct attribute labels and the average number of attributes per entity, i.e. the average size of an entity description $|A(e)|$.

Dataset	#Entities	#Distinct Attribute Labels	$|A(e)| \pm \sigma$
Amazon	115K	28	18.4±3.8
IMdb	859K	32	11.4±6.4
DBpedia	9.1M	39.6K	9±18.2

Table 5.1: Dataset statistics

5.5.2 Queries and Ground Truth

Our goal is to find relevant entities in the target datasets G_t for a given query q_s. In this setting, we can determine the relevant entities in G_t by manually rewriting the query q_s to obtain a structured query q_t adhering to the vocabulary of $G_t \in \mathbf{G}_t$. Figure 5.4 shows such a set of queries, one of the queries serves as the source query q_s and the results of the other two queries capture the ground truth for the retrieval experiments.

---

[3]We thank Julien Gaugaz and the L3S Research Center for providing us their versions of the IMdb and Amazon datasets.

We created three query sets, each containing 23 SPARQL BGP entity queries of different complexities, ranging from 2 to 4 triple patterns that produce a varying number of results, see Table 5.2. Since an ERM is constructed from the results returned by the seed query, Table 5.2 shows also statistics on the number of entities used to build the ERM. The queries represent information needs like retrieve "movies directed by Steven Spielberg", "movies available in English and also in Hebrew", or "movies directed by Rainer Werner Fassbinder, which were released in 1982". The last query is illustrated in Figure 5.4.

Rel. entities	Amazon	IMdb	DBpedia
max	153	834	47
avg.	32.2	114.9	10.9
median	18	21	5
min	1	1	1

Table 5.2: Results per query and dataset.

Source dataset	$|ERM| \pm \sigma$
Amazon	14.1±3.6
IMdb	15.8±6.7
DBpedia	23±5.4

Table 5.3: Average number of fields of an ERM.

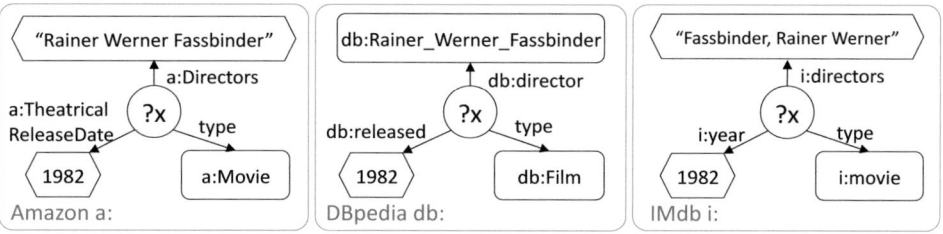

Figure 5.4: Example of manually created, equivalent queries whose results define the ground truth.

125

5.5.3 Systems

We implement three strategies KW, QR, and our approach ERM, as previously discussed in Section 5.3.

Keyword Query (KW). IR style keyword search on Web data has been proposed [36, 159] and implemented as an adoption of Lucene[4], an IR engine, which applies a document and query length adjusted TF/IDF-based ranking function. We use the Semplore implementation [159], which uses a virtual document for every entity description and use the concatenations of attribute labels and attribute values as document terms. In the same way, we transform the structured query into a keyword query by using the concatenations of predicates and constants of the structured query as terms. The resulting keyword query retrieves all virtual documents representing entity descriptions, which contain some of the corresponding terms.

Query Rewriting (QR). This system is based on query rewriting using precomputed schema mappings. We created same-as mappings with the tools Falcon-AO [83] and Aroma [49] using their default configurations. Table 5.4 shows the number of mappings between the datasets. Then, to rewrite constants at runtime as discussed, we apply the KW baseline on top to limit the search results produced by the rewritten query to those that match constants formulated as a keyword query.

Datasets	Falcon-AO [83]	Aroma [49]
Amazon-IMdb	5	8
Amazon-DBpedia	11	11
IMdb-DBpedia	12	4

Table 5.4: Number of mappings.

Hybrid (ERM). Three different versions of *ERM* are studied in our experiments:

- *ERM* computes all mappings on the fly.

- ERM_a relies entirely on the alignment computed upfront by Falcon-AO. This version of ERM can be seen as a combination of our approach and query rewriting that mimics the *QR* baseline. The precomputed mappings are used to obtain a rewritten query, which is processed to obtain results. However instead of using keyword search on top, we use the ERM and apply our approach for ranking.

---

[4]http://lucene.apache.org last retrieved on April 10th 2013

- ERM_q combines these two approaches. It uses pre-computed mappings and creates additional mappings on the fly for those attributes, which could not be mapped upfront.

5.5.4 Search Effectiveness

We use the standard IR measures precision, recall, mean average precision (MAP) and mean reciprocal rank (MRR). We retrieve the top five thousand entities using the initial keyword search, rank them, and compute the metrics based on the top one thousand entities returned by each system. The results for six different retrieval settings are shown in Figure 5.7 and Precision-Recall curves are given in Figure 5.5 and 5.6.

On-the-fly alignments. First, we examine the scenario without prior data integration. Here, finding relevant entities in the target dataset is only possible with *KW* or *ERM*. When comparing their results (Figure 5.7), we observe that *ERM* outperforms *KW* across all metrics and retrieval settings and improves over *KW* by 120% on average in terms of MAP. Looking at the different retrieval settings, we can see that *ERM* performs best between IMdb and Amazon (i.e. when IMdb or Amazon are either source or target dataset), where MAP are 0.8 and 0.95, respectively. The reason for this is that both datasets hold only entities from similar domains, movies and DVD/Videos, and describe them using similar attributes. DBpedia seems to be the most difficult one, mainly due to its schema complexity: It is very heterogeneous, containing information about different types of entities. Thus, whereas only one type has to be considered in the other datasets, identifying the relevant types out of a much larger set of possible candidates is also part of the retrieval problem here. Further, entities in DBpedia often exhibit redundant attributes with same values, e.g. *name*, *title* and *rdfs:label*, which leads to higher ambiguity during the computation of mappings. Across all retrieval settings, *ERM* yields MAP above 0.5. Also similarly good performance could be achieved for MRR and P@10, which consider the top of the ranked results. The retrieval performance of *ERM* can be observed in Figures 5.5 and 5.6, which show the interpolated precision across the recall levels. It can be observed that precision is fairly stable over different recall levels. One exception is the setting with IMdb as the target and DBpedia as the source dataset (Figure 5.6b). Here, performance decreases notably at recall levels above 0.3. This is because there are some outlier queries, which have much more relevant entities than others, and the rank of some entities obtained for these queries were relatively very low.

127

However, P@R, where R is the number of relevant entities, is still above 0.5 even for this setting (Figure 5.7c).

Precomputed alignments. In the next scenario, we examine the performance in the presence of precomputed alignments. Now, applying QR to retrieve entities is possible. This system considerably outperforms KW. Using pre-computed alignments with the approach ERM_a yields slightly better performance than ERM on average (see Figure 5.7). Both, ERM and ERM_a outperform QR on average by 54%, respectively 59% in terms of MAP. The performance of ERM_a is worse than ERM in terms of MAP, if IMdb and Amazon are involved, because creating on-the-fly mappings used by ERM works very well in this setting as we will see in Figure 5.8a in the next section and moreover there are only 5 mappings used by ERM_a as we have seen in Table 5.4. ERM_a is better in the other retrieval settings, most notably in those with IMdb and DBpedia, see Figure 5.6a, 5.6a, and 5.7a. ERM_a outperforms ERM in these cases, because the alignment problem that has to be solved as part of searching is more difficult due to the higher ambiguity and complexity introduced by DBpedia. For the same reason the rewritten query QR using precomputed mappings to produce candidate results yields slightly better performance than ERM, if DBpedia is the target dataset, see Figure 5.7a.

Precomputed and on-the-fly alignments. The strategy of combining the advantages of pre-computed mappings and computing alignments on the fly implemented by ERM_q outperforms the others across all metrics on average (see Figure 5.7).

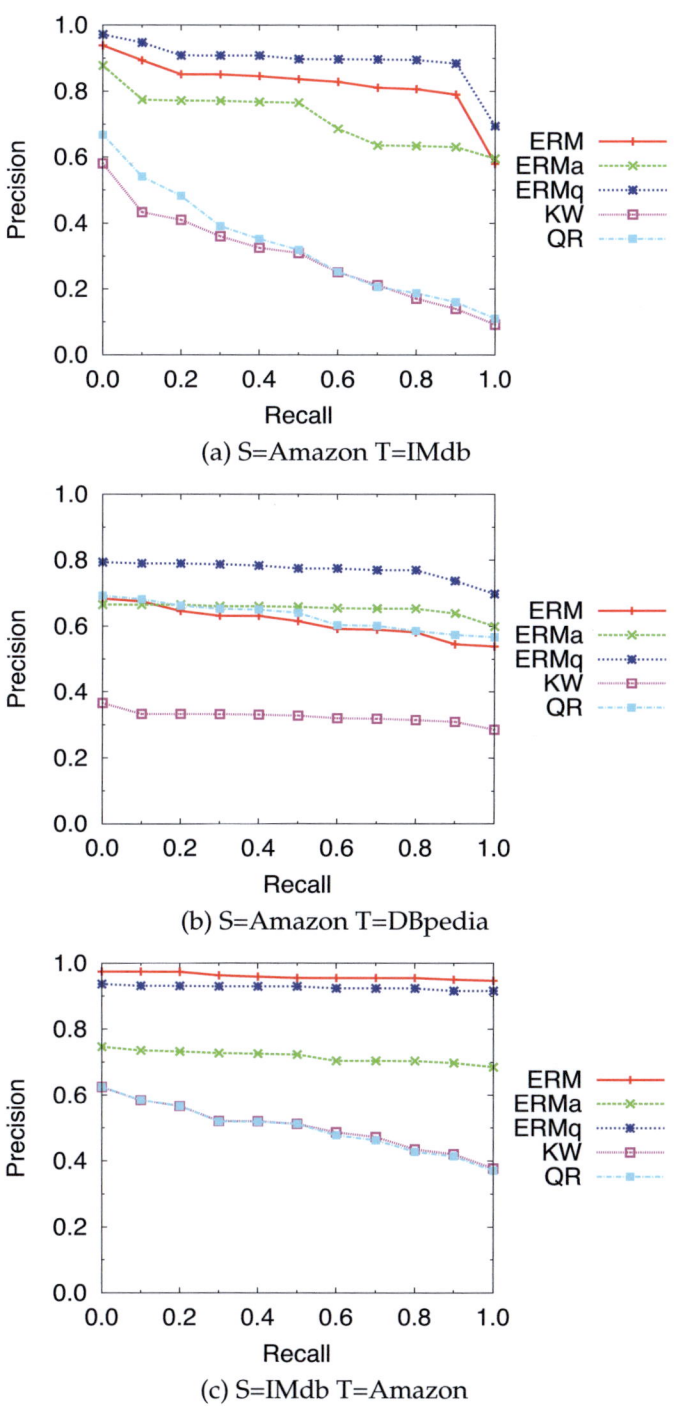

(a) S=Amazon T=IMdb

(b) S=Amazon T=DBpedia

(c) S=IMdb T=Amazon

Figure 5.5: Precision-recall curves for source (S) and target dataset (T). Part I/II

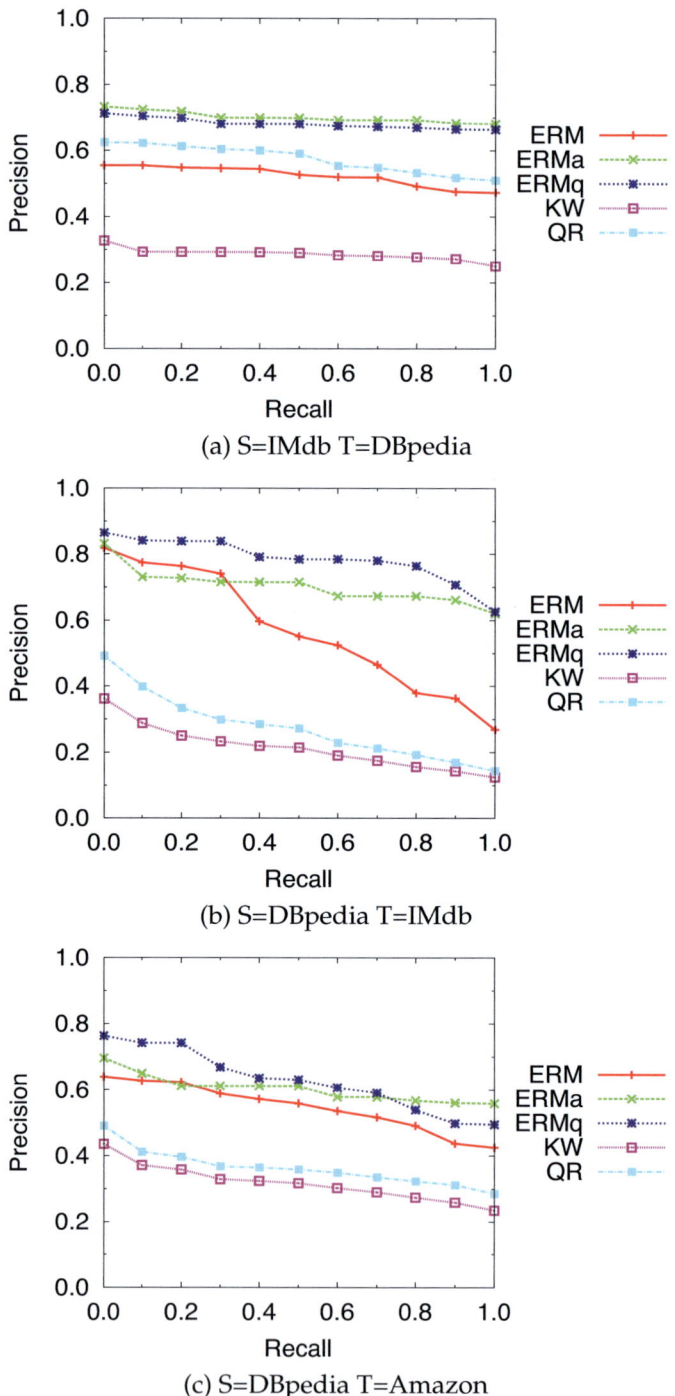

Figure 5.6: Precision-recall curves for source (S) and target dataset (T). Part II/II

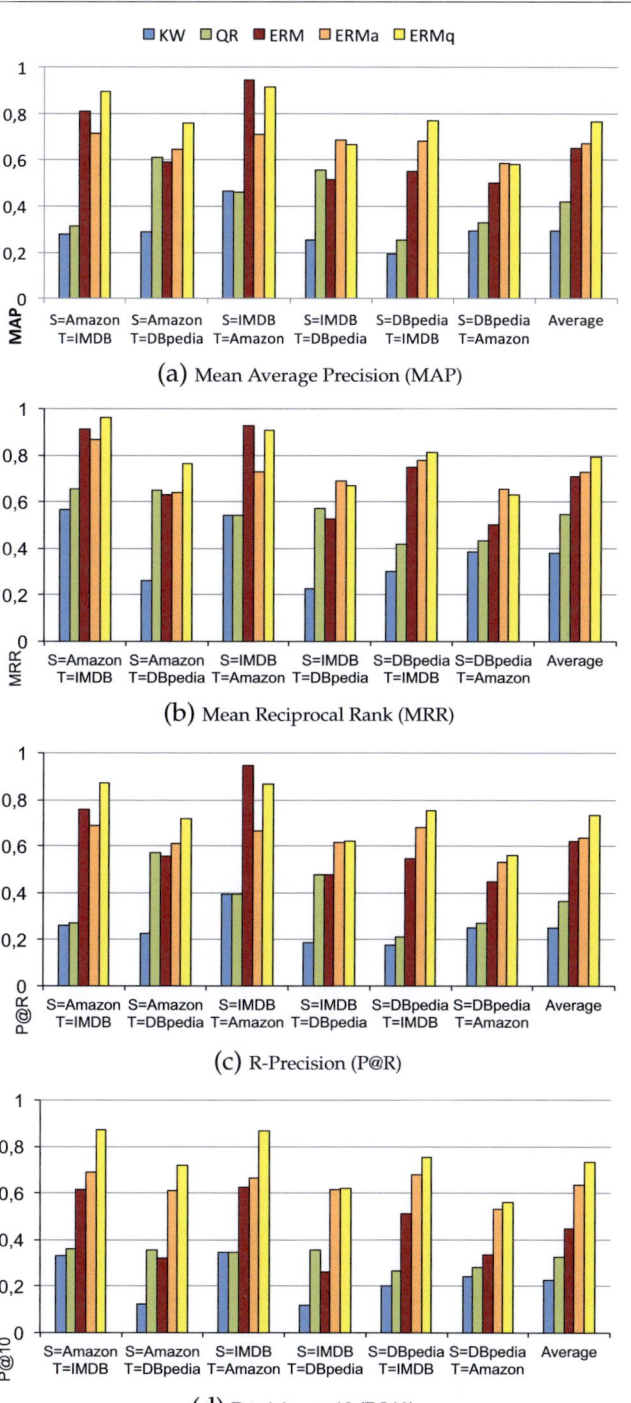

(a) Mean Average Precision (MAP)

(b) Mean Reciprocal Rank (MRR)

(c) R-Precision (P@R)

(d) Precision at 10 (P@10)

Figure 5.7: Retrieval performance between source dataset (S) and target dataset (T).

5.5.5 On The Fly Mappings

We assessed the mappings computed on the fly during the previously discussed experiments. First, we collected all mappings and manually determined the ground truth based on the pooled mappings. Since we operate on heterogeneous datasets, multiple correct mappings for one attribute are possible, e.g. *title* in one dataset might correctly corresponds to *title, name* and *label* in another dataset. Given this ground truth, we computed precision and recall of the mappings created between the fields of an ERM and the attributes of an entity. Table 5.3 shows the average size of an ERM and Table 5.1 provides the average description size of an entity. Precision and Recall are here defined as follows:

$$Precision = \frac{|\{\text{correct mappings}\}|}{|\{\text{created mappings}\}|} \tag{5.7}$$

$$Recall = \frac{|\{\text{correct mappings}\}|}{|\{\text{possible, correct mappings}\}|} \tag{5.8}$$

where $\{possible, correct\ mappings\}$ is the set of mappings, which could be established between the ERM and an entity as captured by the ground truth. We computed precision and recall for each individual entity considered during search, averaged over the query and finally over the entire query set. Overall, mappings obtained for 115k entities and the ERMs are taken into account. Figure 5.8a shows precision and recall for the different retrieval settings. Averaging over all entities, precision is 0.46 and recall is 0.12. However, we are primarily interested in the entities, which are actually relevant. Therefore, we examine precision and recall only for these relevant entities. Here, the average over all scenarios is 0.70 for precision and 0.30 for recall, as shown in Figure 5.8a. Figure 5.8b gives the average number of actual mappings created between the ERM and entities, and between the ERM and relevant entities. Clearly, better results can be achieved for relevant entities. This is important for our search task, which is focused on finding these relevant entities.

Intuitively, the search performance depends on the quality of the alignment. We verified this intuition by computing the Pearson correlation coefficient ρ between the search performance of the different settings captured by MAP, as reported in Figure 5.7a, and the alignment quality in terms of precision and recall for relevant entities, as reported in Figure 5.8a. ρ takes vales in $(-1, 1)$, with $\rho = 1$ indicating linear correlation, $\rho = 0$ indicating no correlation, and $\rho = -1$ states an inverse linear correlation.

In our case, the calculation resulted in $\rho(\text{MAP, Precision-Rel}) = 0.98$ and $\rho(\text{MAP, Recall-Rel}) = 0.97$ indicating a strong linear dependency between quality of the mappings and search performance.

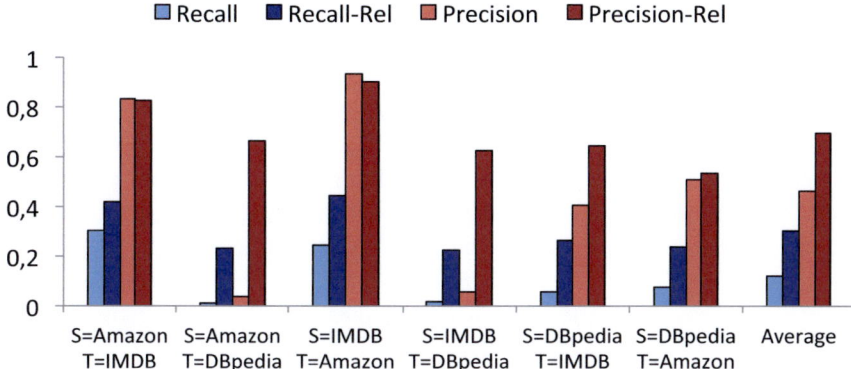

(a) Precision and recall of the mappings created on the fly between ERM and entities, respectively relevant entities (Rel).

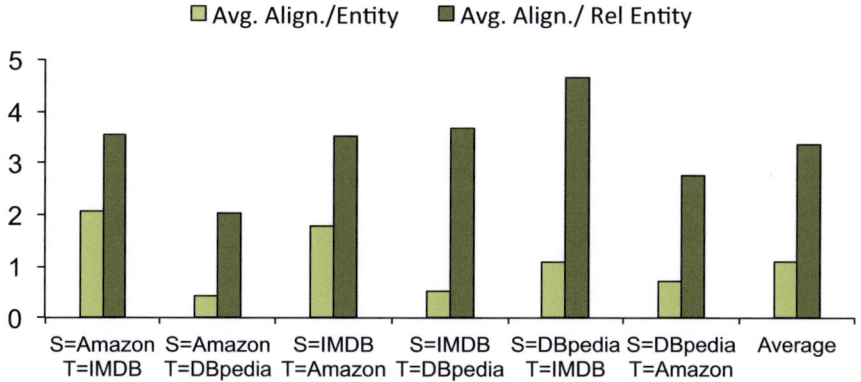

(b) Average number of mappings created on the fly between ERM and entities, respectively relevant entities (Rel).

Figure 5.8: Evaluation of the mappings created on the fly.

5.5.6 Parameter Analysis

The hybrid approach relies on three parameters: b for boosting fields (attributes) in the seed query (Equation 5.5), the alignment threshold t and the threshold c for pruning fields of the ERM (Section 5.4.3). We analyze the robustness of search effectiveness in terms of MAP for the six retrieval scenarios by varying one parameter while keeping the others fixed at the levels we used for the experiments. The results are shown in Figure 5.9. We observed that boosting helps to improve the performance when dealing with similar datasets (i.e. Amazon and IMDB) but has a negative effect when a different and diverse dataset like DBpedia is involved. However, performance is rather insensitive to this parameter when $b > 10$ (thus we chose $b = 10$). Regarding the alignment threshold t, we observed that performance is fairly stable when t is within the range $[0.2, 0.8]$. Pruning fields has almost no effect on effectiveness.

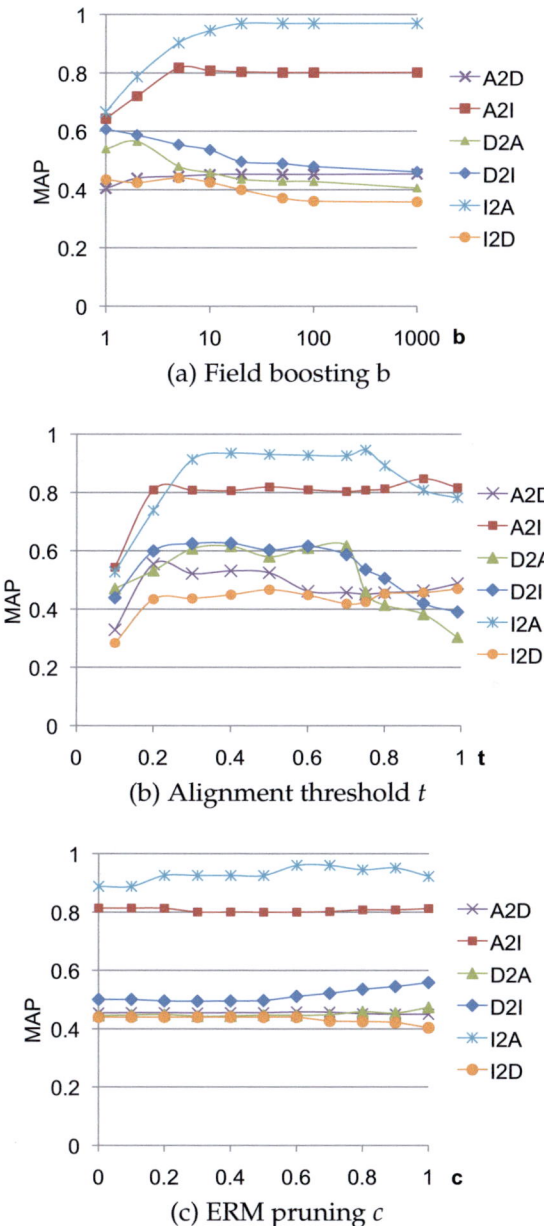

Figure 5.9: Parameter sensitivity analysis. The legend 'A2D' stands for source dataset=Amazon (A), target dataset=DBpedia (D), 'I2A' stands for source=IMdb (I), target=Amazon, etc.

5.5.7 Runtime Performance

To analyze the performance of the hybrid approach, we measured query execution time for *ERM* across all six retrieval scenarios, i.e. for a total of 138 queries. Figure 5.10a shows the min, max and average time in seconds for each retrieval scenario. The times reported cover all steps of the retrieval process, i.e. executing q_s to obtain results for the source dataset, computing *ERM*, retrieving results for target datasets, computing models for each candidate entity, establishing mappings and ranking. Such a retrieval process takes less than 13 secs on average for the above configuration. We

The performance can be improved by increasing the pruning parameter c as shown in Figure 5.10b, which shows the min, max, and average query execution time over all six scenarios for different values of c. For these runtime experiments, we use a standard laptop with Intel Core 2 Duo 2.4 GHz CPU, 4 GB RAM, Serial-ATA HDD@5400rpm, MacOS 10.6, and implemented our approach using Java 6 and Lucene 3.0 for indexing and retrieval. Computing the language models from the term-frequency vectors was performed at runtime. These tasks can also be performed at indexing time. Still, these preliminary results suggest that the hybrid approach is promising, given that not only search results but also on the fly mappings are obtained during the process.

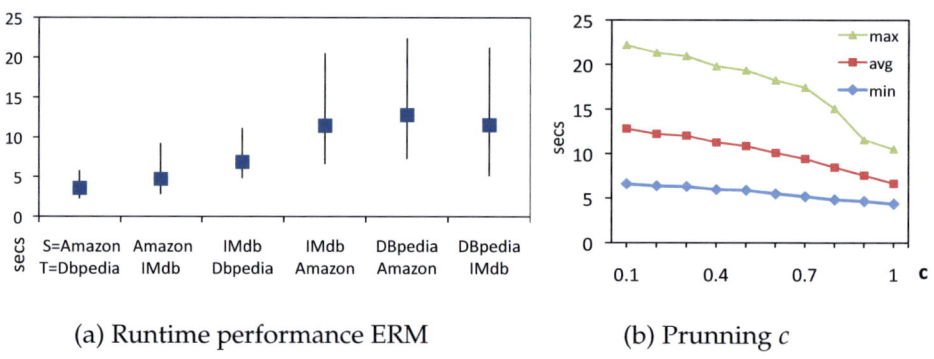

(a) Runtime performance ERM   (b) Prunning c

Figure 5.10: Runtime performance analysis

5.6 Related Work

We have discussed related work throughout the chapter. Basically, there are two existing lines of approaches, one that is based on keyword search [27,

36, 159] and the other one is structured query rewriting [28, 56, 169]. The latter type of approaches uses precomputed mappings, finds duplicates [169] or uses precomputed relaxations of the query constraints [56] to bridge differences in syntactical representation. The keyword search approaches rely on matches on the level of terms. Besides the pure 'bag-of-word' approaches [36, 159], a recent study showed that using a minimal structure by classifying attributes into *important* and *unimportant* fields improves keyword search for entities [27].

Our approach represents a novel combination which combines the flexibility of keyword search with the power of structured querying. Just like keyword search, it does not rely on precomputed mappings. However, it is able to exploit the fine-grained structure of query and results, which is the primary advantage of structured query rewriting. In addition, it can leverage existing mappings created by alignment tools like [49, 83]. We presented the general idea of our approach and preliminary results in [79].

Our work leverages several ideas that are have been proposed for IR tasks. In fact, the model underlying our approach originates from the concept of language models [129], which have been proposed for modeling resources and queries as multinomial distributions over the vocabulary terms, and for ranking based on the distance between the two models, e.g. using KL-divergence [166] or cross entropy [101] as measures. More precisely, the foundation of our work is established by Lavrenko et al.[101], who propose relevance-based language models to directly capture the relevance behind document and queries. Also, structure information has been exploited for constructing structured relevance models [102] (SRM). This is the one mostly related to ERM. The difference is that while the goal of SRM is to predict values of empty fields in a single dataset scenario, ERM targets searching in a completely different setting involving multiple heterogeneous datasets. Thus, we build on well studied concepts and investigate them in a scenario different from the traditional IR settings. Instead of searching documents using keyword queries, we show how to use structured language models to process structured queries against structured data residing in external Web datasets. In this scenario, we also need to take structure mismatches (i.e. differences at the schema level) into account and thus, propose on the fly integration to deal with this problem.

The proposed technique is in principle similar to existing work on schema matching, e.g. [54], to the extent that it relies on the same features, i.e. values of attributes. However, the use of language models for representing these features as well as the similarity calculation based on entropy is common for retrieval tasks, but we have not seen them applied to the schema mapping problem before. We consider this as a promising approach for embedding the pay-as-you-go data integration paradigm [108] into the search process.

5.7 Conclusion

Summary. We have proposed a novel approach for searching heterogeneous Web datasets using one single structured seed query that adheres to the vocabulary of just one of the datasets. We have introduced the entity relevance model which captures the structure and content of relevant results obtained for a seed query. The entity relevance model is used for matching and ranking results from external datasets, as well as for performing data integration on the fly. Our approach combines the flexibility of keyword search in the sense that no upfront integration is required, with the power of structured querying that comes from the use of the fine-grained structure of query and results. Extensive experiments conducted with real-world datasets show the effectiveness and feasibility of our approach. Using our approach allows to take advantage of the structured data available numerously as Linked Data on the Web by incorporating these data sources into existing vertical search capabilities. The experiments showed that our approach outperforms both the keyword search and the query rewriting baselines by 120%, respectively 54% in terms of Mean Average Precision.

Conclusions. We have investigated Research Question 3 and showed how remote structured data can be integrated into a local search process. In particular, we have investigated Hypothesis 3.1 and Hypothesis 3.2. Hypothesis 3.1 assumes that coping with the heterogeneity of Web data is feasible on-the-fly at query time. We have examined our approach with respect to its capabilities of establishing mappings between schema elements that are subsequently used in the retrieval process. The results obtained in our experiments as discussed in Section 5.5.5 allow to confirm this hypothesis. Moreover, the results achieved with respect to the following Hypothesis 3.2, which would not have been possible without the query time integration, fosters this conclusion on Hypothesis 3.1. Regarding Hypothesis 3.2, we have investigated the exploiting of structure for ranking results with the help of the alignments established at query time and showed in Section 5.5.4 that our approach outperforms unstructured keyword search and the query rewriting baseline. Hence, we consider the above hypothesis as confirmed. Overall, we consider the results promising and will apply the general concepts of query time data integration also in the next chapter.

Outlook. The work presented in this chapter can be extended in several directions. First, extending the approach to allow more general queries yielding more complex results, e.g. involving entities of different types possibly connected over long paths, is one way to expand its applicability. Another direction is to improve efficiency of our approach. Besides the examined pruning of fields to improve the performance, one can assume that during the execution time of a query the schema remains stable and hence not each entity has to be aligned individually, but just the first k entities to save time during the alignment step.

Chapter 6

Federated Entity Search using On-The-Fly Consolidation

Nowadays, search on the Web goes beyond the retrieval of textual Web sites and increasingly, takes advantage of the growing amount of structured data. Of particular interest is entity search, where the units of retrieval are structured entities instead of textual documents. These entities reside in different sources, which may provide only limited information about their content and hence are called *uncooperative* in the context of distributed information retrieval. Further, these sources capture complementary but also redundant information about entities. In this environment of uncooperative sources, we study the problem of *federated entity search*, where redundant information about entities is reduced on-the-fly through *entity consolidation* performed at query time. We propose a novel method for entity consolidation that is based on using language models and completely unsupervised, hence more suitable for this on-the-fly uncooperative setting than state-of-the-art methods that require training data. Thus, we apply the same language model technique to deal with the federated search problem of ranking results returned from different sources. Particular novel are the mechanisms we propose to incorporate consolidation results into this ranking. We perform experiments using real Web queries and data sources, showing that our approach for federated entity search with on-the-fly consolidation improves upon the performance of a state-of-the-art method for federated search. We show these improvements are due both to the proposed ranking model and the incorporation of consolidated entities.

6

Outline. After the introduction in Section 6.1, we start the research question, the hypotheses derived thereof and outline the contributions of this chapter in Section 6.2. We provide an overview of the research area, the challenges and our approach in Section 6.3. In Section 6.4 we detail our consolidation procedure and in Section 6.5 we present our ranking model and how it incorporates co-references. Experiments on consolidation and ranking using real-world queries and data are presented in Section 6.6 and related work is discussed in Section 6.7 before we conclude in Section 6.8.

6.1 Introduction

Taking advantage of the growing amount of structured data on the Web has been recognized as a promising way to improve the effectiveness of search, and has therefore gained the interest of researchers and industry [11]. This development is also driven by the demand from Web search users, whose most dominant search task is the search for entities. Recent studies showed that about 70% of Web search queries contain entities [66] and that the intent of about 40% of unique Web queries is to find a particular entity [130]. Structured data representing entities are abundant on the Web. However, they often reside in different sources. These sources capture redundant but also complementary information about entities. Hence, consolidating co-referent entities referring to the same real-world object and providing *search functionalities over co-referent entities* is a crucial step towards exploiting structured data sources for Web search.

To this end, a centralized approach can be adopted that relies on one single index over the sources. This approach constitutes the dominant solution for textual Web search. For searching over structured data, it is however not always applicable. On the one hand, this is due to accessibility constraints. That is, while most providers make some parts of their data sources available over APIs, crawling the entire data is not always possible. Further, many structured data sources are highly dynamic, imposing a high burden on the centralized solution to keep up with frequent changes and to provide fresh information for time sensitive applications such as search over movies, stock quotes and timetables. The alternative to the centralized solution is direct search over distributed data sources, called *federated search*. This solution can be seen as a 'meta' search engine (or broker), which routes the query to distributed data sources (APIs providing access over the sources), and merges the results and their ranks obtained from these sources.

For federated search, the IR literature distinguishes between cooperative and uncooperative environments [29, 139]. In *cooperative environments*, the broker has (full) control and information over data sources to make informed decisions such as how to route the query and how to learn the optimal ranking of merged results. In *uncooperative environments*, full information and training data cannot be assumed. In the extreme case, no information is available such that for searching over the sources, all decisions have to be made on-the-fly without prior information.

6.2 Research Question and Contribution

In this chapter we address the following Research Question 4:

Research Question 4. *Can we detect co-referent entities during the search process over multiple data sources without using training examples, i.e. in an unsupervised way and does consolidation of co-referent entities increase the effectiveness of search by considering co-references in the ranking procedure?*

This research question comprises several aspects. The first requirement is to detect co-references during the search process without using training examples. This aspect targets the setting of uncooperative sources on the Web where up-front data integration or training is not possible. We will assume such a setting in the subsequent discussion. Further, the search process covers multiple data sources, called federated search, which has been studied for document retrieval [29, 139]. We will study it for entity search over structured data and investigate whether covering more data can also lead to more effective search, i.e. whether the ranking can be improved. Hence, we state the first hypothesis of our investigation in this chapter as follows:

Hypothesis 4.1. *Federated entity search, i.e. the search over multiple data sources, improves search effectiveness upon search over single data sources.*

The second part of the research question above addressed the consolidation of co-referent entities. Before consolidation takes place, co-references have to be identified or provided from external services. We will propose a consolidation technique later and then investigate its effect on ranking. We assume that consolidating co-referent results will lead to a higher search effectiveness and hence state the following hypothesis:

Hypothesis 4.2. *Establishing co-references on the fly in an unsupervised way through measuring the similarity between attribute values of entities and using these co-references for consolidation improves search effectiveness compared to unconsolidated search.*

There are several ways of what consolidation can actually mean. We will investigate different ways of considering co-references for consolidated search and explain these different systems later in Section 6.6.4. Regarding the above hypotheses in the defined context, we provide the following contribution in this chapter:

Contribution 4. *Federated Entity Search using On-The-Fly Consolidation*

In this chapter, we aim to address the problem of *federated entity search in uncooperative environments* on the Web. We observe that while more and more links between co-referent entities in different sources are established as a result of initiatives such as Linking Open Data, the full coverage of all entity co-references cannot be assumed. Thus, entity consolidation should be done on-the-fly, i.e. at query time, to combine all entity-related information from different sources and to reduce entity information redundancy, respectively. Towards these goals, this chapter presents three main contributions:

- We propose a novel method for entity consolidation that is based on using language models (LM) for representing entities and a LM-oriented metric for computing the similarity between entities. This LM-based approach has an advantage compared to common string comparisons in that not only entire values or the words contained in them are captured but also their probability of being observed. More importantly, this approach is completely unsupervised, which is a requirement for an uncooperative setting where training data is not available. To the best of our knowledge, we are the first to propose on-the-fly unsupervised entity consolidation for federated entity search.

- We reuse these LM-based representation of entities also for addressing the search problem. In particular, we show how this entity representation in combination with structured relevance models [80, 100] can be used to obtain a combined ranking of results returned from the sources. The mechanisms we propose to incorporate consolidation results into this ranking are particularly novel.

- In the experiments, we employ real-world Web queries and data sources and investigate the effects of federated search in combination with consolidation. We show that our approach exceeds a state-of-the-art preference aggregation method for federated search [154] and show the advantages of consolidation for search in the federated search setting.

The work presented in this chapter was conducted during a research stay at Yahoo! Labs Barcelona.

145

6.3 Overview

In this section, we describe the research problem, point out the challenges
and give an overview of our solution.

Entity Search. We follow the definition by [130] and define *entity search*,
also known as *object search*, as the task of answering arbitrary information
needs related to particular aspects of entities, expressed in unconstrained
natural language and resolved using a collection of structured data.

The key difference to traditional document search is that the units of
retrieval are general entities described via attributes and corresponding
values as well as relations to other entities. These entities are captured by
structured data stored in relational databases, XML data collections or other
kinds of structured data. In this chapter, we focus on Web data for which the
RDF model has been proposed as a W3C standard for data representation
and interchange. Hence, this model is of primary interest. It is a general
graph-structured data model that has been used to capture different kinds
of structured data. For example, relational data can be mapped to RDF
by representing tuple ids as RDF resource nodes (referred to as entities in
this work), other tuple values as RDF literal nodes that are connected to
resource nodes, and foreign key relationships as relations between resource
nodes. For the sake of generality, we omit RDF specific features, like blank
nodes, and employ a general graph-structured data model as in previous
work [80]. In this model, entity nodes stand for RDF resources, literal nodes
correspond to RDF literals, attributes are RDF properties, and edges capture
RDF triples:

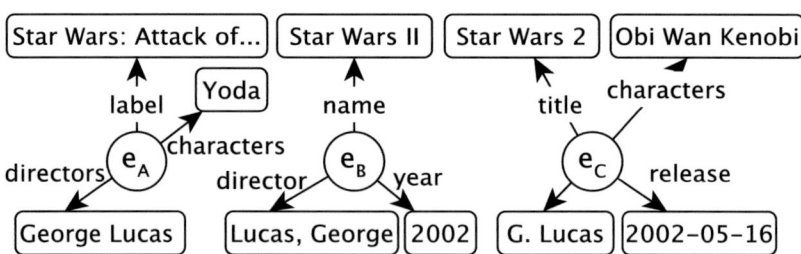

Figure 6.1: Heterogenous Web entities: Three co-referent entities from different data sources.

A *data source* is a directed and labeled data graph $G = (N, E)$ as defined
in Defintion 2.1. The data graph consists of entities according to the Definitions 2.2, 2.3, and 2.4. In our Web scenario, each data source is repre-

sented by a graph G_X, for example Figure 6.2 illustrates three data sources $X = \{A, B, C\}$. Although arbitrary edges can connect entities across data graphs, we are only interested in edges denoting that two entities are co-referent, i.e. $a_{\text{same}}(e_X, e_Y), e_X \in G_X, e_Y \in G_Y$. The attribute $a_s ame$ represents the property `owl:sameAs`[1] defined in Web Ontology Language (OWL), which is frequently used in the Web of Data.

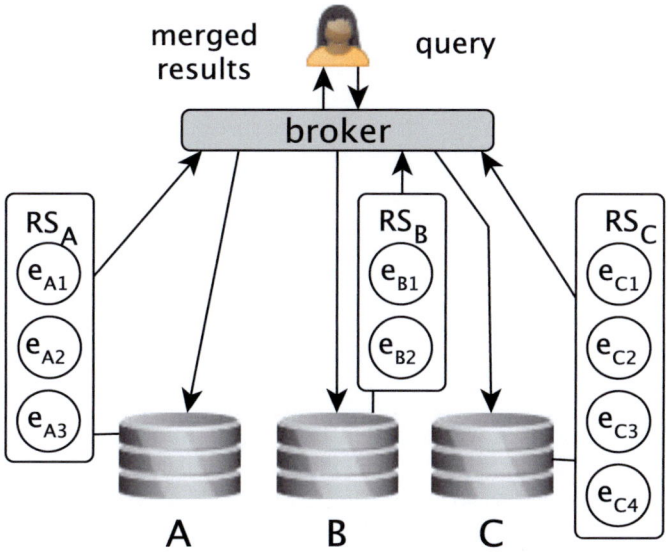

Figure 6.2: Federated search in an uncooperative setting: The broker obtains only the ranked result lists RS_A, RS_B, RS_C from each data source and merges them into one single ranked list.

Federation. We address a particular kind of entity search, namely the search over multiple data sources. This is called *federated search*, also known as distributed information retrieval [29, 139], which entails the three main problems of *source representation*, *source selection*, and *result merging* [29, 139]. Federated search can be executed in a *cooperative setting*, where there is control over the data sources such that we can decide what kinds of information are collected to model the sources and how to select them based upon these source models. Given full control and complete information, this federated search amounts to search over multiple data graphs, where all data captured by the graphs is known, and all the relevant graphs as well as the constituent data representing the results can be determined by

---

[1]`http://www.w3.org/TR/owl-ref/#sameAs-def` last retrieved on April 10th 2013

the broker. On the other hand, information and control is limited in the *uncooperative setting*, where data sources might have to be treated as black boxes. Here, the broker simply forwards the issued query to all sources to retrieve ranked result lists. Federated search boils down to the online problem of merging ranked result lists to return one integrated view to the user as illustrated in Figure 6.2 – without making any assumptions about the sources and the data they capture.

Federation and On-the-Fly Consolidation. In this chapter, we focus on *federated entity search in the uncooperative setting* where ranked result lists obtained from each sources comprise entity descriptions. As discussed in the following, the problem solved goes beyond the pure merging of the individual result lists and their ranking information, but also, requires consolidation. That is, we address *consolidated entity search* where entities representing the same real-world object, called *co-referent entities* and illustrated in Figure 6.1, are identified, linked and incorporated into ranking to avoid redundant results returned by different sources.

6.3.1 Challenges

Targeting this consolidated federated entity search problem, we aim to solve the following main challenges:

Redundancy. Data sources on the Web may overlap with respect to the entity descriptions they contain, especially when they cover the same domain. They may have substantial overlaps as well as complementary information that might be the subject of federated search queries. An example of redundancy in search results is shown in Figure 6.3, which shows a result page of `sindice.com` [126], a Linked Data search engine. The results page has only four distinct entities among the top ten results for the query "aifb".

Our hypothesis, as stated before, is that by detecting these overlaps, i.e. co-referent entities, and merging them into one single result, we can improve the quality of search and the ranking of results in particular.

Heterogeneity. Finding co-referent entities however, is not straightforward on the Web, where providers may share overlapping information on the same real-world object, but use different representations. These schema vocabulary differences are illustrated in Figure 6.1, which depicts three co-referent entities representing the same real-world object, but using a varying number of attributes, different attribute labels and also different values on the data level to describe them. We note that heterogeneity may arise not only at the data but also at the schema level. This problem is increasingly recognized and tackled by Web data providers, who, in addition to the data,

Figure 6.3: Search result page of the Data Web search engine `sindice.com` showing four distinct real-world entities among the top10 results for the query "aifb" (as of Feb 2 2013). There are four co-refenent entities for the "Institute AIFB" and three co-references of the ""SEAL Project"", which marked by the arrows in the figure.

also publish `owl:sameAs` links that connect co-referent elements across data sources. Compared to the data, the schema is usually much smaller in size and also, is less subject to frequent changes. Thus, while `owl:sameAs` links might be used for detecting co-referent elements at the schema-level, they cannot be assumed to be complete at the data level, i.e. capture all co-referent entities.

Limited Information. Another challenge for both consolidation and ranking consolidated entities is the absence of information that results from the uncooperative setting. Given the data graphs representing the sources (or some sufficient statistics about them) and training data, state-of-the-art methods for learning entity consolidation rules [35], or learning the best combination of ranking features [47] can be applied. This is not possible in our setting where only the query-specific lists of results returned by the sources are available. Instead of offline learning and processing, consolidation and ranking have to be performed completely on-the-fly.

6.3.2 Overview of our Approach

We address the above challenges in our approach as follows. During the retrieval process, we perform on-the-fly consolidation to detect co-referent entities. They are linked through `owl:sameAs`, and the resulting consolidated entities are used in the merge of ranked results to avoid redundancy. In order to cope with heterogeneity, we address the consolidation problem using an IR-inspired model for representing entities and for measuring the similarity between entities. It is based on the notion of structured language models [80, 121], where each entity is represented by several multinomial distributions over vocabulary words that in combination, capture both the entity content and structure; and similarity is then derived from the overlap between the entities' LMs. Not only the language models but also their weights representing their importance on the similarity are derived for each query completely on-the-fly – without making any assumption about the sources or the availability of training data. In the next step, the same language models are reused for ranking purposes, which to compute the similarity between an entity and a query. Here, we study different ranking strategies, which take advantage of the consolidation results, i.e. `owl:sameAs` links between co-referent entities.

6.4 On-the-fly Entity Consolidation

Entity consolidation is typically performed through the main steps of *representing entities* as attribute value pairs, and finding the appropriate *similarity metric* and *threshold* to determine whether two given entity representations refer to the same object or not, i.e. when the similarity computed using the metric exceeds the threshold. Since several attributes are typically used, state-of-the-art methods employ machine learning techniques to learn the weights for attributes. In fact, based on training data, supervised learning techniques might be used not only to determine the weights but also to the (attribute-specific) metrics and thresholds [35]. In this section, we (1) represent attribute values as language models, (2) employ a specific notion of distance for LMs as the similarity metric, and (3) propose an unsupervised technique to estimate the weight associated with each attribute LM. In our approach, all the steps needed to derive the LM-based entity representation as well as the actual detection of consolidated entities is performed on-the-fly during the execution of a query.

6.4.1 Entity Representation

We apply the same entity modeling and representation as in the previous chapter, i.e. we model an entity e as a composite model $e = (A', \mathcal{P})$, with $A'(e)$ is the model of e (Definition 2.4) and $\mathcal{P}_t$ is a set of language models, one for each attribute in A' as previously discussed in Section 5.4.2. Each language model $P_e(w|a) \in \mathcal{P}$ of entity e for attribute $a \in A'$ is computed as previously defined in Equation 5.3 with the only difference that we now use the subscript to denote the entity of which the language model is part of.

6.4.2 Similarity Metric

Given two entities in the result lists, $e_X \in RS_X$ and $e_Y \in RS_Y$, we determine whether they are co-referent or not using a similarity metric. Standard metrics used by consolidation methods include *edit distance* and *Jaccard similarity*, which can be applied to two given attribute values. The former captures the number of edit operations needed to transform one value to the other while the latter is based on the word overlaps between the two values.

Since we apply language model to captures values, we measure the overlap of the language models with the *Jensen-Shannon divergence* (JSD), which we discussed in Section 2.2.6 and defined in Equation 2.6. More precisely, we use the square root of the JSD in the computation of the distance d between two entities e_X and e_Y. The distance $d(e_X,e_Y)$ is calculated over the language models constructed for all attributes a that both entities have in common and each overlap measured by the JSD is weighted by $w(a)$ as defined in Equation 6.1. We discuss the weights in the next section.

$$d(e_X,e_Y) = \frac{1}{\sum w(a)} \sum_{a \in A'(e_X) \cap A'(e_Y)} w(a) \, JSD(P_{e_X}(w|a)||P_{e_Y}(w|a))^{\frac{1}{2}} \qquad (6.1)$$

6.4.3 Estimating Weights

The weight $w(a)$ expresses how discriminative and identifying an attribute a is. We determine $w(a)$ w.r.t. the result lists RS_X and RS_Y. First, we construct a language model $P_X(w|a)$ analog to Equation 5.3. However, $P_X(w|a)$ captures the value nodes of all the entities in RS_X instead of a single entity, i.e. $N_a(RS_X) = \{e|a(e_X,e), e_X \in RS_X\}$ instead of $N_a(e)$. Then, we compute the entropy $H(P) = -\sum_w P(w) \log_2 P(w)$ and set $w(a)$ to:

$$w(a) = \frac{1}{2}H(P_X)H(P_Y) \qquad (6.2)$$

The rationale behind this formulation is that the entropy is high, if the bag $N_a(RS_X)$ contains many diverse values, and it is low, if $N_a(RS_X)$ contains similar and hence less discriminative values. Attributes with more diverse values are associated with higher weights because they provide more discriminate information to distinguish entities.

6.4.4 Entity Similarity

Given the above distance function and two result lists $RS_X = (e_{X1}, e_{X2}, ..., e_{Xi}, ...)$ and $RS_Y = (e_{Y1}, e_{Y2}, ..., e_{Yj}, ...)$, we consider two entities $e_X \in RS_X$ and $e_Y \in RS_Y$ as co-referent, if their distance is below a threshold t and if they are mutually the closest to each other, see Equation 6.3. The latter condition assures that only co-references are established, if a candidate entity is favored over all alternatives. Note, that we also compare each source with itself, i.e. $X = Y$, to find co-references within a source.

$$d(e_X,e_Y) < t \wedge d(e_X,e_Y) = \min_i d(e_{Xi},e_Y) = \min_j d(e_X,e_{Yj}) \qquad (6.3)$$

6.5 Ranking Consolidated Entities

We assume the following situation. There are ranked lists of entities RS_X, one for each data source X, and a set of edges A_{same} linking co-referent entities. Figure 6.4(a) depicts this situation with three result lists and four $a_{\text{same}} \in A_{\text{same}}$ edges (arrows). Co-referent entities share the same dashed line style in Figure 6.4 and the subscripts of the entities denote the data source and the original rank, e.g. entity e_{C2} is ranked second by datasource B, see Figure 6.4(a). The co-references A_{same} are either obtained through the consolidation process described in the previous section, are already part of the data returned by the data sources, or provided by external sources or services such as `http://sameas.org`. We aim at merging these entities into one ranked list while taking the co-references into account. In the following we present our ranking model for consolidated entities and then show our strategy for exploiting co-references.

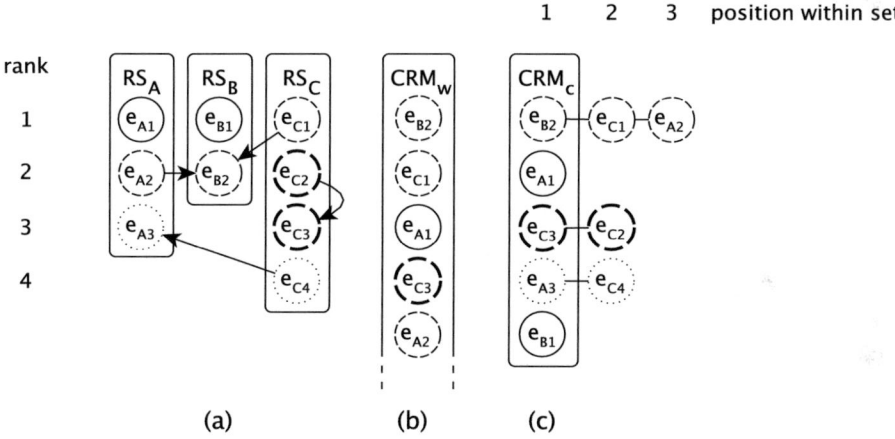

Figure 6.4: (a) Three lists RS_X with four a_{same} edges (b) Ranked list (c) Consolidated ranked list.

6.5.1 Ranking for Structured Web Data

The general concept we apply for ranking is pseudo-relevance feedback based ranking [100]. We adapt this idea and apply it to federated entity search. In line with this concept, we build two models, one Query Model (QM) capturing the information need with the help of relevance feedback and Resource Models (RM) representing results to be ranked. For ranking, each RM is scored against QM and sorted by this score into the final result list.

Both models, QM and RM, share in general the same structure as entities, as described in Section 6.4.1, i.e. they contain a set of attribute labels A' and a corresponding language model $P \in \mathcal{P}$ for each attribute. Formally, the model $M \in \{QM, RM\}$ is a 3-tuple $M = (\mathcal{E}, A', \mathcal{P})$. We denote the set of entities $\mathcal{E}$ of model M as $\mathcal{E}(M)$ and the set of attributes A' of model M as $A'(M) = \{a|a \in A'(e), \exists e \in \mathcal{E}(M)\}$. As previously for the consolidation, we use the *JSD*, Equation 2.6, to measure the distance between two corresponding language models for all attributes that QM and RM have in common.

$$Score(QM||RM) = \sum_{a \in \bigcap_X A'(RS_X)} JSD(P_{QM}(w|a)||P_{RM}(w|a))^{\frac{1}{2}} \qquad (6.4)$$

The language models of QM and RM, see Equation 6.5, are computed from the respective language models of the entities that are comprised by the model and each entity language model P_e (Equation 5.3) is weighted with an entity specific weight $\mu(e)$:

$$P_M(w|a) = \frac{\sum_{e \in \mathcal{E}(M)} \mu(e) P_e(w|a)}{\sum_{e \in \mathcal{E}(M)} \mu(e)} \qquad (6.5)$$

The weight μ is the crucial part of the query model QM. For RM the weight is constant $\mu = 1$. The weight allows to control the impact of each entity on the query model. With the weight μ, we adapt the ranking framework to the federated search setting and exploit the ranking of the individual data sources. We use the discounted rank of the entity e_X in the result list RS_X of its data source X to weight its influence on the query model:

$$\mu(e_X) = \frac{1}{\log(1 + rank(e_X, RS_X))} \qquad (6.6)$$

By using the ranks in μ, we take advantage of the ranking functions of the data sources. Although the data sources do not provide any information explicitly about themselves, all their knowledge, such as domain expertise, popularity, click-data, and other signals, are incorporated in their ranking function and thereby implicitly conveyed in the ranking. Moreover, we tie the importance of an entity represented by its rank to the content and the structure of the entity, which is captured by the language model of the entity.

For QM, we use all entities returned by the sources, i.e. $\mathcal{E}(QM) = \bigcup_X RS_X$ and we construct one RM for each entity.

Note that an advantage of the above ranking technique is that it is entirely parameter free. The whole ranking procedure takes all its ingredients from the results returned by the data sources for the initial query. This is an important feature for dynamic web environments, where data sources may (dis-)appear frequently and a prior integration into the federated search process is not possible.

6.5.2 Ranking consolidation

We start with a common ranking procedure, illustrated in Figure 6.4(a). Given, the result sets RS_X we consider each entity $e \in \bigcup_X RS_X$ individually and construct a corresponding model RM out of each entity. Then, we score each RM and because each RM represents one entity, we obtain a ranked list of entities. This ranked list contains all entities in $\bigcup_X RS_X$, one entity on each rank as depicted in Figure 6.4(b) and labeled with CRM_w. At this point we have a ranked list without taking advantage of the co-references. In the experimental Section 6.6, we will also refer to this stage as CRM_w. Now, we allow sets of entities on each rank instead of a single entity. We iterate through the ranked list from the best to the last ranked entity. During this iteration we make use of the co-references A_{same}. If we observe an entity that has co-references, we position the set of all co-referent entities on this rank and remove them from their original ranks. Within each consolidated set, the entity previously ranked highest is first and then we order the co-referent entities by their previous ranks in CRM_w. Figure 6.4(c) illustrates such a consolidated ranking labeled with CRM_c. We see that all co-referent entities are grouped into sets and each set is positioned on a rank, e.g. the set of co-referent entities $\{e_{C2}, e_{C3}\}$ are on rank 3 and within this set e_{C3} is on position 1, because e_{C3} is the highest ranked entity of its co-reference set in CRM_w. The result of this strategy is a list of ranked sets. In the next section, we also refer to the consolidated ranking strategy as CRM_c.

6.6 Experiments

We conducted experiments on the two tasks, consolidation and ranking, in two real-world scenarios. In one scenario users search for movies and in the another one for scientific publications. We used publicly accessible APIs available on the Web as sources of entities. These sources were accessed via requests in the form `http://api.url.com?q="keyword query"`.

Table 6.1 lists the used data sources for both scenarios. We used Yahoo! Dapper[2] to mimic an API using the site search of Citeseer and ACM.

`netflix.com`	`arxiv.org`
`rottentomatoes.com`	`dl.acm.org`
`moviedb.com`	`citeseerx.ist.psu.edu`
	`academic.research.microsoft.com`

Table 6.1: Data sources (APIs) used for *movie* (left) and *publication* scenario (right).

6.6.1 Real-World Web Search Queries

We extracted real Web search queries from the Yahoo! US Search query log from Jan 1ˢᵗ until July 31ˢᵗ 2012. For each scenario, we manually created a list of more than ten hostnames, which contains those of the data sources and highly popular sites like `imdb.com` for movies and `dblp.org` for publications. We sampled only queries having at least two clicks on one of these hostnames to obtain queries for our experiments. For the publication scenario, these queries were from many different scientific disciplines, e.g. medicine. Since our judges' expertise is in the computer science domain, we manually picked 181 queries related to computer science from the initial sample. We issued the sampled queries to the data sources and requested 100 results. We encountered the problem that for many queries no results were found. In particular for the movie scenario, where for almost half of the 624 initially sampled queries at least one data source returned no results. The reason for this behavior seems to be that some movie data sources require all keywords to be present in an entity description (AND conjunction of keywords). With the goal of minimizing queries with empty results, we sampled a set of 50 queries for each scenario and used these sets for our experiments. Table 6.2 provides the following details on the query sets: The number of queries (#q), terms per query and standard deviation ($|q|$), maximal number of entities per result list (max $|RS|$), average number of entities per result list ($avg|RS|$) and how often an empty result list was returned ($|RS| = \varnothing$) for each source. Ten queries of each set are shown in Table 6.3.

Heterogeneity. The entities returned exhibit heterogeneity in terms of varying entity description sizes A'. Table 6.4 provides statistics on the

---

[2] `www.open.dapper.net` last retrieved on April 10th 2013

	Source	#q	$|q| \pm \sigma$	max$|RS|$	$avg|RS| \pm \sigma$	$|RS| = \emptyset$
Movie	MovieDb	50	2.58±1.3	20	6.18±7.22	6
	Netflix	50	2.58±1.3	100	81.7±30.4	0
	RT	50	2.58±1.3	50	12.0±15.5	0
Publ.	Arxiv	50	4.4±2.1	100	83.2±36.2	0
	ACM	50	4.4±2.1	20	18.6±4.21	0
	Citeseer	50	4.4±2.1	10	9.2±2.51	3
	MS	50	4.4±2.1	100	89.0±27.3	0

Table 6.2: Query sets and corresponding result lists *RS*.

mission impossible 4	parameter selection in particle swarm optimization
the debt	mobility models in inter-vehicle communications literature
hobbit	computer effective to academic learning
cowboys and aliens 2011	bivariate f distribution
the hunters 2011	werner krandick
red tails	using truth tables to evaluate arguments
just go with it	non linear multiple centrality corrections interior point algorithm
prison break	subpixel location
soul surfer	examples of chi-square problems
thor	analytical target cascading feinberg

Table 6.3: Example queries with *movie-related* intend (left) and *scientific* intend (right).

entities returned for the query sets described above. As expected we see that each source uses a varying number of attributes to describe entities. In particular, for the movie scenario, we observe larger differences compared to the publication scenario, where the usage of schema elements is more consistent, (i.e. mostly the same attributes are used, mainly title, authors, abstract and date). Besides these schema differences, the vocabularies differ as well, as already illustrated in Figure 6.1.

6.6.2 Ground Truth

We obtained the ground truth for both tasks through expert judgments. A sub-sample of subjects was judged several times in order to measure an inter-rater agreement.

For the consolidation evaluation, we showed two entity descriptions to a rater, who had to decide whether the two entities are co-referent or

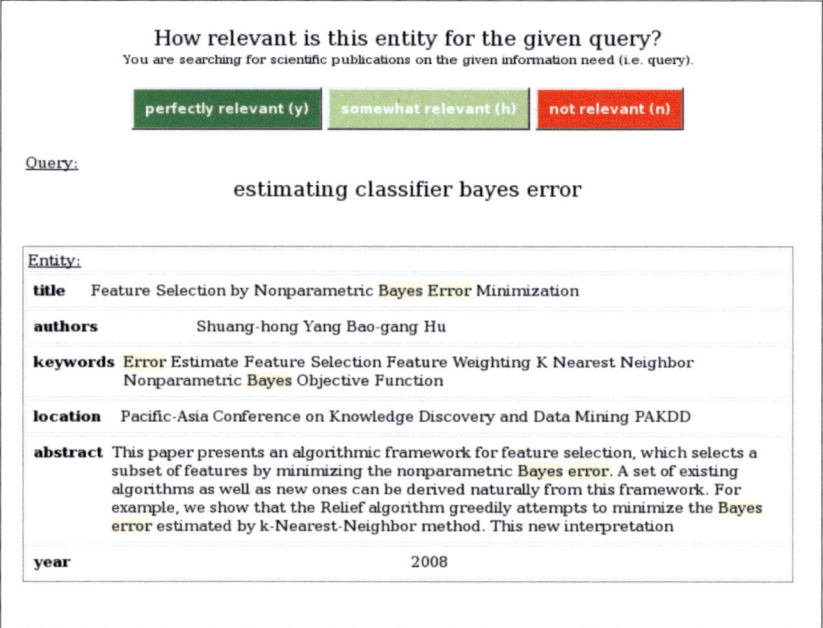

(a) Relevance assessment task

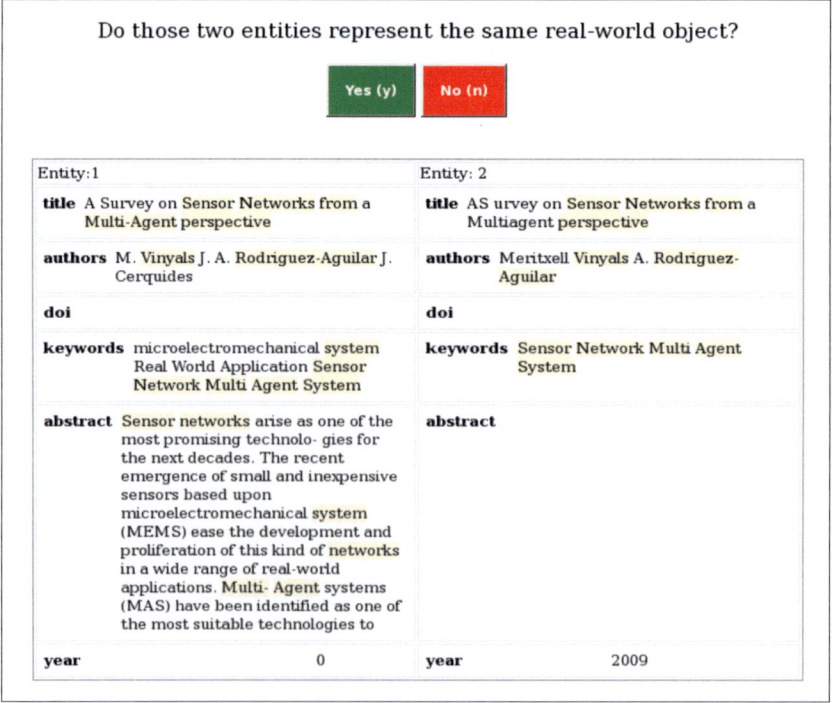

(b) Consolidation assessment task

Figure 6.5: Screenshots of the assessment tasks shown to the judges.

	Source	$avg|A'(e)| \pm \sigma$	$\max A'(e)$	$\min A'(e)$
Movie	MovieDb	11.2±3.4	16	2
	Netflix	5.7±0.6	6	4
	RT	7.4±2.1	11	3
Publ.	Arxiv	6.1±0.6	7	5
	ACM	5.5±0.8	6	3
	Citeseer	4.5±0.6	5	3
	MS	6.8±0.4	7	6

Table 6.4: Statistics on entities descriptions.

	Raters	Subjects	Ratings	Overlap	$\alpha_{ordinal}$
Consolidation					
Publications	6	3076	4246	1170	**0.7596**
Movie	3	5783	6061	278	**0.8204**
Relevance					
Publications	6	2736	3022	286	**0.7051**
Movie	3	1616	1992	376	**0.6919**

Table 6.5: Ground truth: Number of raters, subjects rated, subjects rated several times (overlap), and inter-rater agreement measured by Krippendorff's α [74].

not. We pooled the established co-references over all experimental runs, which resulted in 5783 entity pairs for the movie, respectively 3076 for the publication scenario. A considerable amount of these pairs - 636 (movie), 725 (publication) - are true co-references, which indicates that taking co-references into account is important. In Table 6.6, the distributions of the co-references between the sources are given for the two scenarios. We can observe that co-references exist not just between but also within the results of a data source. Noteworthy, one source (MS) is dominant in the publication scenario and is part of 83% of the co-references.

We apply the methodology introduced in Chapter 3 to obtain relevance judgments for the ranking evaluation, i.e. we showed the query together with an entity description to a rater, who had to decide on a 3-point scale whether the entity is *perfectly relevant*, *somewhat relevant* or *not relevant* to the query. For all experimental runs, we rated the top-10 results for each query, which resulted in 2736 ratings for the publication scenario, and 1616 judgments for the movie scenario. In total, there are 604 relevant entities for the movie scenario, which are distributed among the sources as follows: RT: 40%, Netflix: 36%, MovieDb:23 %. For the publication scenario, the raters judged 997 entities as at least *somewhat relevant*. However, the distribution of the relevant results is here highly skewed. MS returned 53% of the relevant results, ACM 24%, Arxiv 15%, and Citeseer 8%.

Figure 6.5 displays an example of both tasks shown to the judges. Details on the ground truth are shown in Table 6.5, in particular the inter-rater agreement measured with Krippendorff's *alpha* for ordinal values [74]. Overall, we consider the agreement of $\alpha_{ordinal} > 0.66$ high enough to rely on the ground truth for our experiments [96].

	MovieDb	RT	Netflix
MovieDb	4		
RT	179	33	
Netflix	162	248	10
	Total:	636	

(a) movie scenario

	ACM	Arxiv	Citeseer	MS
ACM	25			
Arxiv	14	62		
Citeseer	13	1	5	
MS	239	75	59	232
			Total:	725

(b) publication scenario

Table 6.6: Number of co-references between sources based on the ground truth.

6.6.3 Consolidation Results

The main focus of our work is on the ranking of consolidated entities, which requires co-references. In order to obtain co-references, we applied the procedure described in Section 6.4. In Figure 6.6 we see the effect of the threshold t, the only parameter necessary in our approach, on the the metrics *F1*, *Precision*, and *Recall*. As we have seen in the previous section, many co-references exist also within one data source. We can assume that within a source the same vocabulary is used and therefore entities are inherently closer to each other in terms of our similarity metric compared to entities of different sources. Hence, a lower threshold is needed when consolidating entities of the same source. As a consequence, we reduce t by 0.2 in this case and report evaluation results for $t_{movie} = 0.7$ and $t_{pub} = 0.6$ for the respective scenario. We evaluate consolidation from two perspectives. First,

160

we look at each single co-reference link and second, we evaluate the entire co-reference sets created from these links. Each co-reference is classified as true/false positive/negative (abbr. TP, FP, TN,FN). In Table 6.7 we see the confusion matrix for both scenarios over the entire query set. The consolidation performance as an average of the co-references created for each query is reported in Table 6.8a, which shows the precision, recall, accuracy and F1-measure. Details on the sets created from the co-references are shown in Table 6.8b.

Overall, the performance numbers are high; although a direct comparison is not possible, the numbers are in the same order of magnitudes as previously reported for supervised consolidation [48]. We now apply these co-references for consolidated retrieval as described in the next section.

Movies	
TP: 556	FP: 166
FN: 80	TN: 286571

Publications	
TP: 518	FP: 77
FN: 207	TN: 1049954

(a) Movie (b) Publications

Table 6.7: Confusion matrix for consolidation results.

Avg. per query	Movie	Publ.
F1-score	0.8233	0.7672
Accuracy	0.9982	0.9996
Precision	0.8063	0.8636
Recall	0.8781	0.7118

Avg. per query	Movie	Publ.
#Co-ref Sets	6.9	9.7
#Co-ref Sets@10	3.6	2.9
Set size	2.5	2.1
Set Purity	0.7737	0.8713

(a) Co-references (b) Sets of co-references

Table 6.8: Consolidation performance on average per query.

6.6.4 Ranking Evaluation

In this section we present our experimental results on the ranking performance. The goal of these experiments is to answer two questions. First, what are the effects of federated search on retrieval performance and under what conditions does federated search improve retrieval? And second, does federated and consolidated search improve retrieval performance?

We assess the ranking using standard retrieval metrics. Based on binary relevance, where the relevance levels *perfect* and *somewhat relevant* are both

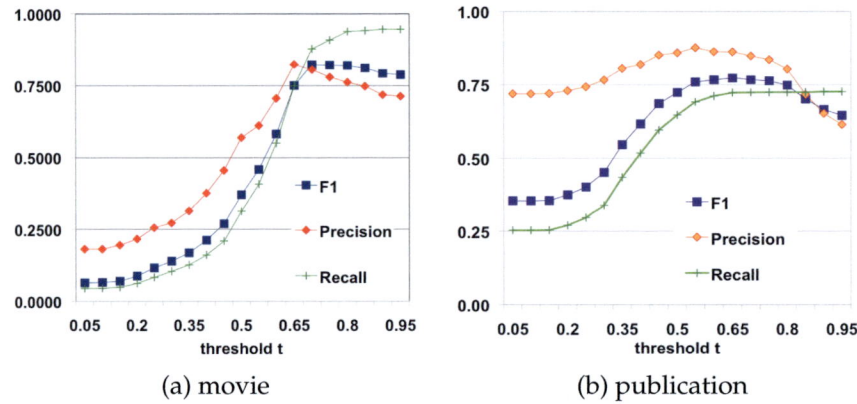

(a) movie   (b) publication

Figure 6.6: Consolidation performance over threshold t.

treated as relevant, we compute Mean Average Precision (*MAP*), Precision (*P@10*) and Mean Reciprocal Rank (*MRR*). More crucial for our analysis and the conclusions derived from it is the standard Normalized Discounted Cumulative Gain (*NDCG*) metric, which in contrast to the other metrics above, is able to take advantage of the graded 3-point relevance scale. As discussed, only the first ten results were assessed to construct the ground truth. Besides these metrics, we also report the number of relevant results retrieved by each approach computed as a total over all queries (*rel_ret*) and report statistically significant differences w.r.t. *NDCG* using Fisher's two-sided, paired randomization test [140].

Systems. We implement our approach, called *Consolidated Relevance Model (CRM)*, in two different ways, in order to address the two questions stated above. First, we employ a federated version *without* using co-references (CRM_w) and second, a federated and *consolidated* version using co-references (CRM_c) as described in Section 6.5. We compare these approaches against two baselines. The first set of baselines are the individual rankings of the data sources. Each returns a ranked list, which we compare against the merged results produced by our approach. The second baseline is a state-of-the-art rank aggregation strategy for federated search [154], which exploits the ranking of the individual sources for rank and result merging. It treats the ranks returned by the sources as preference judgments over the returned results and aggregates these judgments into a consensus ranking. In the experiment, several versions of this *Multinomial Preference Model (MPM)* has been studied, including those assuming training for the supervised learning of parameters [154]. We use an implementation of the unsupervised MPM,

162

i.e. without the supervised adherence parameter [154], and study two different encodings of preferences. The first preference encoding $C(e_i, e_j)$ is binary (the corresponding run is labeled *MPM*), where one result e_i is preferred over one other e_j when it has higher rank ($r(e)$ denotes the rank of e in the result list RS):

$$C(e_i, e_j) = \begin{cases} 1 & \text{if } r(e_i) < r(e_j) \\ 0 & \text{otherwise} \end{cases} \qquad (6.7)$$

In the other encoding, the difference in the ranks is exploited to express the degree of how much e_i is preferred over e_j. It is common, e.g. in the NDCG metric see Section 2.3.1, to discount the ranks by $\frac{1}{\log(1+r(e))}$. The encoding using this discount is defined and runs using this discounted preferences are labeled with the subscript d as MPM_d.

$$C_d(e_i, e_j) = \begin{cases} \frac{1}{\log(1+r(e_i))} - \frac{1}{\log(1+r(e_j))} & \text{if } r(e_i) < r(e_j) \\ 0 & \text{otherwise} \end{cases} \qquad (6.8)$$

Evaluation Settings. Note that all systems return a ranked list of individual entities except those that make use of consolidation. In particular, each result in the ranked list returned by MPM, MPM_d and CRM_c and represent a set of entities, instead of single entities as illustrated in Figure 6.4(c). In order to assess the relevance of such a set, we use the best ranked entity within that set as the representative element, called the label. The relevance of the set is determined based on the relevance of its label. Using the ground truth and this way of assessing relevance, we evaluate the systems in three different settings:

Standard **Setting.** First, we assess the results in the standard way where possible redundancy in the result lists are not taken into account. That is, we go through the result lists as they are returned by the systems and simply assess the degree of relevance of each result using the established ground truth.

NRel **Setting.** In the previous setting, results might be considered relevant even when the same results (i.e. co-referent entities) have been seen before in the list. This redundancy occurs especially with systems that do not perform consolidation. As discussed in previous work [48], this setting accounts for redundancy by considering subsequent occurrences of co-referent entities as non-relevant (*nrel*). That is, even when a result is relevant according to the ground truth, it is considered here as not relevant when a co-reference has already been seen, thus rendering this result redundant.

Expand **Setting.** This setting is similar to the standard setting in that redundant results are not punished in the relevance assessment, i.e. the assessment is based on the ground truth only. However, it gives special treatment to the systems MPM, MPM_d and CRM_c that perform consolidation. In the standard setting, relevance assessment of these systems is simply based on the labels of their results. In this *expand* setting, we assess the results in the way proposed for clustered IR [104]. The idea is that a user goes from the top to the bottom of the result list, and checks the label of each cluster (set of results in this case). If a label is considered relevant, the set is expanded and each entity in the set is assessed individually. So whereas only the label of the set is considered in the standard setting, other results in the set obtained through the expansion of the label are taken into account in the assessment here.

System	rel_ret	MRR	P@10	MAP	**NDCG**
MovieDb	120	0.8700	0.2400	0.2134	0.4128
RT	180	0.9722	0.3600	0.3168	**0.5360**
Netflix	164	0.9633	0.3280	0.3094	0.5191
CRM_w	301	0.9900	0.6020	0.7035	**0.8699**[†]
MPM	157	0.9520	0.3140	0.2876	0.4936
MPM_d	168	0.9629	0.3360	0.3096	0.5232
CRM_c	209	0.9900	0.4180	0.3798	**0.5787**[†*]

[†]stat. diff. to RT at sig. level < 0.05

[*]stat. diff. to MPM,MPM_d at sig. level <0.05

Table 6.9: Standard retrieval performance for the *movie* scenario

Results in the *Standard* Setting. We investigate the systems described above in the movie and the publication scenario. For the publication scenario, we look at two different setups. One setup has the three sources Arxiv, ACM and Citeseer that share about the same amount of co-references and relevant results. In addition to these three sources, the second setup uses MS, which is 'an outlier' because it contains 53% of the relevant results and is part of 83% of the co-references, as described in Section 6.6.2.

System	rel_ret	MRR	P@10	MAP	NDCG
Arxiv	101	0.4810	0.2020	0.0722	0.1824
ACM	189	0.5857	0.3780	0.1203	**0.3537**
Citeseer	84	0.3367	0.1680	0.0510	0.1630

Publ. scenario with 3 sources (Arxiv, ACM, Citeseer)

CRM_w	182	0.6979	0.3640	0.1238	**0.3592**
MPM	132	0.4912	0.2640	0.0847	0.2273
MPM_d	144	0.5502	0.2880	0.0915	0.2541
CRM_c	179	0.6989	0.3580	0.1201	**0.3524**[†]

[†]stat. diff. to MPM, MPM_d at sig. level < 0.01

Publ. scenario with 4 sources (Arxiv, ACM, Citeseer, MS)

MS	319	0.7967	0.6380	0.2777	**0.6474**
CRM_w	275	0.7457	0.5500	0.2200	0.5463
MPM	239	0.6640	0.4780	0.1790	0.4568
MPM_d	244	0.7697	0.4880	0.1938	0.4869
CRM_c	259	0.7457	0.5180	0.2013	**0.5096**

Table 6.10: Standard retrieval performance for the *publication* scenario.

First, we look at the effect of federation. In the movie scenario, when comparing the performance of the single sources, shown in the first three lines in Table 6.9, we observe that RT performs best with a NDCG of 0.53. Further, note that the performance differences among these sources are relatively small. Compared to these numbers, we see that our federation approach CRM_w largely outperforms the individual results by 62% with a NDCG of 0.87. When we look at the publication scenario with 3 sources, we observe a different initial situation (see Table 6.10). The best single source ACM performs with a NDCG of 0.3537 about twice as good as the second best source Arxiv. Given this unbalanced situation, our federation approach CRM_w performs marginally better than the best source with a NDCG of 0.3592. When we look at the publication scenario with 4 sources (see the lower part of Table 6.10), we observe that the source MS with a NDCG of 0.64 is again twice as good as the previously best source ACM and consequently four times as good as the other two sources. First, we observe that adding MS to the pool of sources, improves the performance of CRM_w. However in this skewed setting, the federated approach CRM_w performs not as good as the best source MS, but better than the three other sources. In summary for the standard setting, we observe that federation improves retrieval if the sources do not largely vary in their performances in terms of NDCG. Otherwise, it yields improvements over most sources but cannot guarantee the best performance. Particularly, improvements over those sources are difficult, which already capture a large fraction of relevant results such that considering other sources cannot provide additional values.

Next, we investigate the effect of federation in combination with consolidation. As described above, we assess the labels of each co-reference set for the systems MPM, MPM_d and CRM_c. Through consolidation, entities are grouped into sets. As a consequence, there are less (relevant) results, i.e. (relevant) set labels, in the ranked list after consolidation than entities in the list before consolidation. In the movie case, where more co-reference sets exist (3.6 per query in the top10 ranks), we observe as expected that NDCG is much lower for the setting with than without consolidation. The same holds for the publication scenario although the difference is smaller because there are fewer and smaller co-reference sets (2.9 per query in the top10 ranks, see Table 6.8b). Overall, we observe that federation without consolidation performs best when assessing relevance using the *standard* method. We note that however, since the ranked list with consolidation contains sets of entities, it actually captures much more (relevant) results that are not considered when only assessing their labels.

If we compare among the systems with consolidation, we see that CRM_c outperforms MPM and MPM_d across all scenarios and setups. Further, we observe that the discounted preference encoding MPM_d improves over MPM.

Results in the *NRel* Setting. We perform the same analysis as before, but now regard redundant results as not relevant. We start with the effect of federation. The initial situation is similar to the above setting for the movie scenario (see Table 6.11). RT performs best with a NDCG of 0.5166 and is only marginally better than Netflix. However, now we observe that the federated system CRM_w-nrel performs with a NDCG of 0.50 worse than the best single data source RT. Compared to the standard setting, where a NCDG of 0.87 was achieved, the result is much lower in this setting. This indicates there were many co-referent results (redundancy) that are not reflected in the computation of NCDG in the standard setting. For the publication scenario with 3 sources (see Table 6.12) we also have an initial situation that is similar to the standard setting. ACM performs best and about twice as good as the next best data source. We observe also here that CRM_w-nrel performs worse than the best single source, although it was about as good as the best source in the *standard* setting. In the 4 sources case, the performance of CRM_w-nrel is as before, also below the best single source. In summary, when taking redundancy into account, we observe that federation alone no longer improves the single data sources.

If we investigate the combined effect of federation and consolidation with the system MPM-nrel, MPM_d-nrel, and CRM_c-nrel, we now observe a different result. In the movie case (see Table 6.11) we observe that consolidated CRM_c-nrel improves the non-consolidated CRM_w-nrel. Further, we see that CRM_w-nrel improves upon both the preference aggregation models. For the publication scenario with 3 sources (Table 6.12), we observe the same general picture. The consolidated CRM_c-nrel outperforms the runs without consolidation and also both the MPM models (both do not outperform the non-consolidated run). For the 4 sources publication scenario, we see that the consolidated run improves upon the non-consolidated runs, but not upon the outlier source MS. In all, we observed that consolidation helps federated search when redundant results are considered non-relevant.

System	rel_ret	MRR	P@10	MAP	**NDCG**
MovieDb-nrel	116	0.8700	0.2320	0.2046	0.4025
RT-nrel	170	0.9722	0.3400	0.2953	**0.5165**
Netflix-nrel	160	0.9633	0.3200	0.3064	0.5141
CRM_w-nrel	173	0.9900	0.3460	0.2891	**0.4992**
MPM-nrel	159	0.9620	0.3180	0.2930	0.5037
MPM_d-nrel	166	0.9629	0.3320	0.3090	0.5232
CRM_c-nrel	196	0.9900	0.3920	0.3538	**0.5515[†⋆]**

[†]stat. diff. to MPM at sig. level < 0.05

[⋆]stat. diff. to CRM_w at sig. level < 0.01

Table 6.11: NRel-Retrieval performance for the *movie* scenario.

Results in the *Expand* Setting. When applying the evaluation proposed for clustered retrieval [104], not just their labels but also the content of the sets are taken into account. Just like the standard setting, this one does not 'punish' redundancy. As opposed to that setting, it however does not exclude relevant elements in the sets. Figure 6.7 shows a screenshot of the prototype with three expanded sets of co-referent entities. We now discuss the combined effect of federation and consolidation in this setting (the effect of federation alone does not make sense in this setting because it assumes consolidated results in the form of sets). In Table 6.13 we observe that CRM_c-expand consistently improves upon the MPM models. That is, our approach also outperforms the preference aggregation baseline in this setting.

System	rel_ret	MRR	P@10	MAP	**NDCG**
Arxiv-nrel	97	0.4794	0.1940	0.0668	0.1737
ACM-nrel	183	0.5857	0.3660	0.1152	**0.3455**
Citeseer-nrel	80	0.3367	0.1600	0.0484	0.1551

Publ. scenario with 3 sources (Arxiv, ACM, Citeseer)

System	rel_ret	MRR	P@10	MAP	**NDCG**
CRM_w-nrel	165	0.6979	0.3300	0.1114	**0.3310**
MPM-nrel	131	0.4912	0.2620	0.0843	0.2273
MPM_d-nrel	143	0.5502	0.2860	0.0910	0.2542
CRM_c-nrel	175	0.6989	0.3500	0.1179	**0.3462**[†]

[†] stat. diff. to MPM, MPM_d, CRM_w at sig. level < 0.01

Publ. scenario with 4 sources (Arxiv, ACM, Citeseer, MS)

System	rel_ret	MRR	P@10	MAP	**NDCG**
MS-nrel	289	0.7964	0.5780	0.2465	**0.5976**
CRM_w-nrel	216	0.7457	0.4320	0.1608	0.4430
MPM-nrel	219	0.6529	0.4380	0.1558	0.4230
MPM_d-nrel	233	0.7697	0.4660	0.1841	0.4743
CRM_c-nrel	243	0.7457	0.4860	0.1848	**0.4822**[†]

[†] stat. diff. to CRM_w at sig. level < 0.01

Table 6.12: NRel-Retrieval performance for the *publication* scenario.

To see the effect of expanding the sets as opposed to only using their labels, we compare the results here with the best results obtained in the standard setting, where federated search without consolidation, CRM_w, performed best. We observe that CRM_c-expand also slightly improves upon CRM_w (for both scenarios). This means that consolidated federated search, CRM_c-expand, actually outperforms federated search, CRM_w, when the sets' content representing consolidation results are taken into account (i.e. when using CRM_c-expand instead of CRM_c). That is, consolidation can also be useful even when redundancy is not taken into account in the evaluation procedure.

System	rel_ret	MRR	P@10	MAP	**NDCG**
MPM-expand	263	0.9620	0.5260	0.6175	0.8070
MPM_d-expand	274	0.9629	0.5480	0.6389	0.8366
CRM_c-expand	301	0.9900	0.6020	0.7121	**0.8744**[†]

[†] stat. diff. to MPM at sig. level < 0.01

Table 6.13: Expand-Retrieval performance for the *movie* scenario.

System	rel_ret	MRR	P@10	MAP	**NDCG**
Publ. scenario with 3 sources (Arxiv, ACM, Citeseer)					
MPM-expand	138	0.4912	0.2760	0.0931	0.2434
MPM_d-expand	151	0.5502	0.3020	0.0988	0.2697
CRM_c-expand	187	0.6989	0.3740	0.1280	**0.3697**[†]

[†]stat. diff. to MPM, MPM_d at sig. level < 0.01

System	rel_ret	MRR	P@10	MAP	**NDCG**
Publ. scenario with 4 sources (Arxiv, ACM, Citeseer, MS)					
MPM-expand	252	0.6422	0.5040	0.1937	0.4894
MPM_d-expand	261	0.7697	0.5220	0.2148	0.5291
CRM_c-expand	285	0.7457	0.5700	0.2314	**0.5604**

Table 6.14: Expand-Retrieval performance for the *publication* scenario.

6.6.5 Discussion on Ranking Performance

Regarding federated search, we have seen that the distribution of the performances of the single sources determine the performance of the federated ranking. If the sources perform equally well (movie scenario, Standard setting), they re-enforce each other. As a result, federated search outperforms single sources. However, the more the performance of the sources differ, the less helpful is federated search. In the extreme case where one source captures all relevant results, other sources cannot contribute any useful information. We have observed that our CRM_c strategy, which uses the content as well as the rank of the results outperforms the preference aggregation strategy MPM that relies on the ranks only. As a consequence, MPM is more sensitive to ranked results representing outlier [154].

With respect to consolidation, we have observed in both scenarios that consolidation improves the search results when redundancy is undesirable or when users can expand relevant sets. In the latter case, they do not have to inspect sets with non relevant labels, thus can cover more data with the same effort.

6.6.6 Runtime Performance

The main focus of our work is the effectiveness of ranking strategies. We measured the runtime performance of our implementation of CRM_c on a standard laptop with Intel Core 2 Duo 2.4 GHz CPU and 4 GB memory. On average, consolidation took 0.7s for an average of 117 entities per query in the movie scenario, and 2.2s for 206 entities in the publication scenario. Ranking took 0.4s for the movie scenario and 1.4s for the publication scenario. These run times are small compared to the amount of time necessary for remote API calls, which took 4s for the publication case and 31s for the movie case. In the latter case, the time includes several API calls because some movie sources return a list of IDs for a query and then each ID has to be fetched individually. This is because these APIs were in fact designed for a different use case and are thus, not suitable for online search. In addition, we used developer keys, which may have a lower priority than production keys when requesting data.

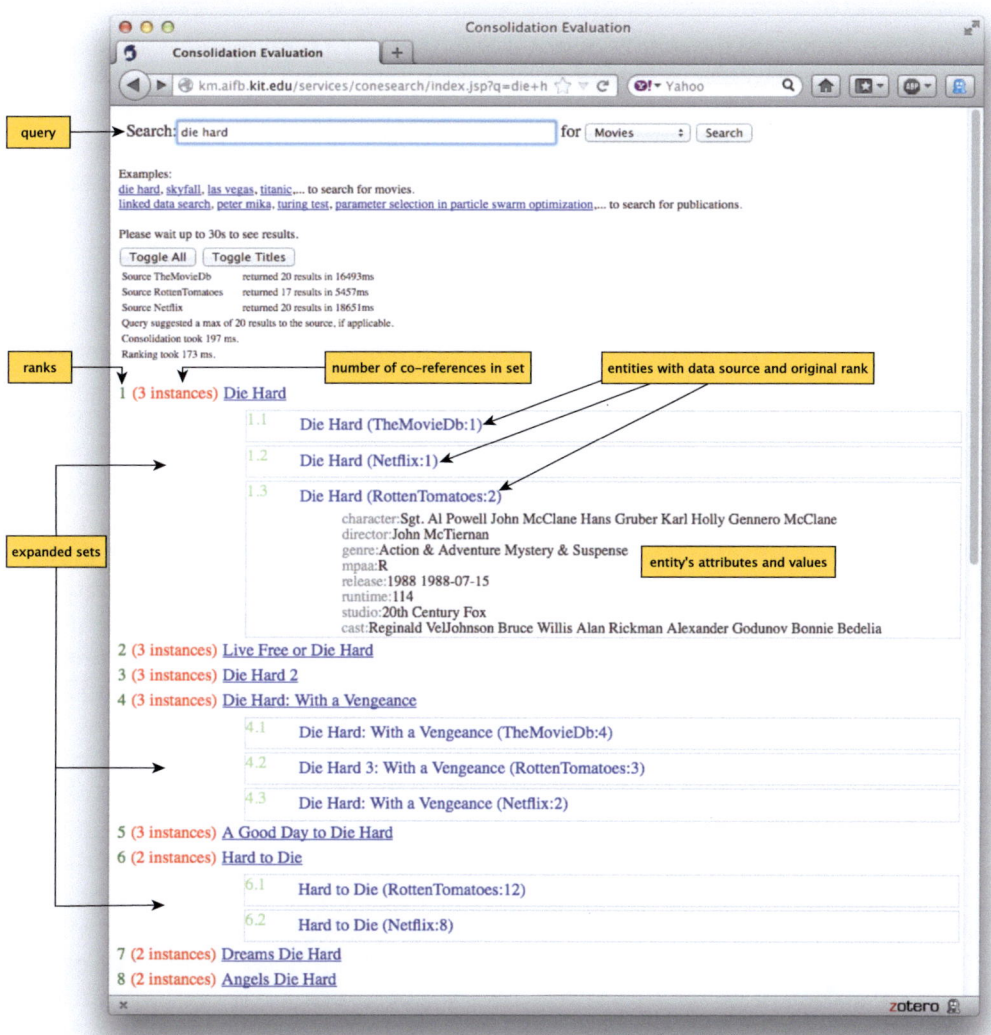

Figure 6.7: Screenshot of the consolidation prototype showing the result page for the query "die hard". The three sets of co-referent entities on rank 1, rank 4, and rank 6 are expanded. The other sets are not expanded. The attributes of the third entity in the set on rank 1 are shown.

6.7 Related Work

We have discussed the related work throughout the chapter and now present further approaches in the main related research areas.

Entity consolidation. The task is different from near-duplicate detection of documents in Web search [109], where hashing techniques for unstructured data are applied. Entity consolidation is rather concerned with structured data, which is also referred to as record linkage, instance matching or object de-duplication (see [53, 57, 95] for recent surveys). Most related to our solution is the recent work on consolidating entities for Web search [48], which show that consolidation improves search performance by achieving more diverse and less redundant search results. While they use a *supervised* approach relying on training examples, we propose an *unsupervised* approach that is more suitable to the uncooperative setting where information and especially training data cannot be assumed.

A considerable amount of work on unsupervised entity consolidation has been done [84, 103, 107, 143]. In the context of heterogeneous Web data, an unsupervised approaches for learning type specific blocking keys for entity consolidation has been proposed, which outperforms supervised techniques [107]. For establishing `owl:sameAs` links in the Semantic Web context, statistics from the entire datasets have been used to derive simple consolidation rules, which are then refined through a self-learning approach [143]. However, all these unsupervised approaches are not targeting at search, but have the goal to integrate entire datasets. Hence, they require access to the full datasets, while our approach only uses data retrieved for a given search query.

On-the-fly data integration. Related to entity consolidation are studies on *query-time* data integration. Given the enormous size and the dynamic changes of data on the Web, the *pay-as-you-go paradigm* has been become a popular way for data integration in this setting [108]. It avoids to go through the entire data to get results and allows to get results early during runtime and in a demand driven way. This paradigm has also been applied for entity consolidation [162] with the goal to report entity matches during the runtime of the consolidation algorithm. An alternative approach to entity consolidation relying on user interactions during the entity search in a pay-as-you fashion has been proposed recently [151], which collects the clicks of users and infers co-references during runtime. We have investigated online schema alignments for Web search in the previous Chapter 5. However, we aligned the schema only and did not consolidate single entities. Consolidating entities in databases at query time has been studied by [20], who propose an 'expand and resolve' algorithm to identify and consolidate records helpful to process the query. Their main goal is in line to our work, but the database setting and database-oriented approach is different to our Web setting using an information retrieval approach based on language models. Similarity join algorithms and efficient indexes have been proposed for faster consolidation [116]. To the best of our knowledge, we are the first to study a language model based approach for representing and computing co-refernces between entities in the consolidation context at query-time.

Entity search. Entity search as one of the most frequent search task has been studied in many approaches [11, 12, 27, 37, 47, 58, 80]. Searching entities extracted from Web pages and ranking them with the help of impressions has been investigated by [37]. All the aforementioned approaches to entity search assume a central index comprising the entire data collection. Integrating the data of several sources has been studied in vertical search [6], where the results of different verticals are integrated at the front-end level but not at the level of the search algorithms.

Federated search. Exploiting several sources for document search has been studied as *federated search (distributed IR)* in the IR community [29, 139]. Combining several sources in one search process for entity search has been investigated by [58], who focus on *query translation* and use source specific query generators to adapt a structured query to each source. [12] proposes *source selection* and ranking algorithms for federated entity search, but do not consider entity consolidation. Source selection for structured queries using light weight source descriptions has been proposed by [152]. Most related is the *rank aggregation* strategy for federated search [154], which we use as baseline in the experiment. It requires the presence of overlapping results to form a consensus ranking. Since no content analysis is performed these methods are fast but also more sensitive to outlying preferences, especially when the sources are not weighted as we have seen in our experiments. Mainly, our work differs from the federated approaches above with respect to the consolidation of entities at query-time.

6.8 Conclusion

Summary. We have presented the first unsupervised solution for federated entity search using on-the-fly consolidation for uncooperative environments. Our consolidation as well as our ranking technique are entirely incorporated into the language model based information retrieval framework and operate without prior knowledge or training examples. Both strategies work only on the data obtained for one query and hence are suitable for search over Web data sources with data access through APIs. Our extensive experiments in two real-world application scenarios investigate the effects of both, consolidation and federated search, on retrieval performance in three different setups. The results show that our approach outperforms a state-of-the-art preference aggregation strategy and that consolidation improves the retrieval performance if redundancy is taken into account. Further, when considering the consolidation results alone, our unsupervised approach achieves results in the same order of magnitudes as previously reported for supervised consolidation.

Conclusions. We addressed Research Question 4 is this chapter. Based on this question, we have proposed a consolidation technique and ranking strategy for federated entity search in uncooperative environments, as summarized above. We investigated our proposed techniques with respect to Hypotheses 4.1 and 4.2 through experiments as described Section 6.6. Given the results obtained for the two domains, *movies* and *publications*, and the three different evaluation methods, *std*, *nrel*, and *expand*, we conclude that for our approach we can confirm Hypotheses 4.1, if the single sources have about the same retrieval performance in terms of NDCG. However, we can not uphold it, if the retrieval performance of the single data sources is highly skewed. Hypothesis 4.2 has been investigated in experiments reported in Section 6.6.4. Based on the obtained results, we confirm this hypothesis, if redundancy is taken into account (*nrel*) or if sets of relevant co-references are considered entirely (*expand*). In order to foster our results, we also compared our approach against a state-of-the-art preference aggregation strategy and observed that our approach consistently exceeded this baseline. Overall, we summarize the results reported in this chapter as Contribution 4.

Outlook. Our investigation have raised further questions worth to be explored. One of them is a result of the observation regarding Hypothesis 4.1 on federated search. Can federated search improve upon the single sources even though they exhibit a highly skewed retrieval performance without using up-front data integration or learning supervised parameters? Especially the latter condition of unsupervised methods and avoiding the usage of expensive training examples is important for the ad-hoc integration in Web scenarios. If training examples are provided and learning a parameter for each search up-front is within the acceptable bounds, this question has already been investigated, e.g. Volkovs and Zemel [154] model the skewed performances as deviations from the consensus ranking and learn a supervised adherence parameter.

Also further research studying the effect of consolidation on retrieval performance is feasible in several directions. One of them is to study ad-hoc consolidation for more complex results than for single entities, such as combinations of related entities.

Chapter 7

Conclusion

We conclude this thesis by summing up the research questions, achieved results and conclusions drawn thereof. Further, we briefly discuss the ethical usage of the developed methods and point out sensitive application areas. Finally, we provide an outlook on further research and directions for future work.

7.1 Summary

Based on the observation that an increasing amount of structured data is published on the Web as described in Chapter 1 and detailed in Chapter 2, we raised the following principal question and investigated it in this thesis:

> *How can ranking techniques leverage structured Web data for effective search?*

We identified four challenges in Chapter 1 that are major obstacles to answering this question. Hence, we broke this question down into four specific research questions each addressing one challenge, investigated all of them in depth through experiments and provided a scientific contribution on each question, as stated in Section 1.5.

Basis for all experimental research is a rigorous analysis using well-defined evaluation metrics. In order to establish such an evaluation methodology for the new task of search over structured Web data, we addressed first the question on evaluation and started in Chapter 3 by creating an evaluation framework using crowd-sourced relevance assessments and investigated it in detail on its repeatability and reliability.

In Chapter 4, the question on a ranking method unifying structured and unstructured data and taking advantage of structured elements in the queries was addressed by developing such a ranking model, which is based conceptually on the language model framework and relevance feedback. The concepts behind this ranking model has been applied in the remainder for the challenges concerning the messiness of the Web of data - heterogeneity and redundancy.

How to cope with the heterogeneity of the Web of data for ranking, the core of Research Question 3, has been shown in Chapter 5, where an approach for integrating remote data sources into the local search process despite schema and data level differences has been presented. The approach overcomes the differences by combining unstructured keyword search and structured ranking based on query-time data integration techniques. The latter is in particular suited for Web scenarios, where large data volumes and changing environments prohibit up-front batch integration, which is the prevailing way for integrating data. The experiments show that our approach improves upon two existing strategies relying on either unstructured keyword search or up-front data integration.

As soon as several data source can be search at once, the problem of redundant results is encountered. How redundant results effect the retrieval performance is studied in detail in Chapter 6 as a consequence of Research Question 4. In order to address the problem of redundancy, we develop a query-time consolidation strategy incorporated into the language model retrieval framework. Our consolidation approach build upon the methods and concepts introduced in the previous chapters and extends them with the capabilities to identify and consolidate co-referent entities referring to the same real world entity. Experimental results obtained for two different domains and three different evaluation settings showed the improvements through consolidation and the applicability of our approach especially for uncooperative distributed Web data scenarios.

7.2 Conclusions

Overall, we have shown in different settings from different perspectives how structured Web data can be leveraged for search. In particular, we examined the effectiveness of search by evaluating its ranking in terms of positioning most relevant results first. Our approach to ranking is based in the language model framework and uses relevance feedback. Further, we employed query-time data integration to overcome heterogeneity and redundancy. Moreover, we presented experimental results regarding all hypotheses put forward as a consequence of the initially posed research questions. In a nutshell, we showed one way how ranking techniques can leverage structured Web data for more effective search.

7.3 Considerations on Ethical Usage

The methods introduced in this thesis allow effective retrieval and data integration of previously unseen data sources. The experiments in this thesis were conducted with data holding publicly accessible information that is not considered to be sensitive with respect to privacy concerns nor prone to misuse. However, the methods are general in nature and can be applied in any domain, e.g. clinical, personal healthcare records and social data. Therefore, we briefly discuss some implications of their usage with respect to ethics and KIT's ethical guidelines [51].

The primary risk for misuse or unintended harm of data integration techniques is the breach of privacy. Due to frequent news on privacy attacks and sensitive data leakages as well as the misunderstanding of "having nothing to hide" [142], often lead to an indifferent attitude and unawareness of privacy issues. With respect to data integration, several studies have shown that integrating even small parts of data across several data sources or within social networks in combination with statistical means to estimate correlations can reveal sensitive private information [88, 168].

Hence, considerations on privacy are required before using the developed methods on sensitive data. Identifying such situations is not always obvious, however a general sensitivity to privacy and considering the trade off between advantages and risk of data integration has to be taken. Still, how these methods and data integration can be used in a privacy-preserving way is an important research question. First steps towards the goal of privacy-preserving data integration has already been taken [21, 44] and are worth be further investigated.

7.4 Outlook

There are three major direction for future work building on top of this thesis: technical, social and economical. From a technical perspective, besides the security and privacy concerning directions that we have described above, we have pointed out several aspects worth of further investigation in the conclusions of each chapter. One promising topic for search on the Web is the continuation of query time data integration techniques as presented in Chapter 5 and 6, e.g. the investigation of the combination of up-front and query time integration, data integration for more complex queries and results, as well as additional constraints such as temporal intervals may improve search over Web data. Room for improvements is also on the exploitation of annotations for document search as discussed in Chapter 4 and here in particular on overcoming the problem of low recall of annotator techniques as well as how hybrid queries are constructed. The latter leads to the question whether new findings in social aspects of search such as new interactive paradigms and user-centric designed query construction may lead to more effective search. Finally, an open question is how to quantify the economical value of search and in particular to assess the monetary benefits of the improvements due to considering structured data in search.

Bibliography

[1] James Allan. HARD Track Overview in TREC 2005 High Accuracy Retrieval from Documents. In Ellen M. Voorhees and Lori P. Buckland, editors, *TREC*, volume Special Publication 500-266. National Institute of Standards and Technology (NIST), 2005.

[2] Omar Alonso, Daniel E. Rose, and Benjamin Stewart. Crowdsourcing for relevance evaluation. *SIGIR Forum*, 42(2):9–15, 2008. ISSN 0163-5840. doi: http://doi.acm.org/10.1145/1480506.1480508.

[3] Omar Alonso, Ralf Schenkel, and Martin Theobald. Crowdsourcing Assessments for XML Ranked Retrieval. In Cathal Gurrin, Yulan He, Gabriella Kazai, Udo Kruschwitz, Suzanne Little, Thomas Roelleke, Stefan M. Rüger, and Keith van Rijsbergen, editors, *32nd European Conference on IR Research (ECIR)*, volume 5993 of *Lecture Notes in Computer Science*, pages 602–606. Springer, 2010. ISBN 978-3-642-12274-3.

[4] Sihem Amer-Yahia, Djoerd Hiemstra, Thomas Roelleke, Divesh Srivastava, and Gerhard Weikum. DB&IR Integration: Report on the Dagstuhl Seminar "Ranked XML Querying". *SIGIR Forum*, 42(2):84–89, 2008.

[5] Marcelo Arenas, Alexandre Bertails, Eric Prud'hommeaux, and Juan Sequeda. A Direct Mapping of Relational Data to RDF, September 2012. URL http://www.w3.org/TR/sparql11-query/. W3C Recommendation as of 27 Sept 2012.

[6] Jaime Arguello, Fernando Diaz, and Jamie Callan. Learning to Aggregate Vertical Results into Web Search Results. In Craig Macdonald, Iadh Ounis, and Ian Ruthven, editors, *Proceedings of the 20th ACM Conference on Information and Knowledge Management (CIKM)*, pages 201–210. ACM, 2011. ISBN 978-1-4503-0717-8.

[7] Ricardo A. Baeza-Yates and Berthier A. Ribeiro-Neto. *Modern Information Retrieval - the concepts and technology behind search, Second edition*. Pearson Education Ltd., Harlow, England, 2011. ISBN 978-0-321-41691-9.

[8] Peter Bailey, Nick Craswell, Ian Soboroff, Paul Thomas, Arjen P. de Vries, and Emine Yilmaz. Relevance assessment: are judges exchangeable and does it matter. In *International ACM SIGIR Conference on Research and Development in Information Retrieval*, pages 667–674, New York, NY, USA, 2008. ACM. ISBN 978-1-60558-164-4. doi: http://doi.acm.org/10.1145/1390334.1390447.

[9] Krisztian Balog, Arjen P. de Vries, Pavel Serdyukov, Paul Thomas, and Thijs Westerveld. Overview of the TREC 2009 Entity Track. In Ellen M. Voorhees and Lori P. Buckland, editors, *TREC*, volume Special Publication 500-278. National Institute of Standards and Technology (NIST), 2009.

[10] Krisztian Balog, Pavel Serdyukov, and Arjen P. de Vries. Overview of the TREC 2010 Entity Track. In Ellen M. Voorhees and Lori P. Buckland, editors, *TREC*. National Institute of Standards and Technology (NIST), 2010.

[11] Krisztian Balog, David Carmel, Arjen P. de Vries, Daniel M. Herzig, Peter Mika, Haggai Roitman, Ralf Schenkel, Pavel Serdyukov, and Thanh Tran Duc, editors. *Proceedings of the first Joint International Workshop on Entity-Oriented and Semantic Search (JIWES)*, JIWES, International ACM SIGIR Conference on Research and Development in Information Retrieval, 2012. ISBN 978-1-4503-1601-9.

[12] Krisztian Balog, Robert Neumayer, and Kjetil Nørvåg. Collection Ranking and Selection for Federated Entity Search. In Liliana Calderón-Benavides, Cristina N. González-Caro, Edgar Chávez, and Nivio Ziviani, editors, *International Symposium on String Processing and Information Retrieval (SPIRE)*, volume 7608 of *Lecture Notes in Computer Science*, pages 73–85. Springer, 2012. ISBN 978-3-642-34108-3.

[13] H. Bast and I. Weber. The CompleteSearch Engine: Interactive, Efficient, and Towards IR&DB integration. In *Conference on Innovative Data Systems Research (CIDR)*, pages 88–95. www.cidrdb.org, 2007.

[14] Hannah Bast, Florian Bäurle, Björn Buchhold, and Elmar Haussmann. A Case for Semantic Full-Text Search. In *Proceedings of the 1st Joint International Workshop on Entity-Oriented and Semantic Search*, JIWES '12, pages 4:1–3, New York, NY, USA, 2012. ACM. ISBN 978-1-4503-1601-9. doi: 10.1145/2379307.2379311. URL http://doi.acm.org/10.1145/2379307.2379311.

[15] Hannah Bast, Florian Bäurle, Björn Buchhold, and Elmar Haussmann. Broccoli: Semantic Full-Text Search at your Fingertips. *Computing Research Repository (CoRR)*, abs/1207.2615, 2012. URL http://arxiv.org/abs/1207.2615.

[16] Dave Beckett. RDF/XML Syntax Specification (Revised), Feburary 2004. URL http://www.w3.org/TR/rdf-syntax-grammar. W3C Recommendation as of 10 Feb 2004.

[17] David Beckett, Tim Berners-Lee, Eric Prud'hommeaux, and Gavin Carothers. Turtle - Terse RDF Triple Language, February 2013. URL http://www.w3.org/TR/turtle/. W3C Candidate Recommendation 19 February 2013.

[18] T. Berners-Lee, R. Fielding, and L. Masinter. Uniform Resource Identifier (URI): Generic Syntax. Internet RFC 3986, January 2005. URL http://www.ietf.org/rfc/rfc3986.txt.

[19] Tim Berners-Lee, James Hendler, and Ora Lassila. The Semantic Web. *Scientific american*, 284(5):28–37, 2001.

[20] Indrajit Bhattacharya and Lise Getoor. Query-time Entity Resolution. *Journal of Artificial Intelligence Research*, 30:621–657, 2007.

[21] Sourav S. Bhowmick, Le Gruenwald, Mizuho Iwaihara, and Somchai Chatvichien-chai. PRIVATE-IYE: A Framework for Privacy Preserving Data Integration. In Roger S. Barga and Xiaofang Zhou, editors, *International Conference on Data Engineering (ICDE) Workshops*, page 91. IEEE Computer Society, 2006.

[22] Veli Bicer, Thanh Tran, and Radoslav Nedkov. Ranking support for keyword search on structured data using relevance models. In Craig Macdonald, Iadh Ounis, and Ian Ruthven, editors, *ACM CIKM International Conference on Information and Knowledge Management*, pages 1669–1678. ACM, 2011. ISBN 978-1-4503-0717-8.

[23] Christian Bizer and Peter Mika. The Semantic Web Challenge, 2009. *Journal of Web Semantics*, 8(4):341, 2010.

[24] Roi Blanco, Harry Halpin, Daniel M. Herzig, Peter Mika, Jeffrey Pound, Henry S. Thompson, and Duc Thanh Tran. Repeatable and Reliable Semantic Search Evaluation. *Journal of Web Semantics: Science, Services and Agents on the World Wide Web*, (to appear) 2013. (accepted for publication).

[25] Roi Blanco, Harry Halpin, Daniel M. Herzig, Peter Mika, Jeffrey Pound, Henry S. Thompson, and Duc Thanh Tran. Repeatable and reliable search system evaluation using crowdsourcing. In Wei-Ying Ma, Jian-Yun Nie, Ricardo A. Baeza-Yates, Tat-Seng Chua, and W. Bruce Croft, editors, *International ACM SIGIR Conference on Research and Development in Information Retrieval*, pages 923–932. ACM, 2011. ISBN 978-1-4503-0757-4.

[26] Roi Blanco, Harry Halpin, Daniel M. Herzig, Peter Mika, Jeffrey Pound, Henry S. Thompson, and Duc Thanh Tran. Entity Search Evaluation over Structured Web Data. In *Proc. of the 1st Int. Workshop on Entity-Oriented Search (EOS 2011) at SIGIR*, 2011. URL http://research.microsoft.com/en-us/um/beijing/events/eos2011/20.pdf.

[27] Roi Blanco, Peter Mika, and Sebastiano Vigna. Effective and Efficient Entity Search in RDF Data. In Lora Aroyo, Chris Welty, Harith Alani, Jamie Taylor, Abraham Bernstein, Lalana Kagal, Natasha Fridman Noy, and Eva Blomqvist, editors, *International Semantic Web Conference*, volume 7031 of *Lecture Notes in Computer Science*, pages 83–97. Springer, 2011. ISBN 978-3-642-25072-9.

[28] Andrea Calì, Domenico Lembo, and Riccardo Rosati. Query rewriting and answering under constraints in data integration systems. In Georg Gottlob and Toby Walsh, editors, *International Joint Conference on Artificial Intelligence*, pages 16–21. Morgan Kaufmann, 2003.

[29] Jamie Callan. Distributed Information Retrieval. In W.Bruce Croft, editor, *Advances in Information Retrieval*, volume 7 of *The Information Retrieval Series*, pages 127–150. Springer US, 2002. ISBN 978-0-7923-7812-9. doi: 10.1007/0-306-47019-5_5. URL http://dx.doi.org/10.1007/0-306-47019-5_5.

[30] Chris Callison-Burch. Fast, Cheap, and Creative: Evaluating Translation Quality Using Amazon's Mechanical Turk. In *Proceedings of the 2009 Conference on Empirical Methods in Natural Language Processing*, pages 286–295, Singapore, August

2009. Association for Computational Linguistics. URL `http://www.aclweb.org/anthology/D/D09/D09-1030`.

[31] Bob Carpenter. Multilevel Bayesian Models of Categorical Data Annotation. Technical Report. Technical report, Alias-I, 2008. URL `http://lingpipe.files.wordpress.com/2008/11/carp-bayesian-multilevel-annotation.pdf`.

[32] Pablo Castells, Miriam Fernández, and David Vallet. An Adaptation of the Vector-Space Model for Ontology-Based information retrieval. *IEEE Trans. Knowl. Data Eng.*, 19(2):261–272, 2007.

[33] Sung-Hyuk Cha. Comprehensive survey on distance/similarity measures between probability density functions. *International Journal of Mathematical Models and Methods in Applied Sciences*, 1(4):300–307, 2007.

[34] Surajit Chaudhuri, Raghu Ramakrishnan, and Gerhard Weikum. Integrating DB and IR Technologies: What is the Sound of One Hand Clapping? In *Conference on Innovative Data Systems Research (CIDR)*, pages 1–12, 2005.

[35] Surajit Chaudhuri, Bee-Chung Chen, Venkatesh Ganti, and Raghav Kaushik. Example-driven design of efficient record matching queries. In Christoph Koch, Johannes Gehrke, Minos N. Garofalakis, Divesh Srivastava, Karl Aberer, Anand Deshpande, Daniela Florescu, Chee Yong Chan, Venkatesh Ganti, Carl-Christian Kanne, Wolfgang Klas, and Erich J. Neuhold, editors, *VLDB*, pages 327–338. ACM, 2007. ISBN 978-1-59593-649-3.

[36] Gong Cheng and Yuzhong Qu. Searching Linked Objects with Falcons: Approach, Implementation and evaluation. *Int. J. Semantic Web Inf. Syst.*, 5(3):49–70, 2009.

[37] Tao Cheng, Xifeng Yan, and Kevin Chen-Chuan Chang. EntityRank: Searching Entities Directly and Holistically. In Christoph Koch, Johannes Gehrke, Minos N. Garofalakis, Divesh Srivastava, Karl Aberer, Anand Deshpande, Daniela Florescu, Chee Yong Chan, Venkatesh Ganti, Carl-Christian Kanne, Wolfgang Klas, and Erich J. Neuhold, editors, *VLDB*, pages 387–398. ACM, 2007. ISBN 978-1-59593-649-3.

[38] Jennifer Chu-Carroll and John M. Prager. An experimental study of the impact of information extraction accuracy on semantic search performance. In Mário J. Silva, Alberto H. F. Laender, Ricardo A. Baeza-Yates, Deborah L. McGuinness, Bjørn Olstad, Øystein Haug Olsen, and André O. Falcão, editors, *ACM CIKM International Conference on Information and Knowledge Management*, pages 505–514. ACM, 2007. ISBN 978-1-59593-803-9.

[39] Jennifer Chu-Carroll, John M. Prager, Krzysztof Czuba, David A. Ferrucci, and Pablo Ariel Duboué. Semantic search via XML fragments: a high-precision approach to ir. In Efthimis N. Efthimiadis, Susan T. Dumais, David Hawking, and Kalervo Järvelin, editors, *International ACM SIGIR Conference on Research and Development in Information Retrieval*, pages 445–452. ACM, 2006. ISBN 1-59593-369-7.

[40] Marek Ciglan, Kjetil Nørvåg, and Ladislav Hluchý. The SemSets model for ad-hoc semantic list search. In Alain Mille, Fabien L. Gandon, Jacques Misselis, Michael Rabinovich, and Steffen Staab, editors, *International World Wide Web Conference (WWW)*, pages 131–140. ACM, 2012. ISBN 978-1-4503-1229-5.

[41] Cyril W. Cleverdon. The CRANFIELD Tests on Index Language Devices. *Aslib Proceedings*, 19(6), 1967.

[42] Cyril W. Cleverdon. The Significance of the Cranfield Tests on Index Languages. In Abraham Bookstein, Yves Chiaramella, Gerard Salton, and Vijay V. Raghavan, editors, *SIGIR*, pages 3–12. ACM, 1991. ISBN 0-89791-448-1.

[43] Cyril W. Cleverdon and Michael Keen. Factors Determining the Performance of Indexing Systems. In *Aslib Cranfield Research Project, Cranfield, England*, volume 2, 1966. URL http://dspace.lib.cranfield.ac.uk/handle/1826/863.

[44] Chris Clifton, Murat Kantarcioglu, AnHai Doan, Gunther Schadow, Jaideep Vaidya, Ahmed K. Elmagarmid, and Dan Suciu. Privacy-preserving data integration and sharing. In Gautam Das, Bing Liu, and Philip S. Yu, editors, *ACM SIGMOD Workshop on Research Issues in Data Mining and Knowledge Discovery (DMKD)*, pages 19–26. ACM, 2004. ISBN 1-58113-908-X.

[45] Joel Coffman and Alfred C. Weaver. A framework for evaluating database keyword search strategies. In Jimmy Huang, Nick Koudas, Gareth J. F. Jones, Xindong Wu, Kevyn Collins-Thompson, and Aijun An, editors, *ACM CIKM International Conference on Information and Knowledge Management*, pages 729–738. ACM, 2010. ISBN 978-1-4503-0099-5.

[46] Jacob Cohen. A Coefficient of Agreement for Nominal Scales. *Educational and psychological measurement*, 20(1):37–46, 1960.

[47] Lorand Dali, Blaz Fortuna, Duc Thanh Tran, and Dunja Mladenic. Query-Independent Learning to Rank for RDF Entity Search. In Elena Simperl, Philipp Cimiano, Axel Polleres, Óscar Corcho, and Valentina Presutti, editors, *Extended Semantic Web Conference (ESWC)*, volume 7295 of *Lecture Notes in Computer Science*, pages 484–498. Springer, 2012. ISBN 978-3-642-30283-1.

[48] Jeffrey Dalton, Roi Blanco, and Peter Mika. Coreference aware web object retrieval. In Craig Macdonald, Iadh Ounis, and Ian Ruthven, editors, *ACM CIKM International Conference on Information and Knowledge Management*, pages 211–220. ACM, 2011. ISBN 978-1-4503-0717-8.

[49] Jérôme David. AROMA Results for OAEI 2009. In Pavel Shvaiko, Jérôme Euzenat, Fausto Giunchiglia, Heiner Stuckenschmidt, Natalya Fridman Noy, and Arnon Rosenthal, editors, *Ontology Matching Workshop, International Semantic Web Confernce*, volume 551 of *CEUR Workshop Proceedings*. CEUR-WS.org, 2009. URL http://ceur-ws.org/Vol-551/oaei09_paper3.pdf.

[50] Gianluca Demartini, Tereza Iofciu, and Arjen P. De Vries. Overview of the INEX 2009 entity ranking track. In *Proceedings of the Focused retrieval and evaluation, and 8th international conference on Initiative for the evaluation of XML retrieval*, INEX'09, pages 254–264, Berlin, Heidelberg, 2010. Springer-Verlag.

[51] Senat des Karlsruher Instituts für Technologie. Leitlinien für ethische Grundsätze des Karlsruher Instituts für Technologie (KIT), May 2012. URL http://www.kit.edu/downloads/KIT_Ethische_Leitlinien.pdf. beschlossene Version vom 21.05.2012.

[52] Fernando Diaz and James Allan. When Less is More: Relevance Feedback Falls Short and Term Expansion Succeeds at HARD 2005. In Ellen M. Voorhees and Lori P. Buckland, editors, *TREC*, volume Special Publication 500-266. National Institute of Standards and Technology (NIST), 2005.

[53] AnHai Doan and Alon Y. Halevy. Semantic Integration Research in the Database Community: A brief survey. *AI Magazine*, 26(1):83–94, 2005.

[54] Songyun Duan, Achille Fokoue, and Kavitha Srinivas. One Size Does Not Fit All: Customizing Ontology Alignment using user feedback. In Peter F. Patel-Schneider, Yue Pan, Pascal Hitzler, Peter Mika, Lei Zhang, Jeff Z. Pan, Ian Horrocks, and Birte Glimm, editors, *International Semantic Web Conference (ISWC)*, volume 6496 of *Lecture Notes in Computer Science*, pages 177–192. Springer, 2010. ISBN 978-3-642-17745-3.

[55] Shady Elbassuoni, Maya Ramanath, Ralf Schenkel, Marcin Sydow, and Gerhard Weikum. Language-model-based ranking for queries on RDF-graphs. In David Wai-Lok Cheung, Il-Yeol Song, Wesley W. Chu, Xiaohua Hu, and Jimmy J. Lin, editors, *ACM CIKM International Conference on Information and Knowledge Management*, pages 977–986. ACM, 2009. ISBN 978-1-60558-512-3.

[56] Shady Elbassuoni, Maya Ramanath, and Gerhard Weikum. Query Relaxation for Entity-Relationship Search. In Grigoris Antoniou, Marko Grobelnik, Elena Paslaru Bontas Simperl, Bijan Parsia, Dimitris Plexousakis, Pieter De Leenheer, and Jeff Z. Pan, editors, *Extended Semantic Web Conference (ESWC)*, volume 6644 of *Lecture Notes in Computer Science*, pages 62–76. Springer, 2011. ISBN 978-3-642-21063-1.

[57] Ahmed K. Elmagarmid, Panagiotis G. Ipeirotis, and Vassilios S. Verykios. Duplicate Record Detection: A Survey. *IEEE Trans. Knowl. Data Eng.*, 19(1):1–16, 2007.

[58] Stefan Endrullis, Andreas Thor, and Erhard Rahm. Entity Search Strategies for Mashup Applications. In Anastasios Kementsietsidis and Marcos Antonio Vaz Salles, editors, *ICDE*, pages 66–77. IEEE Computer Society, 2012. ISBN 978-0-7685-4747-3.

[59] Hui Fang and ChengXiang Zhai. An exploration of axiomatic approaches to information retrieval. In Ricardo A. Baeza-Yates, Nivio Ziviani, Gary Marchionini, Alistair Moffat, and John Tait, editors, *International ACM SIGIR Conference on Research and Development in Information Retrieval*, pages 480–487. ACM, 2005. ISBN 1-59593-034-5.

[60] Joseph L. Fleiss. Measuring nominal scale agreement among many raters. *Psychological bulletin*, 76(5):378–382, 1971.

[61] B. Fuglede and F. Topsoe. Jensen-Shannon divergence and Hilbert space embedding. In *Proceedings of the International Symposium on Information Theory (ISIT 2004)*, page 31, 2004. doi: 10.1109/ISIT.2004.1365067.

[62] Jianfeng Gao, Haoliang Qi, Xinsong Xia, and Jian-Yun Nie. Linear discriminant model for information retrieval. In Ricardo A. Baeza-Yates, Nivio Ziviani, Gary Marchionini, Alistair Moffat, and John Tait, editors, *International ACM SIGIR Conference on Research and Development in Information Retrieval*, pages 290–297. ACM, 2005. ISBN 1-59593-034-5.

[63] Jan Grant and Dave Beckett. RDF Test Cases, February 2004. URL http://www.w3.org/TR/rdf-testcases/. W3C Recommendation 10 February 2004.

[64] W3C OWL Working Group. OWL 2 Web Ontology Language Document Overview (Second Edition), 2012. URL http://www.w3.org/TR/owl2-overview/. W3C Recommendation 11 December 2012.

[65] Ramanathan V. Guha, Rob McCool, and Eric Miller. Semantic Search. In *International World Wide Web Conference (WWW)*, pages 700–709, 2003.

[66] Jiafeng Guo, Gu Xu, Xueqi Cheng, and Hang Li. Named entity recognition in query. In James Allan, Javed A. Aslam, Mark Sanderson, ChengXiang Zhai, and Justin Zobel, editors, *International ACM SIGIR Conference on Research and Development in Information Retrieval*, pages 267–274. ACM, 2009. ISBN 978-1-60558-483-6.

[67] Kevin Haas, Peter Mika, Paul Tarjan, and Roi Blanco. Enhanced results for web search. In Wei-Ying Ma, Jian-Yun Nie, Ricardo A. Baeza-Yates, Tat-Seng Chua, and W. Bruce Croft, editors, *International ACM SIGIR Conference on Research and Development in Information Retrieval*, pages 725–734. ACM, 2011. ISBN 978-1-4503-0757-4.

[68] Peter Haase, Daniel M. Herzig, Mark A. Musen, and Thanh Tran. Semantic Wiki Search. In Lora Aroyo, Paolo Traverso, Fabio Ciravegna, Philipp Cimiano, Tom Heath, Eero Hyvönen, Riichiro Mizoguchi, Eyal Oren, Marta Sabou, and Elena Paslaru Bontas Simperl, editors, *European Semantic Web Conference (ESWC)*, volume 5554 of *Lecture Notes in Computer Science*, pages 445–460. Springer, 2009. ISBN 978-3-642-02120-6.

[69] Harry Halpin. A Query-Driven Characterization of Linked Data. In *Proceedings of the WWW Workshop on Linked Data on the Web*, Madrid, Spain, 2009.

[70] Harry Halpin, Daniel M. Herzig, Peter Mika, Roi Blanco, Jeffrey Pound, Henry S. Thompson, and Duc Thanh Tran. Evaluating Ad-Hoc Object Retrieval. In *Int. Workshop on Evaluation of Semantic Technologies (IWEST 2010) at ISWC*, 2010. URL http://people.csail.mit.edu/pcm/tempISWC/workshops/IWEST2010/paper9.pdf.

[71] Donna Harman. Relevance Feedback Revisited. In Nicholas J. Belkin, Peter Ingwersen, and Annelise Mark Pejtersen, editors, *International ACM SIGIR Conference on Research and Development in Information Retrieval*, pages 1–10. ACM, 1992. ISBN 0-89791-523-2.

[72] Steve Harris and Andy Seaborne. SPARQL 1.1 Query Language, November 2012. URL http://www.w3.org/TR/sparql11-query/. W3C Proposed Recommendation as of 08 Nov 2012.

[73] Stephen P. Harter. Variations in relevance assessments and the measurement of retrieval effectiveness. *J. Am. Soc. Inf. Sci.*, 47(1):37–49, 1996. ISSN 0002-8231. doi: http://dx.doi.org/10.1002/(SICI)1097-4571(199601)47:1<37::AID-ASI4>3.3.CO;2-I.

[74] Andrew F. Hayes and Klaus Krippendorff. Answering the Call for a Standard Reliability Measure for Coding Data. *Communication Methods and Measures*, 1(1): 77–89, 2007. doi: 10.1080/19312450709336664. URL http://www.tandfonline.com/doi/abs/10.1080/19312450709336664.

[75] Tom Heath and Christian Bizer. *Linked Data: Evolving the Web into a Global Data Space*. Morgan & Claypool, 1st edition, 2011. ISBN 9781608454303. URL http://linkeddatabook.com/.

[76] Daniel M. Herzig. Hybrid Search Ranking for Structured and Unstructured Data. In Grigoris Antoniou, Marko Grobelnik, Elena Paslaru Bontas Simperl, Bijan Parsia, Dimitris Plexousakis, Pieter De Leenheer, and Jeff Z. Pan, editors, *PhD Symposium, Extended Semantic Web Conference (ESWC)*, volume 6644 of *Lecture Notes in Computer Science*, pages 518–522. Springer, 2011. ISBN 978-3-642-21063-1.

[77] Daniel M. Herzig and Basil Ell. Semantic MediaWiki in Operation: Experiences with Building a Semantic Portal. In Peter F. Patel-Schneider, Yue Pan, Pascal Hitzler, Peter Mika, Lei Zhang, Jeff Z. Pan, Ian Horrocks, and Birte Glimm, editors, *International Semantic Web Conference (ISWC)*, volume 6497 of *Lecture Notes in Computer Science*, pages 114–128. Springer, 2010. ISBN 978-3-642-17748-4.

[78] Daniel M. Herzig and Hristina Taneva. Multilingual Expert Search using Linked Open Data as Interlingual Representation. In Martin Braschler, Donna Harman, and Emanuele Pianta, editors, *CLEF (Notebook Papers/LABs/Workshops)*, 2010. ISBN 978-88-904810-0-0.

[79] Daniel M. Herzig and Thanh Tran. One Query to Bind Them All. In Olaf Hartig, Andreas Harth, and Juan Sequeda, editors, *Proc. of the Second International Workshop on Consuming Linked Data (COLD2011)*, volume 782 of *CEUR Workshop Proceedings*. CEUR-WS.org, 2011.

[80] Daniel M. Herzig and Thanh Tran. Heterogeneous Web Data Search Using Relevance-based On-The-Fly Data Integration. In Alain Mille, Fabien L. Gandon, Jacques Misselis, Michael Rabinovich, and Steffen Staab, editors, *International World Wide Web Conference (WWW)*, pages 141–150. ACM, 2012. ISBN 978-1-4503-1229-5.

[81] Alan R. Hevner, Salvatore T. March, Jinsoo Park, and Sudha Ram. Design Science in Information Systems Research. *MIS Quarterly*, 28(1):75–105, 2004.

[82] Aidan Hogan, Jürgen Umbrich, Andreas Harth, Richard Cyganiak, Axel Polleres, and Stefan Decker. An empirical survey of Linked Data conformance. *Journal of Web Semantics: Science, Services and Agents on the World Wide Web*, 14:14–44, 2012.

[83] Wei Hu and Yuzhong Qu. Falcon-AO: A practical ontology matching system. *Journal of Web Semantics: Science, Services and Agents on the World Wide Web*, 6(3):237–239, 2008.

[84] Wei Hu, Jianfeng Chen, and Yuzhong Qu. A self-training approach for resolving object coreference on the semantic web. In Sadagopan Srinivasan, Krithi Ramamritham, Arun Kumar, M. P. Ravindra, Elisa Bertino, and Ravi Kumar, editors, *International World Wide Web Conference (WWW)*, pages 87–96. ACM, 2011. ISBN 978-1-4503-0632-4.

[85] Heasoo Hwang, Vagelis Hristidis, and Yannis Papakonstantinou. ObjectRank: a system for authority-based search on databases. In Surajit Chaudhuri, Vagelis Hristidis, and Neoklis Polyzotis, editors, *SIGMOD Conference*, pages 796–798. ACM, 2006. ISBN 1-59593-256-9.

[86] Kelly Y. Itakura and Charles L. A. Clarke. A framework for BM25F-based XML retrieval. In Fabio Crestani, Stéphane Marchand-Maillet, Hsin-Hsi Chen, Efthimis N. Efthimiadis, and Jacques Savoy, editors, *International ACM SIGIR Conference on Research and Development in Information Retrieval*, pages 843–844. ACM, 2010. ISBN 978-1-4503-0153-4.

[87] Kalervo Järvelin and Jaana Kekäläinen. Cumulated gain-based evaluation of IR techniques. *ACM Transactions of Information Systems*, 20(4):422–446, 2002.

[88] Carter Jernigan and Behram F. T. Mistree. Gaydar: Facebook Friendships Expose Sexual Orientation. *First Monday*, 14(10), 2009.

[89] Daniel Jurafsky and James H. Martin. *Speech and Language Processing: An Introduction to Natural Language Processing, Computational Linguistics, and Speech Recognition*. Prentice Hall PTR, Upper Saddle River, NJ, USA, 2nd edition, 2009. ISBN 0-13-504196-1.

[90] Varun Kacholia, Shashank Pandit, Soumen Chakrabarti, S. Sudarshan, Rushi Desai, and Hrishikesh Karambelkar. Bidirectional Expansion For Keyword Search on Graph Databases. In Klemens Böhm, Christian S. Jensen, Laura M. Haas, Martin L. Kersten, Per-Åke Larson, and Beng Chin Ooi, editors, *VLDB*, pages 505–516. ACM, 2005. ISBN 1-59593-154-6, 1-59593-177-5.

[91] Jaap Kamps, Shlomo Geva, Andrew Trotman, Alan Woodley, and Marijn Koolen. Overview of the INEX 2008 Ad Hoc Track. *Advances in Focused Retrieval: 7th International Workshop of the Initiative for the Evaluation of XML Retrieval, INEX 2008*, pages 1–28, 2009.

[92] Jaana Kekäläinen. Binary and graded relevance in ir evaluations–comparison of the effects on ranking of ir systems. *Inf. Process. Manage.*, 41(5):1019–1033, 2005.

[93] Graham Klyne and Jeremy J. Carroll. Resource Description Framework (RDF):Concepts and Abstract Syntax, February 2004. URL http://www.w3.org/TR/rdf-concepts/. W3C Recommendation 10 February 2004.

[94] Donald E. Knuth. *The Art of Computer Programming, Volume III: Sorting and Searching*. Addison-Wesley, 1973. ISBN 0-201-03803-X.

List of Abbreviations

[95] Hanna Köpcke and Erhard Rahm. Frameworks for entity matching: A comparison. *Data Knowl. Eng.*, 69(2):197–210, 2010.

[96] Klaus Krippendorff. Reliability in Content Analysis: Some Common Misconceptions and Recommendations. *Human Communication Research*, 30(3): 411–433, 2004. URL http://onlinelibrary.wiley.com/doi/10.1111/j.1468-2958.2004.tb00738.x/abstract.

[97] Klaus Krippendorff. Computing Krippendorff's Alpha Reliability. Departmental papers (asc), University of Pennsylvania, 2011. URL http://repository.upenn.edu/asc_papers/43/. Version of Jan 25th 2011.

[98] Markus Krötzsch, Denny Vrandečić, and Max Völkel. Semantic mediawiki. In Isabel F. Cruz, Stefan Decker, Dean Allemang, Chris Preist, Daniel Schwabe, Peter Mika, Michael Uschold, and Lora Aroyo, editors, *International Semantic Web Conference (ISWC)*, volume 4273 of *Lecture Notes in Computer Science*, pages 935–942. Springer, 2006. ISBN 3-540-49029-9.

[99] Günter Ladwig. *Efficient Optimization and Processing of Queries over Text-Rich Graph-Structured Data*. PhD thesis, Karlsruhe Institute of Technology, Feburary 2013.

[100] Victor Lavrenko. *A generative theory of relevance*. Springer, Berlin, 2009. ISBN 9783540893639.

[101] Victor Lavrenko and W. Bruce Croft. Relevance-Based Language Models. In W. Bruce Croft, David J. Harper, Donald H. Kraft, and Justin Zobel, editors, *International ACM SIGIR Conference on Research and Development in Information Retrieval*, pages 120–127. ACM, 2001. ISBN 1-58113-331-6.

[102] Victor Lavrenko, Xing Yi, and James Allan. Information Retrieval On Empty Fields. In Candace L. Sidner, Tanja Schultz, Matthew Stone, and ChengXiang Zhai, editors, *HLT-NAACL*, pages 89–96. The Association for Computational Linguistics, 2007.

[103] Luís Leitão and Pável Calado. Duplicate detection through structure optimization. In Craig Macdonald, Iadh Ounis, and Ian Ruthven, editors, *ACM CIKM International Conference on Information and Knowledge Management*, pages 443–452. ACM, 2011. ISBN 978-1-4503-0717-8.

[104] Anton Leuski. Evaluating Document Clustering for Interactive Information retrieval. In *ACM CIKM International Conference on Information and Knowledge Management*, pages 33–40. ACM, 2001. ISBN 1-58113-436-3.

[105] Fang Liu, Clement T. Yu, Weiyi Meng, and Abdur Chowdhury. Effective keyword search in relational databases. In Surajit Chaudhuri, Vagelis Hristidis, and Neoklis Polyzotis, editors, *SIGMOD Conference*, pages 563–574. ACM, 2006. ISBN 1-59593-256-9.

[106] Yi Luo, Wei Wang, and Xuemin Lin. SPARK: A Keyword Search Engine on Relational Databases. In Gustavo Alonso, José A. Blakeley, and Arbee L. P. Chen, editors, *ICDE*, pages 1552–1555. IEEE, 2008.

[107] Yongtao Ma and Thanh Tran. Typimatch: type-specific unsupervised learning of keys and key values for heterogeneous web data integration. In Stefano Leonardi, Alessandro Panconesi, Paolo Ferragina, and Aristides Gionis, editors, *WSDM*, pages 325–334. ACM, 2013. ISBN 978-1-4503-1869-3.

[108] Jayant Madhavan, Shirley Cohen, Xin Luna Dong, Alon Y. Halevy, Shawn R. Jeffery, David Ko, and Cong Yu. Web-Scale Data Integration: You can afford to Pay as You go. In *Conference on Innovative Data Systems Research (CIDR)*, pages 342–350. www.cidrdb.org, 2007.

[109] Gurmeet Singh Manku, Arvind Jain, and Anish Das Sarma. Detecting near-duplicates for web crawling. In Carey L. Williamson, Mary Ellen Zurko, Peter F. Patel-Schneider, and Prashant J. Shenoy, editors, *International World Wide Web Conference (WWW)*, pages 141–150. ACM, 2007. ISBN 978-1-59593-654-7.

[110] Christopher D. Manning and Hinrich Schütze. *Foundations of statistical natural language processing*. MIT Press, 2001. ISBN 978-0-262-13360-9.

[111] Christopher D. Manning, Prabhakar Raghavan, and Hinrich Schütze. *Introduction to Information Retrieval*. Cambridge University Press, 2008. ISBN 978-0-521-86571-5.

[112] Frank Manola and Eric Miller. RDF Primer, February 2004. URL http://www.w3.org/TR/rdf-primer/. W3C Recommendation 10 February 2004.

[113] Alexander Markowetz and Vagelis Hristidis, editors. *Proceedings of the Second International Workshop on Keyword Search on Structured Data, KEYS 2010, Indianapolis, Indiana, USA, June 6, 2010*, 2010. ACM.

[114] Winter Mason and Duncan J. Watts. Financial Incentives and the "Performance of Crowds". In *Human Computation Workshop (HComp2009)*, 2009.

[115] Frank McSherry and Marc Najork. Computing Information Retrieval Performance Measures Efficiently in the Presence of Tied Scores. In *Proceedings of the 30th ECIR*, Berlin, Heidelberg, April 2008. Springer-Verlag.

[116] Ahmed Metwally and Christos Faloutsos. V-SMART-Join: A Scalable MapReduce Framework for All-Pair similarity joins of multisets and vectors. *PVLDB*, 5(8):704–715, 2012.

[117] Peter Mika and Tim Potter. Metadata Statistics for a Large Web Corpus. In Christian Bizer, Tom Heath, Tim Berners-Lee, and Michael Hausenblas, editors, *LDOW*, volume 937 of *CEUR Workshop Proceedings*. CEUR-WS.org, 2012.

[118] Andrei Mikheev, Claire Grover, and Marc Moens. Description of the LTG System Used for MUC-7. In *Proceedings of 7th Message Understanding Conference (MUC-7)*, 1998.

[119] D. Milne and I. H. Witten. An open-source toolkit for mining Wikipedia. In *Proc. New Zealand Computer Science Research Student Conf., NZCSRSC*, volume 9, 2009.

[120] Hannes Mühleisen and Christian Bizer. Web Data Commons - Extracting Structured Data from Two Large web corpora. In Christian Bizer, Tom Heath, Tim Berners-Lee, and Michael Hausenblas, editors, *LDOW*, volume 937 of *CEUR Workshop Proceedings*. CEUR-WS.org, 2012.

[121] Robert Neumayer, Krisztian Balog, and Kjetil Nørvåg. On the Modeling of Entities for Ad-Hoc Entity Search in the web of data. In Ricardo A. Baeza-Yates, Arjen P. de Vries, Hugo Zaragoza, Berkant Barla Cambazoglu, Vanessa Murdock, Ronny Lempel, and Fabrizio Silvestri, editors, *ECIR*, volume 7224 of *Lecture Notes in Computer Science*, pages 133–145. Springer, 2012. ISBN 978-3-642-28996-5.

[122] Zaiqing Nie, Yuanzhi Zhang, Ji-Rong Wen, and Wei-Ying Ma. Object-level ranking: bringing order to Web objects. In Allan Ellis and Tatsuya Hagino, editors, *International World Wide Web Conference (WWW)*, pages 567–574. ACM, 2005. ISBN 1-59593-046-9.

[123] Zaiqing Nie, Yunxiao Ma, Shuming Shi, Ji-Rong Wen, and Wei-Ying Ma. Web object retrieval. In Carey L. Williamson, Mary Ellen Zurko, Peter F. Patel-Schneider, and Prashant J. Shenoy, editors, *International World Wide Web Conference (WWW)*, pages 81–90. ACM, 2007. ISBN 978-1-59593-654-7.

[124] Stefanie Nowak and Stefan M. Rüger. How reliable are annotations via crowdsourcing: a study about inter-annotator agreement for multi-label image annotation. In *Multimedia Information Retrieval*, pages 557–566, 2010.

[125] Paul Ogilvie and Jamie Callan. Hierarchical Language Models for XML Component Retrieval. In Norbert Fuhr, Mounia Lalmas, Saadia Malik, and Zoltán Szlávik, editors, *INEX*, volume 3493 of *Lecture Notes in Computer Science*, pages 224–237. Springer, 2004. ISBN 3-540-26166-4.

[126] Eyal Oren, Renaud Delbru, Michele Catasta, Richard Cyganiak, Holger Stenzhorn, and Giovanni Tummarello. Sindice.com: A document-oriented lookup index for open linked data. *International Journal of Metadata, Semantics, and Ontologies*, 3(1): 37–52, 2008.

[127] Ferdinand Österreicher and Igor Vajda. A new class of metric divergences on probability spaces and its applicability in statistics. *Annals of the Institute of Statistical Mathematics*, 55(3):639–653, 2003. ISSN 0020-3157. doi: 10.1007/BF02517812. URL http://dx.doi.org/10.1007/BF02517812.

[128] I. Ounis, G. Amati, V. Plachouras, B. He, C. Macdonald, and C. Lioma. Terrier: A High Performance and Scalable Information Retrieval Platform. In *Proceedings of ACM SIGIR'06 Workshop on Open Source Information Retrieval (OSIR 2006)*, 2006.

[129] Jay M. Ponte and W. Bruce Croft. A Language Modeling Approach to Information Retrieval. In *International ACM SIGIR Conference on Research and Development in Information Retrieval*, pages 275–281. ACM, 1998.

[130] Jeffrey Pound, Peter Mika, and Hugo Zaragoza. Ad-hoc object retrieval in the web of data. In Michael Rappa, Paul Jones, Juliana Freire, and Soumen Chakrabarti, editors,

International World Wide Web Conference (WWW), pages 771–780. ACM, 2010. ISBN 978-1-60558-799-8.

[131] Eric Prud'hommeaux and Andy Seaborne. SPARQL Query Language for RDF. W3c recommendation, W3C, Jan 2008. URL http://www.w3.org/TR/rdf-sparql-query/.

[132] Stephen Robertson and Hugo Zaragoza. The Probabilistic Relevance Framework: BM25 and Beyond. *Foundations and Trends in Information Retrieval*, 3(4):333–389, 2010. ISSN 1554-0669. doi: 10.1561/1500000019. URL http://www.nowpublishers.com/product.aspx?product=INR&doi=1500000019.

[133] Stephen E. Robertson and Steve Walker. Some Simple Effective Approximations to the 2-Poisson Model for probabilistic weighted retrieval. In W. Bruce Croft and C. J. van Rijsbergen, editors, *International ACM SIGIR Conference on Research and Development in Information Retrieval*, pages 232–241. ACM/Springer, 1994. ISBN 3-540-19889-X.

[134] J. J. Rocchio. Relevance feedback in information retrieval. In G. Salton, editor, *The Smart retrieval system - experiments in automatic document processing*, pages 313–323. Englewood Cliffs, NJ: Prentice-Hall, 1971.

[135] Ian Ruthven and Mounia Lalmas. A survey on the use of relevance feedback for information access systems. *The Knowledge Engineering Review*, 18:95–145, 5 2003. ISSN 1469-8005. doi: 10.1017/S0269888903000638. URL http://dx.doi.org/10.1017/S0269888903000638.

[136] G. Salton, A. Wong, and C. S. Yang. A vector space model for automatic indexing. *Commun. ACM*, 18:613–620, November 1975. ISSN 0001-0782. doi: http://doi.acm.org/10.1145/361219.361220. URL http://doi.acm.org/10.1145/361219.361220.

[137] Stefan Schlobach and Craig A. Knoblock. Dealing with the Messiness of the Web of Data. *Web Semantics: Science, Services and Agents on the World Wide Web*, 14(0): 1, 2012. ISSN 1570-8268. doi: 10.1016/j.websem.2012.05.004. URL http://www.sciencedirect.com/science/article/pii/S1570826812000583. Special Issue on Dealing with the Messiness of the Web of Data.

[138] Nigel Shadbolt, Tim Berners-Lee, and Wendy Hall. The Semantic Web Revisited. *IEEE Intelligent Systems*, 21(3):96–101, 2006.

[139] Milad Shokouhi and Luo Si. Federated Search. *Foundations and Trends in Information Retrieval*, 5(1):1–102, 2011.

[140] Mark D. Smucker, James Allan, and Ben Carterette. A comparison of statistical significance tests for information retrieval evaluation. In Mário J. Silva, Alberto H. F. Laender, Ricardo A. Baeza-Yates, Deborah L. McGuinness, Bjørn Olstad, Øystein Haug Olsen, and André O. Falcão, editors, *ACM CIKM International Conference on Information and Knowledge Management*, pages 623–632. ACM, 2007. ISBN 978-1-59593-803-9.

[141] Ian Soboroff and Donna Harman. Novelty detection: the TREC experience. In *HLT '05*, USA, 2005. ACL. doi: http://dx.doi.org/10.3115/1220575.1220589.

[142] Daniel J. Solove. 'I've Got Nothing to Hide' and Other Misunderstandings of Privacy. *San Diego Law Review, GWU Law School Public Law Research Paper*, 44(289), 2007. URL http://ssrn.com/paper=998565.

[143] Dezhao Song and Jeff Heflin. Automatically Generating Data Linkages Using a Domain-Independent candidate selection approach. In Lora Aroyo, Chris Welty, Harith Alani, Jamie Taylor, Abraham Bernstein, Lalana Kagal, Natasha Fridman Noy, and Eva Blomqvist, editors, *International Semantic Web Conference (ISWC)*, volume 7031 of *Lecture Notes in Computer Science*, pages 649–664. Springer, 2011. ISBN 978-3-642-25072-9.

[144] Fei Song and W. Bruce Croft. A General Language Model for Information Retrieval. In *ACM CIKM International Conference on Information and Knowledge Management*, pages 316–321. ACM, 1999. ISBN 1-58113-146-1.

[145] Steffen Staab and Rudi Studer, editors. *Handbook on Ontologies*. International Handbooks on Information Systems. Springer, 2004. ISBN 3-540-40834-7.

[146] Tran Thanh, Stephan Bloehdorn, Philipp Cimiano, and Peter Haase. Expressive Resource Descriptions for Ontology-Based Information Retrieval. In *Proc. of the First International Conference on the Theory of Information Retrieval (ICTIR)*, pages 55–68, 2007.

[147] Martin Theobald, Ralf Schenkel, and Gerhard Weikum. An Efficient and Versatile Query Engine for TopX Search. In Klemens Böhm, Christian S. Jensen, Laura M. Haas, Martin L. Kersten, Per-Åke Larson, and Beng Chin Ooi, editors, *VLDB*, pages 625–636. ACM, 2005. ISBN 1-59593-154-6, 1-59593-177-5.

[148] Alberto Tonon, Gianluca Demartini, and Philippe Cudré-Mauroux. Combining inverted indices and structured search for ad-hoc object retrieval. In William R. Hersh, Jamie Callan, Yoelle Maarek, and Mark Sanderson, editors, *International ACM SIGIR Conference on Research and Development in Information Retrieval*, pages 125–134. ACM, 2012. ISBN 978-1-4503-1472-5.

[149] Thanh Tran, Haofen Wang, and Peter Haase. Hermes: Data Web search on a pay-as-you-go integration infrastructure. *Journal of Web Semantics: Science, Services and Agents on the World Wide Web*, 7(3):189–203, 2009.

[150] Thanh Tran, Daniel M. Herzig, and Günter Ladwig. SemSearchPro - Using semantics throughout the search process. *Journal of Web Semantics: Science, Services and Agents on the World Wide Web*, 9(4):349–364, 2011.

[151] Thanh Tran, Yongtao Ma, and Gong Cheng. Pay-less entity consolidation: exploiting entity search user feedbacks for pay-as-you-go entity data integration. In Noshir S. Contractor, Brian Uzzi, Michael W. Macy, and Wolfgang Nejdl, editors, *WebSci*, pages 317–325. ACM, 2012. ISBN 978-1-4503-1228-8.

[152] Jürgen Umbrich, Katja Hose, Marcel Karnstedt, Andreas Harth, and Axel Polleres. Comparing data summaries for processing live queries over linked data. *World Wide Web*, 14(5-6):495–544, 2011.

[153] Christina Unger, Philipp Cimiano, Vanessa Lopez, and Enrico Motta. QALD-1 Open Challenge, 2011. http://www.sc.cit-ec.uni-bielefeld.de/sites/www.sc.cit-ec.uni-bielefeld.de/files/sharedtask.pdf.

[154] Maksims Volkovs and Richard S. Zemel. A flexible generative model for preference aggregation. In Alain Mille, Fabien L. Gandon, Jacques Misselis, Michael Rabinovich, and Steffen Staab, editors, *International World Wide Web Conference (WWW)*, pages 479–488. ACM, 2012. ISBN 978-1-4503-1229-5.

[155] Ellen Voorhees. The Philosophy of Information Retrieval Evaluation. In *In Proceedings of the The Second Workshop of the Cross-Language Evaluation Forum on Evaluation of Cross-Language Information Retrieval Systems*, pages 355–370. Springer-Verlag, 2001.

[156] Ellen M. Voorhees. Query Expansion Using Lexical-Semantic Relations. In W. Bruce Croft and C. J. van Rijsbergen, editors, *International ACM SIGIR Conference on Research and Development in Information Retrieval*, pages 61–69. ACM/Springer, 1994. ISBN 3-540-19889-X.

[157] Ellen M. Voorhees and Donna K. Harman. *TREC: Experiment and Evaluation in Information Retrieval*. Digital Libraries and Electronic Publishing. MIT Press, September 2005. ISBN 0262220733. URL http://mitpress.mit.edu/catalog/item/default.asp?ttype=2&tid=10667&mode=toc.

[158] Haofen Wang, Thanh Tran, Peter Haase, Thomas Penin, Qiaoling Liu1, Linyun Fu, , and Yong Yu. SearchWebDB: Searching the Billion Triples! In *Semantic Web Challenge, ISWC*, 2008. URL http://www.cs.vu.nl/~pmika/swc-2008/SearchWebDB-paper.pdf.

[159] Haofen Wang, Qiaoling Liu, Thomas Penin, Linyun Fu, Lei Zhang, Thanh Tran, Yong Yu, and Yue Pan. Semplore: A scalable IR approach to search the Web of Data. *Journal of Web Semantics: Science, Services and Agents on the World Wide Web*, 7(3):177–188, 2009.

[160] Haofen Wang, Thanh Tran, Chang Liu, and Linyun Fu. Lightweight integration of IR and DB for scalable hybrid search with integrated ranking support. *Journal of Web Semantics*, 9(4):490–503, 2011.

[161] Gerhard Weikum. DB&IR: both sides now. In Chee Yong Chan, Beng Chin Ooi, and Aoying Zhou, editors, *SIGMOD Conference*, pages 25–30. ACM, 2007. ISBN 978-1-59593-686-8.

[162] Steven Euijong Whang, David Marmaros, and Hector Garcia-Molina. Pay-As-You-Go Entity Resolution. *IEEE Transactions on Knowledge and Data Engineering*, 99, 2012. ISSN 1041-4347. doi: http://doi.ieeecomputersociety.org/10.1109/TKDE.2012.43.

[163] ChengXiang Zhai. *Statistical Language Models for Information Retrieval*. Synthesis Lectures on Human Language Technologies. Morgan & Claypool Publishers, 2008.

[164] ChengXiang Zhai and John D. Lafferty. Model-based Feedback in the Language Modeling Approach to information retrieval. In *ACM CIKM International Conference on Information and Knowledge Management*, pages 403–410. ACM, 2001. ISBN 1-58113-436-3.

[165] ChengXiang Zhai and John D. Lafferty. A study of smoothing methods for language models applied to information retrieval. *ACM Trans. Inf. Syst.*, 22(2):179–214, 2004.

[166] ChengXiang Zhai and John D. Lafferty. A risk minimization framework for information retrieval. *Inf. Process. Manage.*, 42(1):31–55, 2006.

[167] Le Zhao and Jamie Callan. A generative retrieval model for structured documents. In James G. Shanahan, Sihem Amer-Yahia, Ioana Manolescu, Yi Zhang, David A. Evans, Aleksander Kolcz, Key-Sun Choi, and Abdur Chowdhury, editors, *ACM CIKM International Conference on Information and Knowledge Management*, pages 1163–1172. ACM, 2008. ISBN 978-1-59593-991-3.

[168] Elena Zheleva and Lise Getoor. To join or not to join: the illusion of privacy in social networks with mixed public and private user profiles. In Juan Quemada, Gonzalo León, Yoëlle S. Maarek, and Wolfgang Nejdl, editors, *International World Wide Web Conference (WWW)*, pages 531–540. ACM, 2009. ISBN 978-1-60558-487-4.

[169] Xuan Zhou, Julien Gaugaz, Wolf-Tilo Balke, and Wolfgang Nejdl. Query relaxation using malleable schemas. In Chee Yong Chan, Beng Chin Ooi, and Aoying Zhou, editors, *SIGMOD Conference*, pages 545–556. ACM, 2007. ISBN 978-1-59593-686-8.

[170] Justin Zobel. *Writing for Computer Science, 2nd ed*. Springer, 2004. ISBN 978-1-85233-802-2.

List of Figures

PRF Pseudo Relevance Feedback. 21

RDF Resource Description Framework. 12
Recall Recall metric. 27
RKS Relational keyword search. 80, 96
RM Relevance-based Language Model. 96

SDR Structured document retrieval. 80
SPARQL SPARQL Protocol And RDF Query Language. 15
SQL Structured query language for relational database systems. 15

TF/IDF Term frequency (TF) divided by inverse document frequency (IDF). A common ranking function [136]. 61
TREC Text REtrieval Conference (http://trec.nist.gov/). 26

URI Uniform Resource Identifier. 13

W3C World Wide Web Consortium (www.w3.org). 15
Web (*www*) World Wide Web. 11

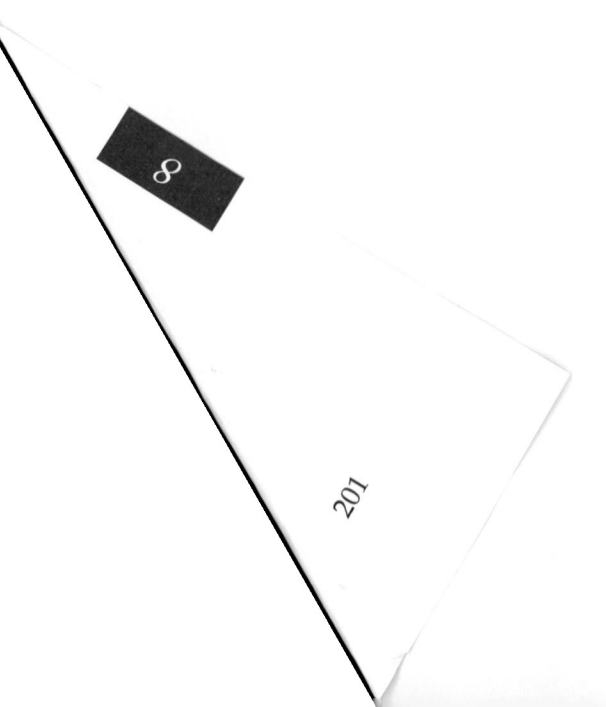

List of Tables

∞